Industrial Innovation, Networks, and Economic Development

T0270770

This book offers an innovative examination of how 'low-technology' industries operate. Based on extensive fieldwork in India, the book fuses economic and sociological perspectives on information sharing by means of informal inter-action in a low-technology cluster in a developing country. In doing so, the book sheds new light on settings where economic relations arise as emergent prop-erties of social relations.

This book examines industrial innovation and microeconomic network behaviour among producers and clusters, perceiving knowledge diffusion to be a socially spatial, as much as a geographically spatial, phenomenon. This is achieved by employing two methods – simulation modelling and (quantitative, qualitative, and historical) social network analysis. The simulation model, based on its findings, motivates two empirical studies – one descriptive case and one network study – of low-tech rural and semi-urban traditional technology clusters in Kerala state in southern India. These cases demonstrate two contrasting stories of how social cohesion either supports or thwarts informal information sharing and learning.

This book pushes towards an economic-sociology approach to understanding knowledge diffusion and technological learning, which perceives innovation and learning as being more social processes than the mainstream view perceives them to be. In doing so, it makes a significant contribution to the literature on defensive innovation and the role of networks in technological innovation and knowledge diffusion, as well as to policy studies of Indian small firm and tradi-tional technology clusters.

Anant Kamath is currently faculty at Azim Premji University, Bangalore, India.

Routledge studies in development economics

Industrial Innovation, Networks, and Economic Development

Informal information sharing in low-technology clusters in India

Anant Kamath

Routledge
Taylor & Francis Group

LONDON AND NEW YORK

First published 2015 by Routledge

2 Park Square, Milton Park, Abingdon, Oxfordshire OX14 4RN
52 Vanderbilt Avenue, New York, NY 10017

Routledge is an imprint of the Taylor & Francis Group, an informa business

First issued in paperback 2019

British Library Cataloguing in Publication Data
A catalogue record for this book is available from the British Library

Library of Congress Cataloging in Publication Data
Kamath, Anant.
Industrial innovation, networks, and economic development : informal
information sharing in low-technology clusters in India / Anant Kamath. –
First Edition.
   pages cm – (Routledge studies in development economics)
   Includes bibliographical references and index.
   1. Technological innovations–India. 2. Social networks–India. I. Title.
   HC440.T4K35 2014
   338.8'70954–dc23   2014021423

ISBN: 978-1-138-81546-9 (hbk)
ISBN: 978-0-367-87110-9 (pbk)

Typeset in Times New Roman
by Wearset Ltd, Boldon, Tyne and Wear

Contents

Figures

Tables

Acknowledgements

The first person who must be accredited with due acknowledgement is Robin Cowan, under whose extraordinary and holistic guidance this work was executed during six years of my doctoral study.

I also deeply thank Sunil Mani, Saurabh Arora, Shyama Ramani, and Pierre Mohnen for their sensitive appreciation of the theme and its treatment, and for suggesting several constructive critiques of the thesis version of this study. Thanks are also due to Adam Szirmai and Michiko Iizuka for their approval of this work.

This work was undertaken during my doctoral research at the United Nations University/MERIT (UNU-MERIT), Maastricht, The Netherlands. Thanks are due, at UNU-MERIT, to Ad Notten, to Luc Soete, and to Shyama Ramani who helped out a great deal in crafting the essentials of the simulation model in this thesis. Special thanks to Eveline in de Braek for help rendered on countless occasions during this period.

A large part of this work was undertaken at the Centre for Development Studies (CDS), Trivandrum, India. Hence, a major acknowledgement is due also to CDS, to Mohanan Pillai, J. Devika, and particularly to Sunil Mani who remains my mentor.

Large parts of the analysis and writing of this thesis were also completed during my affiliation with the Department of Sociology, University of Georgia, Athens GA, United States. I am indebted to this Department, particularly to Dawn Robinson, Joe Hermanowicz, and William Finlay, for providing me with a wonderful work environment and generous infrastructure.

Two libraries, besides the UNU-MERIT/Maastricht University libraries, were greatly exploited for bibliographic material for this work. These are the KN Raj Library at CDS, and the University of Georgia Library. To these libraries, and their staff, I owe deep gratitude.

For the coir cluster study, I thank KN Harilal (CDS), V. Nandamohan (formerly Professor and Head, Department of Futures Studies, University of Kerala), K. Madanan (Director of Coir Development, Government of Kerala), K.T. Rammohan (School of Social Sciences, Mahatma Gandhi University, Kottayam), Anil (NCRMI, Trivandrum), Antoniel Vaz (Coir Board, Cochin), Tomychan (NCT&DC, Aleppey), and N. Ajith Kumar and the CSES at Cochin and Saikumar (Cooperative Coir Weavers' Society, Chirayinkeezh). The study would not have been possible without the help provided by V.R. Prasad (TMMC Pvt. Ltd, Chertala), Shaji and Paul (at Manappuram) and of course, the cooperation given by the households in the Manappuram coir-producing cluster.

For the weavers cluster study, I thank J. Devika (CDS), Mohanakumar, Ramesan (Pallichal Panchayat), Viswambaran (Handloom Palace), Sudhakaran (master weaver) at Balaramapuram; and P.S. Mani (IHCDP, Nemom). Special thanks are due to the Saliyar community at Balaramapuram, particularly Selvaraj, Subramanian and family, and Magesh and family, Paramasivan and Manikandan; and to the handloom weaving community at Payattuvila, particularly Udayan and Thankappan Panicker, and family.

Many others have incrementally guided the path of this work. They include Erkki Kaukonen, Mammo Muchie, Giovanni Dosi, Alice Duhaut, Keshab Das, and Rajeswari Raina.

Azim Premji University at Bangalore provided a most congenial work environment to complete this book. To this organisation and its members I offer deep gratitude.

I owe gratitude to the teams at Routledge and Wearset for all assistance provided. Of course, all errors remain mine.

Many friends and others have provided overwhelming support during this research: Robert Kleinenberg, Diederik Rijkens, Anant Joshi, Andrew Herod, Pappettan and Shaku, Agniva Saha, and Vasantha.

I am ever obliged to my family: to my mother and father, Ammamma, and Umanath, for unconditional support throughout my life. Although I will not be able to show Ammamma and Remakka this work, I know for sure that they can see everything. Thanks also to Neethi's parents for being very accommodating towards the end of the research period.

And, of course, to Neethi, who endured and overcame much travail to see this work reach this stage. With accomplishments of no small significance, Neethi has been the very motive to shape this work into a book. We have travelled, over the past many years, through the eccentric and the eclectic, making considerable progress on our continuing journey towards aestheticism in both life and research.

Anant Kamath
Bangalore, India

1 Introduction and conceptual outline

> The diffusion of new information and knowledge is accelerated by the exchange of knowledge and experiences between the actors within the system. Thereby knowledge is accumulated and capabilities are broadened, which, if economically useful, might lead to more innovation.
>
> (Cantner and Graf, 2008, p. 1)

This book is a study on the nature and characteristics of information sharing by means of informal interaction among small low-technology[1] producers located in clusters. The aims of this study are: (1) to understand intra-cluster interaction channels and dynamics of information sharing among producers in low-tech clusters surviving on defensive innovation, and (2) to study this information sharing in settings where economic relations arise as emergent properties of social relations. These aims are fulfilled by means of employing one simulation model and two empirical studies. The book begins with the simulation model, which motivates the two empirical studies out of its findings – a descriptive case study and a network study of low-tech rural and semi-urban clusters in traditional technology industries in Kerala state in southern India.

The aims and contributions of this book assume significance for several reasons. In a developing country like India, small-unit clusters constitute a large population of industrial clusters which, nevertheless, bring out a range of product and process innovations; however, as these small units do not have the means to conduct formal research and development (R&D), information exchanges and technological learning in these settings often occur in environments where social networks serve as valuable channels of information exchange, providing both opportunities and constraints (Gulati, 1998; Das, 2005; Mani, 2011, 2013). Most studies in Indian academia, when dealing with technological progress and modernisation among small producers or clusters, or even studies on traditional industries, enquire only occasionally into the mechanisms and dynamics of learning through informal interaction among producers, and into the policy and institutional environment conducive to this sort of learning and information sharing. A superficial treatment of these themes in the Indian literature exists despite the ubiquity of this behaviour among industrial and artisan clusters in

India, and awareness of the dominant position of low-technology actors in India's economy.[2] In clusters of tiny low-tech producers within traditional industry sectors, the systematic supply of codified technological know-how is minimal, and necessary updates on new techniques are sourced mainly through informal interactive channels (Bala Subrahmanya *et al.*, 2002; UNIDO, n.d.). Since such producers have little or no external linkages with technology leaders locally or extra-locally, they rely on close contacts, family, kinship ties, and buyers and suppliers to gain new knowledge (Utterback, 1994; von Hippel and Tyre, 1995; Howells, 2002). Stunted information gathering and information sharing, low cooperative behaviour among tiny low-tech producers, or a faulty institutional and policy foundation, can contribute significantly towards technological backwardness. Subdued informal information sharing among producers can threaten to trap them in their obsolete practices, hindering them from sourcing new information and moving towards the technology frontier in the industry at which their peers may be competing. There has been adequate attention paid in the literature outside of India to information sharing by means of interactions through social networks. However, in India this is still only superficial.

This book hence brings this analysis to India where its appreciation is still only superficial. The analysis in the book also delves into studying this informal information sharing in scenarios where social relations drive economic relations among agents. These are the chief motivations and contributions of this book.

One may attribute innovation and learning to only high-tech producers, but this endeavour is, as the literature has demonstrated, very much the prerogative of low- and medium-tech producers too – even of household units in traditional industries in rural India. The perceived role of these small producers has dramatically changed over the past few decades, from merely infinitesimal parts of production chains, to innovators in their own right (see Rothwell and Zegveld, 1982; Rothwell, 1989). Especially in India, broad changes brought about in the early 1990s as a response to the economic crises at the time shifted the focus of industrial policy from a system of planning and protection to one that encouraged entrepreneurial potential among individuals and small producers. The opening up of vast opportunities was intended by the new regime, through enabling the prospects of exploiting one's comparative advantage, freely locating, innovating, tapping local and global information flows, and, above all, participating in a system that rewards adaptation to change and penalises rigidity and isolation. Small producers, whether individual household units or small agglomerations of employees under one roof, were now to control their own innovation and learning processes rather than being simply recipients of new technologies. But this new freedom necessitated new varieties of efforts such as constantly being on the lookout for what's new at the technology horizon and to frantically gather new information. The need for proximity or clustering among small producers became important not only to exploit economies of scale and economies of scope but also for *learning*, since it was increasingly recognised that information can and should be sourced not only from abroad, or from technologically advanced domestic firms, but also from fellow small producers in the vicinity. In other words, small producers, especially low-tech small producers, swiftly recognised the importance of keeping a steadfast lookout for technological developments among their close allies and competitors, especially since they were too insignificant to work in isolation and could not undertake R&D on a large scale or in the formal, conventional sense. It remains important, if small producers wish to be technologically proximate (i.e. similar to peers in terms of technological capability and information stock), that they keep abreast in terms of the velocity of technical change in their immediate vicinity.

There are two strategies to achieve this outcome. One is to ensure geographical proximity to one's peers. Another is to dedicate efforts specifically towards efficient networking, as this is of utmost importance in an environment of continuous innovation, constant learning and a relentless flow of new knowledge. There are few streams of research in innovation studies, and probably in the economics and management literature at large, that have not subscribed to the fact that effective networking remains a most essential activity for economic agents, large or small, high-tech or low-tech; and that economic agents' behaviour and performance may only be understood fully by examining their social, technological and exchange relationships with other agents (Vonortas, 2009).

Following this, it therefore becomes an objective, during the course of investigation into innovation and learning behaviour among low-tech producers, to discover network paths and information transmission channels among even seemingly heterogeneous (or even rival) individuals. This is given the high possibility that these paths – especially short paths that facilitate rapid information transfer between agents – actually exist and can be unearthed (Cowan, 2004; Vega-Redondo, 2007).

But learning and innovation among low-tech producers involves tactics of which geographic proximity and networking are only two out of a distinctive set of strategies that come under the umbrella of *defensive innovation*, which is essentially the spectrum of overlapping possibilities that include being offensive, defensive, imitative, dependent, traditional or opportunist (Freeman and Soete, 1997). Defensive innovation and learning may, or may not, be influenced by social relations among units within the agglomeration. On the one hand, seamless information sharing may occur in a socioeconomically homogeneous or heterogeneous agglomeration with little influence from social demarcations. On the other hand, information sharing may be heavily influenced, for better or for worse, by social demarcations in a heterogeneous environment.

This is what brings us to the objectives of this book espoused at the beginning of this chapter: to understand collective learning and defensive innovation, and to investigate their paths in environments where economic relations are embedded in social relations. This work seeks to provide an understanding of this genre of innovative and learning behaviour – defensive innovation – when it is witnessed in low-technology clusters that experience social embeddedness of information exchange relations.

These explorations commence with a discussion and review of the broad conceptual themes that form the foundations of this book. These include collective invention and defensive innovation, clusters and learning regions, the role of proximity, the role of networks, and themes from economic sociology such as social capital, embeddedness and homophily, most of which are conceptually intertwined with one another. The conceptual discussion and literature review in this chapter are placed under two broad themes: (1) defensive innovation in clusters and the role of networks in informal information sharing, and (2) economic relations within social relations. These are evidently concurrent to the two objectives of this book outlined earlier.

Defensive innovation in clusters, and the role of networks in informal information sharing

Collective invention, defensive innovation and the significance of 'low-tech'

Allen (1983) described a rather strange activity among iron manufacturers in the mid-1800s in the Cleveland region in Britain – producers were sharing new information on the latest and best production practices and technologies, on a continuous basis, free of charge, even to their rivals. In fact, this behaviour was not unique to Cleveland, as similar activities of uninhibited information sharing, even among competitors, were thriving among paper manufacturers in the early 1800s in Berkshire, New England (McGaw, 1987; Cowan and Jonard, 2003). Gault and von Hippel (2009) list a host of studies describing this 'voluntary and intentional spillover' also occurring in the early history of mine-pumping engines, in medical equipment, semiconductor process equipment, library information systems and sporting equipment. This behaviour, considered initially as 'an undesired "leakage" that reduces the incentives to invent' (Allen, 1983, p. 21), is actually neither undesired nor a leakage, and certainly did not reduce the incentive to invent. It was, in fact, as Allen (1983) argued, a proactively pursued *collective invention* practised in the form of freely releasing information, since it was almost impossible and often expensive to keep the new information a secret. In addition, it was often conscious and strategic to actually release the information in the form of a broadcast to other producers in the region through local publications, presentations at meetings, social circles, and through informal channels of word-of-mouth information exchanges (Allen *et al.*, 1983; Cowan, 2004). Individual producers were known to have devoted little time and effort to discovering new information all on their own, relying more on these frequent information releases and the 'buzz' of new ideas and techniques among local groups of producers (Allen, 1983).

As mentioned at the beginning of this chapter, many low-tech and small producers often do not have internal resources dedicated to generating ideas, and are dependent on others for information on new technologies (Allen *et al.*, 1983). They do not favour investing in R&D as much as they favour *satisficing*, i.e. undertaking a conscious local search among their co-located and connected peers for incremental improvements to their present technologies and production practices, especially when they find themselves performing below par compared to peers whom they can easily observe (Nelson and Winter, 1982; Sheffrin, 1996; Romijn, 1999).[3] Learning thus becomes an organisational response rather than a continuing policy commitment and the search for new information becomes conscious, concentrating around one's vicinity in geographical and technological space (Nelson and Winter, 1982). The new knowledge and subsequent technologies that arise due to this collective invention and satisficing behaviour are, like the behaviour itself, imitative (Kauffman and Tödtling, 2003). This brings us to Foray's (2010) recommendation that we should understand innovation itself, in a broader sense, as taking place over an entire spectrum of economic activity and sectors, not just high-tech sectors and those practising formal R&D. This is because innovation in most developing economies is mostly 'incremental, cumulative and mostly informal (without R&D), mainly in "traditional" sectors or in services that do not qualify as "high technology"', generating local spillovers that ultimately affect the productivity of several sectors in the local economy (Foray, 2010, p. 96). In the Indian scenario too, informal R&D of this sort is the preference of the majority of small producers, with suppliers, consultants and friends assuming a principal role in their exploration of new information (Bala Subrahmanya *et al.*, 2002).

Studies by Peter Maskell (see, for example, Maskell, 2001a, 2001b; Maskell and Malmberg, 1999; Malmberg and Maskell, 1997; Maskell *et al.*, 1998) have contributed substantially to the literature on small units watching one another and striving to catch up with local rivals. This body of literature is founded on the basic fact that producers with unsophisticated R&D resources and even traditional industry clusters are not excluded from the rewards and pressures of technological progress, thereby resorting to undertake learning to build their information stock, employing defensive techniques such as imitation and collective invention. Oakey and colleagues (1988) propose that internal R&D and more advanced techniques are only some of the many strategies open to small producers who cannot afford to be left behind or isolated given their size, and have to constantly be on a par with other units around them lest they fall behind. Small producers are always on a treadmill (Freeman and Soete, 1997) where imitating neighbours' strategies and movements and surveying the landscape for niches to which other fellow units are being attracted becomes a survival strategy in a constantly evolving industry environment.

These strategies comprise what is known to be, as mentioned earlier, defensive innovation (Freeman and Soete, 1997), wherein producers seek to be imitative and opportunistic in their environment. Freeman and Soete (1997) propose that defensive behaviour among producers is not the absence of R&D; rather the desire to be well informed about new developments in the environment to which producers need to adapt for survival. This, Freeman and Soete add, is ubiquitous across countries.

However, Smallbone and colleagues (2003) warn that imitation and defensive behaviour among co-localised (low-tech) firms opens up the possibility of pushing groups of firms into suboptimal outcomes that are not conducive to long-term survival. In other words, there is a high probability of a lock-in into an inferior technology or practice when relying too much on strategies of defence and imitation. Small units, especially in the low-tech end of the technological spectrum, may be prone to this probability.

There is substantial evidence for the ubiquity of defensive innovation. Kauffman and Tödtling (2003) find that defensive innovation through observation and imitation was common in an entire spectrum of technological capabilities from Austria to Valencia; they conclude that innovation as such is part of a defensive strategy focusing on market niches, and that innovation strategies of most small firms are characteristically defensive. Bougrain and Haudeville (2002) discover (upon studying projects carried out by over 300 small enterprises in the 1980s) that even 'formal' firms spend a large amount of time on informal innovation activities. Such activities may be hard to estimate, but are very relevant for developing country economies (Maharajh and Kraemer-Mbula, 2010). In a survey by Gault and von Hippel (2009) it was found that over 20 per cent of user-innovators transferred information to other users or suppliers, very often at no charge. Firms that combine the standard R&D processes with a strong focus on interaction, and spreading the information gained by learning-by-doing or learning-by-using, were found to excel in innovation more than those engaging only standard R&D processes (Jensen *et al.*, 2007). Although this is more acute in low-tech firms than in high-tech firms, the combination of competitive pressure, peer pressure and constant comparison (Porter, 1998) is found in all varieties of producers, whether high-tech or low-tech.

But being small or low-tech and adopting defensive innovation strategies need not suggest 'insignificance' with respect to innovation and learning in the larger economy. For example, one set of studies, following the work of Hirsch-Kreinsen,[4] dispute the notion that the term 'low-tech' may suggest that producers are only recipients of information or remain in a semi-starved state for new technologies. Hirsch-Kreinsen *et al.* (2003) refute the notion that high-tech producers are all intensive users of codified knowledge whereas low-tech units deal mainly with tacit knowledge, arguing that there is no such rule-of-thumb correspondence and that there is low-tech outside the domain of tacit knowledge and a tacit knowledge domain outside of low-tech.[5] The notion that the knowledge economy is identified with high-tech and formal R&D firms and industries is also criticised by Hirsch-Kreinsen and Jacobson (2008), who reveal that a large proportion of manufacturing in advanced economies is in low- (and medium-) tech industries, providing goods and services that are not peripheral but *vital* to their economy's functioning. Hirsch-Kreinsen and Jacobson (2008) reveal further that low- and medium-tech industries account for nearly 60 per cent of employment in manufacturing, and are by far the largest contributors to value-added in manufacturing in OECD countries, displaying resilience and stability. In India too, despite a steady increase in the high-tech component in manufactured exports over the years, exports of products originating from low-tech industries dominate more than two-thirds of total manufacturing exports (Mani, 2009).[6]

Clusters and learning regions

The preceding discussion has suggested that collective invention and defensive innovation occur, particularly in *clusters* of small producers. In fact, clustering is now a common characteristic of small producers worldwide, whether high-tech or low-tech (Oakey *et al.*, 1988; MoI, 1997), since it allows for geographical and technological proximity to constantly monitor each other closely and often without cost (Maskell, 2001b), so much so that small units working in clusters are found to perform better than those working individually (van Dijk, 2005). Small producers find it necessary to cluster for face-to-face sharing of experiences, which is not surprising, since knowledge processes are often 'people processes' (Dankbaar, 2004; Dwivedi and Varman, 2005; Das, 2005).

Although research interest on clustering and networking has grown dramatically over recent decades (partly due to the increasing awareness that innovation is driven by effective diffusion through improved information flows among proximate innovating agents (Cowan *et al.*, 2004)), these ideas were advocated in the early literature on economics, such as by Alfred Marshall:

> [S]o great are the advantages which people following the same skilled trade get from near neighbourhood to one another. The mysteries of the trade become no mysteries; but are as it were in the air, and children learn many of them unconsciously ... inventions and improvements in machinery, in processes and the general organization of the business have their merits promptly discussed: if one man starts a new idea, it is taken up by others and combined with suggestions of their own; and thus it becomes the source of further new ideas.
>
> (Marshall, 1895, p. 325)

Even when information is codified and firms are high-tech, the trust, information sharing and teamwork that form the basis for collaborative relations among small producers require a continuous interaction that is easier over short spaces than over long distances (Saxenian, 1991). This is clarified by evidence from Silicon Valley in the United States, where long-distance communication was found to be inadequate for the 'continuous and detailed engineering adjustments required in making technically complex electronics products. Face-to-face interactions allow firms to address the unexpected complications in a supplier relationship that could never be covered by a contract' (Saxenian, 1991, p. 430).

The forces pulling small units into clusters are founded on the necessity to constantly learn from other units in the proximate surroundings, which, if efficiently undertaken, is also the recipe for its long-term innovative capability (Breschi and Malerba, 2005). Clusters enhance cooperation and assist units in combating economic adversity, increasing their flexibility to the changing economic environment (Pedersen *et al.*, 1994).[7] The literature has so adequately elaborated upon the role of clustering in learning and innovation that Bell and Albu (1999), in a prominent study surveying the literature on innovation in clusters, argue that geographically bounded clusters must be viewed not simply as production systems but as *innova-tion systems* in their own right. Basant (2006) and Mytelka (2007) argue that an industrial policy oriented towards knowledge accumulation can convert a cluster-based production system into an innovation system.[8]

Agglomerations thus become not only containers to tap locational advantages but created spaces or *learning regions* that act as forums for collective learning through intense interaction (Maskell and Malmberg, 1999; Maskell *et al.*, 1998). The literature on 'learning regions', a subset of the vaster literature on innovation in clusters, provides strong conceptual propositions which are essential for our understanding on innovation and learning among low-tech small producer clusters.

A 'learning region' is an 'ideal industrial district' in the true sense of the term (van Dijk and Rabellotti, 1997; Ruttan and Boekema, 2007) when regional actors engage in collaboration and coordination for mutual benefit, when there exists an intense set of linkages – backward and forward, horizontal and vertical – based on exchange of tangible goods and information in a cluster, and when there are strong public and private local institutions supporting the linked agents. The literature on learning regions, much like the literature on clusters, is an eclectic mix of concepts from the research on systems of innovation, industrial districts and networks. Hassink (2007) terms the literature on learning regions as 'fuzzy' and often 'squeezed' between systems of innovation and global production net-works, which at first sight may suggest vagueness and excessive breadth, but which in fact can be demarcated to allow for conceptual clarity. Learning regions are of critical importance, according to Ruttan and Boekema (2007), since they provide both space and proximity, contributing to the production, use, distribu-tion and utilisation of the tacit knowledge and the capacity for learning that support innovation. The learning regions concept also reiterates that since tacit knowledge does not travel easily, information sharing between partners becomes essential. Sharing 'sticky' information becomes effective when agents share common codes of communication, share norms and conventions, and have a per-sonal knowledge of one another – all three constituting basic requirements of a learning region in terms of enabling the mutual understanding required between actors for the flow of tacit knowledge (Gertler, 2007). Proponents of the learning regions approach suggest that firms undertake local search, since past interac-tions, word-of-mouth information diffusion and local reputation effects provide an intimate knowledge of other local firms and their capabilities, which improves their chances of finding a 'right match' (Gertler, 2007).

Another term for the learning region is 'local innovation system' (Breschi and Lissoni, 2001) or 'local system of innovation' (McCormick and Oyelaran-Oyeyinka, 2007), which includes, like learning regions, the idea of a cluster exhibiting high rates of collaboration, interaction and learning among its firms, supported by formal and informal institutions, leading to a continuously chang-ing knowledge base. Of course, McCormick and Oyelaran-Oyeyinka (2007) also caution that all clusters do not automatically become innovation systems, since this requires tremendous policy support and explicit investments in time and effort in learning.

The role of proximity

Although, as argued earlier, tacit knowledge and low-tech need not associate with one another as a rule-of-thumb, the truth remains that they often *do* go together. Especially in an era where codified information can be disseminated very quickly, tacit and spatially 'sticky'[9] information remain a basis for comparative advantage,[10] which puts proximity at the forefront (Maskell *et al.*, 1998; Maskell, 2001a).[11] In fact, not only small units, but all categories of economic agents tend to use local information when information is 'sticky' (Lüthje *et al.*, 2005). Tacit knowledge has therefore come to be acknowledged as a prime determinant of the geography of innovative activity, since its role in learning through interaction reinforces the local over the global, as much as geography is known to influence tacit knowledge and innovative activity (Howells, 2002; Gertler, 2007).

Maskell (2001b) notes that 'proximate firms undertaking similar activities find themselves in a situation where every difference in the solutions chosen, however small, can be observed and compared' (Maskell, 2001b, p. 928), and that even the most 'subtle, elusive and complex information of possible relevance' (Maskell, 2001b, p. 929) developed in the cluster is watched, discussed and compared, by which small low-tech firms become engaged in the process of continuous learning and innovation. This behaviour is not uncommon, as White (1981) has noted that competition is often in terms of 'observables', where producers *watch* each other. Porter (1990) also stresses the role of this sort of local interaction, explaining how despite the fact that information on technological advances by far-off firms may be instantly accessible, a visible difference between a firm and its co-located rival creates a more direct pressure to catch up (Maskell *et al.*, 1998), a result of 'the combination of competitive pressure, peer pressure and constant comparison' (Porter, 1998, p. 83) – which is particularly acute in low-tech firms. In addition, even if accessible, some information cannot be simply bought from the far-off innovator by virtue of its tacitness, and co-location is a must for keeping up to date (Malmberg and Maskell, 1997; Maskell, 2001a). Hence, the pressure to keep up with the velocity of technological progress in a cluster by means of constantly *watching* one another is very high among low-tech producers.

Maskell (2001b) also notes that it would be immediately noticed if a firm tries to free ride or overuse asymmetric information to cheat, since news about such misbehaviour would pass on to everyone almost instantly. When a firm becomes a local outcast, it is systematically deprived of local interactions and new information. Given that a large part of information that is shared among low-tech units in a cluster is tacit and 'sticky', such ostracising would prove very costly for any firm trying to misbehave.

Whether for seeking information about new technologies or about news regarding someone's misbehaviour, neighbours (or those in the immediate vicinity) often play a principal role. Even at an organisational level, a great deal of organisational behaviour is shaped by activities of other organisations considered to be exemplars (Powell and Smith-Doerr, 1994). Individuals may choose an action, such as the adoption of an innovation or accepting a new production practice, from a set of options conditioned not only by their own past experience but by gathering information from their neighbours (Bala and Goyal, 1998; Goyal, 2007).[12] Numerous studies on agriculture (e.g. Braguinsky and Rose, 2009) have cited neighbours as being principal sources of new information. Griliches (1957), one of the earliest studies on diffusion of new technologies in agricultural communities, discovered that during the process of the diffusion of hybrid corn in the Midwest United States, the influence of neighbours as chief information providers gained significance as the innovation diffused further. During the first phase of diffusion (about three years), 50 per cent of the farmers were convinced by salesmen and about 20 per cent by neighbours; but after this phase the proportions reversed (Chamley, 2004). Foster and Rosenzweig (2000), in a study of the diffusion of high-yield variety techniques in rural India, found that neighbours turned out to be the most important sources of information not only concerning the innovative use of inputs but also as critical information sources. Further, they found that the decisions made by each farmer depended on past decisions by neighbours as well as their own expectations about future planting decisions. Another study by Dasgupta (1989) demonstrated that neighbours, friends and relatives were the most frequent of information sources in the diffusion of agricultural techniques in rural India, more than even official and formal sources such as Village Level Workers. Personal sources, he reports, were used more frequently by his sample, and often even given greater credibility than impersonal sources. Dasgupta found that while the information was first communicated through institutional channels to more cosmopolite agents in the community, it was then distributed to the community at large mainly through interpersonal channels. Ryan and Gross (1943), in another study on hybrid corn diffusion and the predecessor of Griliches (1957), also found that while seed salesmen were reported in their surveys as the most common original sources of information, neighbours emerged as the most influential in deciding whether or not to implement it (Young, 2009). All this evidence is not surprising, since innovation and diffusion are essentially very social processes involving the role of interpersonal channels, face-to-face information exchanges, and the observation of the experiences of one's proximate peers (Rogers, 1995).

The uncertainty surrounding technologies, the increasing intensity of knowledge being person-embodied, and the need for rapid cooperation and decision making only pushes the need for proximity further (Malmberg and Maskell, 1997). Hence, proximity matters, especially for the kind of economic agents that form the focus of this book – small low-tech units surviving on defensive innovation. Hirsch-Kreinsen *et al.* (2003) cite Alfred Marshall as one of the first proponents of the idea that proximity contributes to the rapid development and diffusion of practical knowledge. The skills that are developed by virtue of being in proximity, according to Marshall, become almost common knowledge and develop a 'hereditary' character, often even passed on to subsequent generations.

Almost every study in the literature on innovation and clusters has stressed the need for geographical proximity, successfully refuting notions that information flows are increasingly becoming spatially unbounded and that geography is 'dying' (Breschi and Malerba, 2005). Despite drastic reductions in transport costs and continuous leaps in speed and in the variety of modes of information transfer, face-to-face contact permitted by proximity has remained central to the coordination of the economy, since it is still a highly efficient mode of communication, allowing personalised screening of agents and economic actors to align commitments (Storper and Venables, 2004). It has now become almost a set of stylised facts that (1) interactive collaboration is less costly and smoother the shorter the distance between units (Malmberg and Maskell, 1997); (2) organisational proximity is a prerequisite for collective learning and invention (Hirsch-Kreinsen *et al.*, 2003); and (3) learning by interacting is the natural follow-up of increasing proximity (Hassink, 2007). The arguments in favour of proximity have reinforced the importance of innovative clusters and regions in policy too (Breschi and Malerba, 2005; Gertler, 2007).

Simultaneously, however, it has been cautioned that geographical proximity is only a necessary and not a sufficient condition for efficient information exchange, since social, organisational and cultural proximity, and, most important of all, effective connectedness, are vital for collective learning (Boschma, 2005; Boschma and ter Wal, 2007; Hassink, 2007; McCormick and Oyelaran-Oyeyinka, 2007).

Informal information sharing and the role of networks

Howard White, who had proposed that competition is in terms of 'observables', also propositioned that 'producers watch each other' (White, 1981), analogising with the experience of how, when Roger Bannister broke the four-minute-mile record, other runners immediately attempted to accomplish the same, out of motives based on pure observation of the defined realities and rewards associated with this achievement. Porter (1990) had also proposed 'watching' among producers in terms of the impact it had on local rivalry; i.e. best practices are set by another producer in the vicinity who is incidentally also well known to the observers, creating a much higher pressure to catch up than an achievement by a producer at a distance (Maskell *et al.*, 1998).[13] But competition in terms of observables may manifest itself in a more interesting form when information about best practices and achievements is exchanged by barter among local producers. Information is offered free of charge, but with the obligation of reciprocity, i.e. one is required to produce and freely share information in order to get new information in the future when the need arises (Malmberg and Maskell, 1997; Maskell and Malmberg, 1999; Cowan and Jonard, 2004).

This harks back to the discussion on collective invention earlier in this chapter, evoking ideas of 'informal and cooperative R&D', involving routine and informal trading of information between even direct rivals (von Hippel, 1987, 1988). Informal and cooperative R&D spreads common understandings of innovative processes and products, as well as skills and technical insights (which are technical elements of tacit knowledge) among those agents exchanging information (Figueiredo, 2001). The work of von Hippel has been meticulously articulate in illustrating this phenomenon. The discussion below draws broadly from his 1988 work *The Sources of Innovation*, as well as from von Hippel (1987, 2005, 2007), Lüthje *et al.* (2005), von Hippel and Tyre (2005), and Gault and von Hippel (2009).

Reciprocity is a central component of most informal information sharing. Although information is distributed freely, it may not always be available to everyone and may be restricted to only those who would willingly offer any new information that they may discover or gather in the future. This is not only at a firm level but even between individuals within firms, and between individuals working for rival firms. Another central component, besides reciprocity, is *vitality*. Keeping information secret may offer little comparative advantage in the local agglomeration, and may even, as discussed in an earlier section, bring out the ire of other producers in the form of ostracising the firm that keeps quiet about its new information. This was argued by Mansfield as well: firms 'may not go to any extent to keep information secret, partly because they believe [and know] that secrecy is going to be futile in any event' (Mansfield, 1985, p. 221). This may be, as von Hippel (2005) proposes, the best practical route for an innovator for long-term profit and reputation. Free revealing, say Gault and von Hippel (2009), encourages innovation through private rewards, without public grants of temporary legal monopolies to innovators. This sort of free revealing has been found even in aerospace firms, waferboard manufacturers and many other industries where one may have assumed strict secrecy of information on innovations.[14] Von Hippel cites Allen *et al.* (1983) to demonstrate how product and process innovations stemmed significantly from information sourced from personal contacts in *rival* firms in the same industry.[15]

Despite the fact that free and informal information sharing is pervasive, Powell and Grodal (2005) and Maharajh and Kraemer-Mbula (2010) lament that there have been few studies and scarce empirical research linking informal information sharing to the innovation process. This is probably due to the fact that these activities are not captured by innovation surveys (Gault and von Hippel, 2009), and there is a bias by quantitative survey-based research and policy deliberations towards innovation processes involving formal scientific and technical information, as well as formal R&D (Jensen *et al.*, 2007; Maharajh and Kraemer-Mbula, 2010). It may not actually be the case that studies are numerically few, as seen in the abundance of evidence and conceptual discussion on defensive innovation and collective innovation shown across this chapter. Powell and Grodal may be referring to the fact (suggested also by Jensen *et al.* (2007) and Maharajh and Kraemer-Mbula (2010)) that attention given to free information sharing in the literature is disproportionate to its occurrence relative to the attention given to formal R&D and formal methods of diffusion of information, such as foreign direct investment and the practice of information secrecy, to its occurrence.

Pavitt (2005) suggests that informal links and information sharing stemming from these linkages deserve greater attention, since informal ties, intentionally or incidentally, can 'undergrid formal ties', and have the potential to significantly contribute to innovation at large (Powell and Grodal, 2005, p. 71). Informal links can also result in 'formal outputs that can in turn trigger more informal contacts' (Pavitt, 2005, p. 94). This may be seen in Figueiredo (2001), who illustrates the free revealing of information and sharing of technical experiences during technical training between Japanese and Brazilian engineers in the 1960s and 1970s in the construction and operations phase of the Brazilian steel company USIMINAS: 'a large group of Japanese were at USIMIAS, where they shared their tacit knowledge to the extent that it was almost squeezed out of them, as the Brazilians were determined to learn how to solve intricate problems' (Figueiredo, 2001, p. 100). This interaction during these meetings not only increased the frequency of the meetings from monthly to weekly; it also gave rise to an 'informal communication system' with established informal network linkages.[16]

Hence, there is overwhelming evidence for the fact that a great deal of information is passed and exchanged through face-to-face personalised contact in a local setting (as opposed to being transmitted over large distances). According to Cowan (2004), space matters for information diffusion, geographical or social, of which social space may be understood best in the context of *networks*.

Agents acquire new information and learn more through their networks than through codified sources such as databases and files, due to which 'whom you know' has a significant bearing on 'what you know' – this being one of the most consistent findings in social science (Cross *et al.*, 2003, p. 8). Cross and colleagues (2003) continue to explain that to improve information flow, knowledge on 'whom one knows' can help identify problematic points that are restricting the dissemination of information (or even the key to success of a particular region such as Silicon Valley). Studying the key to success in Silicon Valley, says Swedberg (2003), cannot be found by investigating single successful firms but by studying the *networks* that are made up by actors from various sectors that participate in the success of the region. Mere clustering and geographical proximity, even if backed by cultural and organisational proximity, is only a necessary condition and may not guarantee a constant flow of new information until and unless there is efficient and strategic *networking*. The nature of a unit's networks directs its business, mitigates market failure, and of course influences the quality and variety of the information it sources (Sorenson, 2005). To fully understand the history and development of a cluster, investigating the networks of that cluster – the manner in which they stitch the community together, the dependencies they create, the channels of information flow they carve, and so on – is critical (Porter *et al.*, 2005). Especially for low-tech producers, networking becomes a lifeline for survival and endurance.

Social network analysis has produced a rich array of analytic concepts and powerful methods for studying the structural features of economic action (Vedres and Stark, 2010). The network perspective allows us to address questions about economic (and other) systems that exhibit interdependent organisation (Brandes *et al.*, 2013). This sort of approach allows for a deeper understanding of almost all that has been discussed hitherto in this chapter – defensive innovation, collective learning, learning regions and informal information sharing. Until network analysis gained prominence in the mainstream, attempts at understanding the individual, or even a collective, were characterised by a disregard for the underyling interaction structure, i.e. the network structure. This myopic understanding of a collective by mainstream empirical social science research has been reflected upon by Freeman (2004), who cites Allen Barton in likening the study of a set of individuals in a sample survey – torn away from their social context and interaction paths – as a 'sociological meatgrinder' (Freeman, 2004):

> For the last thirty years, empirical social research has been dominated by the sample survey. But as usually practiced, using random sampling of individuals, the survey is a sociological meatgrinder, tearing the individual from his social context and guaranteeing that nobody in the study interacts with anyone else in it. It is a little like a biologist putting his experimental animals through a hamburger machine and looking at every hundredth cell through a microscope; anatomy and physiology get lost, structure and function disappear, and one is left with cell biology ... if our aim is to understand people's behaviour rather than simply to record it, we want to know about primary groups, neighbourhoods, organisations, social circles, and communities about interaction, communication, role expectations, and social control – Allen Barton, 1968.
>
> (Freeman, 2004, p. 1)

Social interaction among economic agents through their networks has a clear functional aspect in shaping innovation choices, since the adoption of an innovation by an economic agent often depends on whether those with whom he or she interacts have adopted it; this necessitates a careful look at how interaction patterns between people shape individual choice and innovation (Goyal, 2007). This was also recognised by Allen *et al.* (1983), who said that networks in many industries were developed for the sole purpose of disseminating information. If broadcasting information to 'those you know', 'those you trust' and 'those who are guaranteed to reciprocate' is a vital process of an economy's existence and growth, the structure of the networks that form the economy become vital for performance (Cowan and Jonard, 2003).

Bougrain and Haudeville (2002) describe three major ways in which networks are fundamental to the operation and success of small firms.

1 First, since *information* is the axis around which competition among small units revolves, its complexity becomes a concern for small units due to their disadvantaged position in their ability to gather new information and interpret it to their advantage. Networks allow small units to decode and appropriate large flows of information, since they provide openings to technical assistance and the observation of strategic choices made by peers.

2   Second, and as we have visited earlier in this chapter, personal networks assist in the transfer of *tacit knowledge*; knowing 'who holds the information' is decisive in tough economic situations. 'Members of networks "provide the know-why, know-how, know-when, and know-what necessary for entrepreneurial success" (Malecki and Tootle, 1996, p. 45)' (Bougrain and Haudeville, 2002, p. 739).

3   Third, *uncertainty* being a characteristic of innovation (and thereby making resource allocation all the more risky), there exists a risk of irreversibility of a commitment. This is accentuated by the fact that in many sectors product life cycles are short and technological changes are rapid. Formal and informal networks help small units reduce the uncertainties and costs of irreversible decisions and resource allocations, by having access to new information and to more experienced actors in the arena.

Ceci and Iubatti (2012) also describe, in the same vein, how diffusion of information is enabled by personal relationships, where trust, shared values and mutual objectives buttress potentially risky ventures on innovation adoption.[17]

Networks, in principle, play a central role in the diffusion of tacit knowledge. While codified knowledge can be diffused globally and impersonally, the diffusion of tacit knowledge, especially if broadcast over a small space and over a few selected recipients, is heavily dependent on the structure of and relations within networks, especially localised informal information networks (Cowan and Miller, 1998; Cowan and Jonard, 2003; Cowan, 2004). We know that individuals may adopt innovations or accept new production practices based not only on their own past experience but also by gathering information from those with whom they interact frequently – often neighbours – which on an aggregate shapes innovation and learning in the region (Bala and Goyal, 1998; Goyal, 2007). Networks may even restrict where firms locate and cluster, since it is through network links that entrant firms mobilise and obtain access to tacit knowledge, and financial and human capital (Sorenson, 2005). It may therefore be proposed that (spontaneous) clustering and interactive learning is essentially an emergent property of network structure and relations, especially where agents prefer learning through networks than through codified sources. Network structure provides opportunities (or even constraints) for agents to develop alliances with each other, which, importantly, are amenable to quick transformations and adjustments from time to time; a flexibility that has important behavioural and performance implications (Gulati, 1998). Economic exchanges very often end up riding on interpersonal networks, replacing contractual agreements and hierarchical dictates, as a great deal of information on administrative and technological innovations flows through professional networks among individual professionals and networked organisations, expanding both formal cooperative ventures as well as informal collaborative networks for the future (Powell and Smith-Doerr, 1994). Evidently, networks differ across industries and sectors (thus across knowledge, technology and production space), evolve through time as a result of changing technology, firm and industry characteristics, and reflect the underlying social norms and institutional factors (Malerba and Vonortas, 2009).

We began this chapter by understanding collective learning and defensive innovation, realising that these were common strategies for informal information sharing, learning and innovation. We proceeded to study the role of clusters and proximity in informal information sharing, and finally the role of networks. This forms the conceptual backing to the first objective of this book: to understand intra-cluster interaction channels and dynamics for information sharing among producers in low-tech clusters surviving on defensive innovation. How this is based on social norms and factors, central not only to innovation and learning but also to economic behaviour in general, requires a review of the next family of literature. The discussion that follows engages in a broad debate on the theme of economic relations among agents arising as an emergent property of their underlying social relations.

Economic relations within social relations

The central exercise in this book is to study information sharing by means of informal interaction among economic actors in low-tech settings where social relations steer production relations. The idea that social relations shape business and production relations between economic agents is not new, and rich strands of literature in economic-sociology, management studies, and especially in network analysis, have been devoted to it. The nature of knowledge in an environment where business and information networks are deeply influenced and overlapped by social structures and community relations is essentially tacit, and the valuation of the sharing of information is often contingent on the social identity of the economic agents exchanging it, as work by Brian Uzzi, among others, has illustrated in detail. Hence, production and exchange relations cannot be treated as peripheral to social relations, since they may even develop as emergent properties of these social relations. The social-relational context becomes the social 'architecture' in which even knowing occurs, rendering learning and knowing as both individual and *social* phenomena, or essentially social and cultural processes that are sensitive to social and cultural conditions (Rooney and Schneider, 2005). And since learning is a social phenomenon, innovation also becomes a socially interactive process (Cooke, 2002). Engaging with these themes are three economic-sociology concepts that form conceptual pillars for the rest of this book. These three concepts are social capital, embeddedness and homophily.

Social capital

It has been strongly argued across the social sciences over many decades that the individual economic agent is not detached from his or her social environment but *shaped* by it, and contributes to shaping it in turn. Social relationships enter every stage of the process, from the selection of economic goals to the organisation of relevant means, tying economic agents in a 'multiplex' manner (Portes, 1995, pp. 3, 10). The structure of social relationships determines an agent's choices of trading partners and their interactions (DiMaggio and Louch, 1998, p. 620). In addition, despite the expanding breadth of firms' multinational bases, local geographical factors (and hence local communities) have continued to influence the formation of functional communities for economic agents (Laumann *et al.*, 1978). Social influences in economic behaviour are no more perceived as 'frictional drags' (Grabher, 1993a), since they drive individuals to support and depend on their *social connections* for economic exchanges. These connections and the exchanges entailing them may appear suboptimal, but they often emerge as assets in their own right, assets termed 'social capital' (Burt, 1997a).

Esser (2008) lists David Hume as a proponent of the idea that society, above all, provides the individual with resources that help him overcome economic problems (Esser, 2008, p. 47). But Castiglione and colleagues (2008), prompted by Robert Putnam, cite Lyda Hanifan as the first user of the term 'social capital' in its modern meaning, having identified it with 'the building up of social connections and sociability ... "good will, fellowship, sympathy, and social intercourse"' (Castiglione *et al.*, 2008, p. 2). Castiglione and colleagues (2008) also list James Coleman and Pierre Bourdieu as the first to (independently) systematise the concept, giving it formalised theoretical definitions. Woolcock (1998) and Woolcock and Narayan (2000), on the other hand, credit the pioneering development of this concept to a whole body of contributors, including Lyda Hanifan, Jane Jacobs, Pierre Bourdieu, Jean-Claude Passeron and Glenn Loury, besides James Coleman, Ronald Burt, Robert Putnam and Alejandro Portes.

Akçomak (2009, p. 21) lists several definitions of social capital, including Burt: 'friends, colleagues, and more general contacts through whom you receive opportunities to use your financial and human capital'; Lin: 'investment in social relations by individuals through which they gain access to embedded resources to enhance expected returns of instrumental and expressive actions'; and Bourdieu:

> the aggregate of the actual or potential resources which are linked to possession of a durable network or more less institutionalised relationship of mutual acquaintance and recognition – or in other words, to membership in a group – which provides each of its members with the backing of the collectively owned capital, a 'credential' which entitles them to credit, in the various senses of the word.

Woolcock (1998) defined social capital as a 'broad term encompassing the norms and networks facilitating collective action for mutual benefit'. He argues that one would expect communities blessed with high social capital to be:

> safer, cleaner, wealthier, more literate, better governed, and generally 'happier' than those with low stocks, because their members are able to find

and keep good jobs, initiate projects serving public interests, costlessly monitor one another's behavior, enforce contractual agreements, use existing resources more efficiently, resolve disputes more amicably, and respond to citizens' concerns more promptly.

(Woolcock, 1998, p. 155)

Portes (1998) reviews the origins and definitions by Bourdieu, Loury and Coleman, among others, illustrating how Bourdieu's definition clarifies social capital as divisible into two elements: 'first, the social relationship itself that allows individuals to claim access to resources possessed by their associates, and second, the amount and quality of those resources' (Portes, 1998, p. 4). Portes also explains how, despite the many differences in the way social capital is defined and dissected, there is a consensus that it 'stands for the ability of actors to secure benefits by virtue of membership in social networks or other social structures' (Portes, 1998, p. 6). Dasgupta (2005), concurrently, takes social capital to mean, simply, 'interpersonal networks'; the advantage of this notion being that it does not 'prejudge the asset's quality' and recognises that networks can 'remain inactive or be put to use in socially destructive ways', and that the determinant of their quality is the use to which it is put by members (Dasgupta 2005, p. S10). Hence, the 'capital' in social capital by itself does not yield any results unless it rides on an effective network: 'social capital does not bind or bridge ... it is the nature of the social *networks* that bind, bond or bridge' (Lin, 2008, p. 62, emphasis added).

The network perspective – holistic, structuralist and interdisciplinary in approach – is crucial to the study of social capital, since agents are purposeful, and their motivations, opportunity sets and restrictions are influenced by the network in which they reside (Portes, 1995; García, 2006); so much so that Lin (2008) labels social capital a 'network-based' concept.

But at the same time, the literature has cautioned not to *equate* social capital with social networks, i.e. social networks are necessary for the acquisition, evolution and utilisation of social capital, but are still not sufficient: 'resources by themselves are *not* social capital; the concept refers instead to the individual's ability to mobilise them on demand' (Portes, 1995, p. 12, emphasis in original). Agents' actions are what make the capital, made available by the network, effective (Akçomak, 2009). Hence, the effectiveness of the network that social capital rides on is a source of opportunity and the point where it differs from human capital. In other words, while human capital refers to *individual ability*, social capital refers to *opportunity*, due to which agents with more social capital, positioned to identify and develop more rewarding opportunities, achieve higher returns on their human capital (Vonortas, 2009). In addition, unlike economic capital, social capital depletes if restricted or not used; hence a state of 'equilibrium' in social capital poses a threatening precondition for redundancy and stagnation (Pillay, 2005).

Social capital has strong implications for economic and innovative behaviour. It has been argued that personal-based relationships are central and have superior potential for innovation, with diffusion of innovation allowing for exploiting a large variety of relationships through multiple interpersonal network dimensions (Ceci and Iubatti, 2012). For example, Cooke (2002) describes how social capital emphasises collaboration in competition, where firms benefit from interacting and learning at negligible financial cost; through social capital, businesses also gain scale advantages. Irawati and Rutten (2012) also demonstrate, using the case of the automotive industry in western Java, that some regions and industries perform better than others in terms of learning and innovation simply on account of differences in social capital (though the mechanisms of operation of social capital works vary across different industries and regions). Adam and Westlund (2012) compile a series of studies that argue for the role of social capital in innovation processes at all spatial levels of innovation – from single inventing units to large transnational corporations – through social networks, norms and values, trust, cooperation, etc.

Sources, forms and public good nature

According to Portes and Sensenbrenner (1993), the first of four sources of socially oriented economic action, and of social capital, is *value introjection*, as it prompts individuals to deviate from greed and self-interest, the resulting behaviour and choices becoming appropriable by the collective as a resource. The second is from *reciprocity transactions*, involving the accumulation of 'chits' based on good deeds to others in the past – these deeds encompassing a vast variety of primary transactions of social intangibles like favours, information, approval and so on. The third is *bounded solidarity*, focusing on those circumstances leading to the emergence of principled group-oriented behaviour, which precedes early value introjections. The fourth source is *enforceable trust*, stemming not from sentiments of solidarity due to outward confrontation, but from the social community's internal sanctioning capability. Lin (2008) identifies three sources of social capital: *structural position* (an agent's position in the social hierarchy, i.e. the 'strength of position' proposition), *network locations* (an agent's location in the network, considering closure, openness, bridging, etc., i.e. the 'strength of tie' proposition), and *purposes of action* (for maintaining solidarity, social cohesion and well-being). Woolcock (1998) argues that by virtue of the fact that the sources of social capital may shift over time as transactions increase or decrease in their complexity, there may be different types of social capital, and that collectively they form resources not to be maximised but optimised. Esser (2008) explains two such kinds of social capital. *Relational social capital*, about an agent's personal resource, includes all benefits as a result of direct or indirect relations with other agents. Its value is contingent upon prior investments dedicated to it, due to which it shares many characteristics with human and physical capital investment decisions, including calculations of costs of building and maintaining relations with other actors. *Systemic social capital*, on the other hand, is about the links or relations between actors and not the individual actors themselves, and is not contingent upon individual efforts.[18]

Social capital assumes a public good character and brings along with it the consequent problems associated with public goods. Coleman, one of the chief contributors to the systemic theorisation of social capital, explains how social capital has a distinct public good character unlike human and physical capital (Coleman, 1988). He illustrates how, in many cases, agents in a network who generate social capital manage to capture only a fraction of its benefits, which leads to both free-riding by some and consequent underinvestment by others. Hence, Coleman proposes, most forms of social capital emerge not out of direct action but as by-products of routine activities.[19]

Role of the ethnic environment, and of norms and obligations

When discussing the role of social relations in carving economic relations, we must bear in mind that social capital resides not only within the family but with the entire community, its structure of relations, its institutions, and the relationships the individuals' family maintain with all of these elements (Coleman, 1988). Hence the quality of the ethnic environment in which the parents make their investment is as crucial as the inputs they give to their children (Borjas (1992) provides empirical evidence for this). Coleman's (1988) observation of the Jewish community's involvement in the New York wholesale diamond market shows that 'close ties, through family, community, and religious affiliation, provide the insurance that is necessary to facilitate the transactions in the market' (Coleman, 1988, p. S99), implying, according to Borjas (1992), that it is the culture as a whole in which the agent is raised that shapes his opportunity set and has consequences for behaviour, human capital formation and labour market outcomes – 'skills and labour market outcomes of today's generation depend not only on the skills and labour market experiences of their parents, but also on the average skills and labour market experiences of the ethnic group in the parent's generation' (Borjas, 1992, p. 148). Informal resources available in ethnic communities, a significant category of them falling under 'cultural values' (based heavily on solidarity, communication, monitoring and enforceable trust within the community), are transferred to offspring in abundance many a time, even if only to see them survive and be preserved (Dasgupta, 2005). Even long-established network links shaped along ethnic lines are preserved across generations, which causes them to remain multipurpose, dense and resilient, ruling out any entry or exit (Wintrobe, 1995) and reinforcing their internal economic linkages. Agents are therefore 'locked in' from birth (Dasgupta, 2005, p. S12) and the opportunity cost of making new linkages is high given that old links are inherited, ingrained and based on strong kinship values, which are difficult to sever if inconvenient. Viewed in this respect, 'nodes' and 'ties' in a social network become not simply dots and lines, but the slowly solidified results of historical processes, which include iterated production rules and communication protocols in interactions (Padgett and Powell, 2012, p. 3).

Most studies on these kinds of links draw insights from research on immigrant communities, since they represent 'some of the clearest examples of the bearing contextual factors can have on individual economic action' (Portes and Sensenbrenner, 1993, p. 1322). Studies on immigrant communities and ethnic enclaves[20] (e.g. Aldrich and Waldinger, 1990; Portes, 1995; Fong and Isajiw, 2000) demonstrate how the networks of kinship and friendship within and around ethnic communities have immense influence on their economic and social outcomes and well-being, and how ethnic entrepreneurs manipulate family and communal perseverance and loyalty to their own advantage, but also incur obligations in doing so (Aldrich and Waldinger, 1990, p. 130). Residential clustering builds up a local ethnic market with a 'co-ethnic clientele' (Aldrich and Waldinger, 1990, p. 123), even if not in complete segregation (Fong and Isajiw, 2000).

Cohesiveness and structural holes

One important stimulator of social capital is said to be social cohesion (Coleman, 1988). Cohesiveness permits a shared culture and strong collective identity, necessary for loyalty and long-term stability (Perry, 1999). Cohesively tied actors are said to emulate each other's behaviour, aware of the capacity of social ties as vehicles to carry information, which diminish uncertainty and promote trust (Gulati, 1998). But the literature on cohesion abounds with warnings about its detrimental effects. Burt (1992) points out that cohesion may be a source of rigidity, and may not assist an agent in flexible adaptation to changes in his economic or social environment. In fact, a firm's organisational inertia may not be due to its internal or intrinsic failings, but to its position in a cohesive and rigid network (Walker *et al.*, 1997). Since cohesive contacts are likely to have similar information, redundancy in information benefits is very likely (Burt, 1997a). Strong ties may abrogate alienation but breed cohesion; weak ties hence become indispensable to individuals' opportunities (Granovetter, 1973).

What may therefore be more effective than cohesiveness is the strategic capture of *sparse regions* or *structural holes* (Burt, 1992) in networks, and gainfully exploiting weak links (Granovetter, 1973). Network positions associated with the highest economic returns lie not in densely connected regions but in sparse regions that provide opportunities for brokering information flows and creating the potential for arbitrage (Burt, 1992; Walker *et al.*, 1997).[21] Connections between two agents (or two groups of agents) on either side of the structural hole allow for new information flow as well as operational flexibility in times of change (Burt, 1997a, 1997b; Gargiulo and Benassi, 2000). Agents benefit with regard to social capital by bridging structural holes for personal contacts, discussions and unofficial information flow channels (Burt, 1997b). Cohesion may certainly appear 'safe' – dense and tightly coupled networks guarantee safety, especially when every agent knows every other agent (Perry, 1999) – but safety may not always be the correct strategy while accessing new information. Greater variability in skills, outlooks and capacities, which make for greater innovation opportunities, is lower in tightly coupled networks (Perry, 1999, p. 17). Hence, the more structural holes spanned, the richer the information benefits of the network (Burt, 1997a, p. 341).[22] The agent's role in a fluid task environment, therefore, is to make the right balance or trade-off between rigidity through cohesiveness and flexibility by bridging structural holes, in the manner of a 'tightrope walker' (Gargiulo and Benassi, 2000, p. 194). Highly dense networks with a fair share of weak ties linking them with other networks benefit with the highest level of social capital (García, 2006).

Woolcock and Narayan (2000) seem to have netted the debate by calling social capital a 'double-edged sword', as it provides both a valuable range of services for the networked agents, but also entails a number of costs in terms of obligation and commitment that may overpower economic concerns. Hence, they suggest, both intra-community ties and weak extra-community links are essential to capture the full efficacy of social capital.

Social capital is both a concept as well as a theory, the body of literature dedicated to it spanning a broad spectrum of disciplines, definitions and applications.[23] It is now understood to embrace almost everything, 'ranging from neighbourly help to the civil morality of a globalised world' (Esser, 2008, p. 2). Due to its breadth and by virtue of its large variety of applications and definitions, it has been treated as a 'catch-all term encompassing all social explanations to various socio-economic phenomena' (Akçomak, 2009, p. 18). Lin (2008) even warns about the continuance of social capital as a rigorous concept and theory due to the multiplicity of definitions, conceptualisations and empirical measurements. However, social capital's success as a framework, theory and concept, and the tools that its underpinnings and components provide, are what have prompted a vast literature to be built up around its basis of conceptual multiplicity, and what provide this study, too, to lay it as a foundation for the next two conceptual pillars: embeddedness and homophily.

Embeddedness and homophily

In social networks, the driving forces of economic exchange are neither entirely selfish nor entirely cooperative, neither rational nor irrational, but essentially an emergent property of the social structure in which the economic agents are embedded (Uzzi, 1997). Rogers, in his *Diffusion of Innovations*, had also proposed that the ability of an economic agent to learn or innovate has been found to be affected not only by individual character but also by the nature of the social system of which the agent is a member. That is, economic relations may be, in most cases, *embedded* in social relations.

Embeddedness stands for making choices in a complex environment, since decision making is the result of a multitude of factors, rooted in a variety of settings, and never just a question of simple cost–benefit analysis (Dankbaar, 2004). It implies that 'behaviour and institutions to be analysed are so constrained by ongoing social relations that to construe them as independent is a grievous misunderstanding' (Granovetter, 1985, p. 482), and that 'economic transactions of the most diverse sorts are inserted in overarching social structures that affect their form and their outcomes' (Portes, 1995, p. 6) Social relations increase the credibility of the information shared between agents (especially if fine-grained) and imbue qualities within that information which are beyond immediate perception (Uzzi, 1996). Embeddedness as a concept is based on the same notions as social capital: the unatomised nature of the individual, the weakness of the 'immediate utility' approach in explaining social relations, the logics underlying the formation of institutions and norms, and the fact that these cannot be removed from the social, cultural and cognitive contexts and identities in which they are implanted (Boschma, 2005; Ghezzi and Mingione, 2007). In most low-tech rural and traditional industries, the information shared being mostly uncodified, it becomes imperative that new know-how is sourced chiefly through close social ties; these, over time, overpower even formal (and sometimes cost-free) sources of information such as visual or print media. That is, people may prefer to gather information through their social ties even if it is available free through formal sources (Uzzi and Lancaster, 2003), since social ties have the added advantage of shaping expectations and opportunities that are almost impossible in purely market-based exchanges (Uzzi, 1996, 1997) or through formal sources. In low-tech clusters in developing regions, knowledge networks cannot stand alone, and are embedded in business or social networks (Gebreyeesus and Mohnen, 2013). Social ties dictate individual behaviour so significantly that once the individual's social class and sector are known, everything else may even become automatic due to socialisation (Granovetter, 1985).

Hence, as Woolcock (1998) pointed out, Granovetter's view on embeddedness inclined towards the idea that all economic action was enmeshed in social relations of one configuration or another, and that development brings about a change in the *kind*, and not the *degree*, of embeddedness. Agents may even embed their production and information activities *wholly* in their social groups as a survival strategy, if ethnic barriers are impenetrable, and if strengthening traditional institutions is as much a priority as maintaining the quality of information exchanged (Schnell and Sofer, 2002).

It was Karl Polanyi who first brought forth the idea of social embeddedness in its present understanding. Polanyi (1944, 1957) argued that tacit knowledge is deeply embedded in specific contexts where potential economic exchange partners need to familiarise with each other, or have a common background acquired through socialisation, which is achieved through face-to-face meetings (Storper and Venables, 2004). When economic actions are disembedded from social actions and social structure, the results could be disastrous, and if economy decided society it could lead to tumult and turbulence, which is, as Swedberg (2003) argues, the central problem with capitalism. Polanyi recommended that the economy must therefore be *re-embedded* within the social system. This called for a new paradigm among economists as well as sociologists to keep the social as central to the economic. Economic action by an economic agent had to be perceived as socially oriented, as it could be governed by value introjection, was dependent upon the opinion of others around the agent, and could build up reciprocity expectations through social interactions that constrained the pursuit of gain and profit (Portes, 1995). The economic agent has the ability to affect the incentive structure he or she faces by engaging in social interactions, and at times has the incentive to even act against his or her economic self-interest for the purpose of conforming to the social norms and values ingrained within; investigating community character hence emerges as being as important as investigating individual agent behaviour (Akçomak, 2009).

Weber (1978/1922), as well as Durkheim, conceived of the economic agent, and the individual as such, as not utilitarian and atomised but as 'inserted in diversified networks and institutional contexts, the very subject matter of socio-logical analysis' (Ghezzi and Mingione, 2007, p. 14). More recently, Granovet-ter has also been a significant proponent of this view, his 1985 work having been cited by almost the entire literature on embeddedness ever since. Works by Uzzi have also contributed very significantly in formalising this concept and expand-ing its theoretical underpinnings. Uzzi (1997) has described how embedded rela-tionships comprise three major components regulating exchange partners' present behaviour and future expectations – trust, fine-grained information transfer and joint problem-solving arrangements – components that can be inves-tigated independently, but connected by a common strand by virtue of being ele-ments of social structure. In addition, like 'solidarity', 'embeddedness' is a multidimensional construct relating generally to the importance of social net-works for action (Moody and White, 2003). The concept of embeddedness, as Krippner (2001) reviews, hence 'enjoys a privileged – and as of yet, largely unchallenged position as the central organizing principle of economic sociology' (Krippner, 2001, p. 775).[24] This is echoed by Woolcock and Narayan (2000), who credit embeddedness as the most influential concept to emerge from economic-sociology, and also by Hass (2007), who terms it the central idea of economic-sociology.

But, at the same time, Krippner (2001) as well as Moody and White (2003) warn that one must not over-socialise the economic agent into being a 'socially automated' being, lest one commits the sociological version of 'over-atomising' and 'rationalising' the agent. Grabher (1993a) warns about another common slip of reducing embeddedness to 'dyadic reductionism' (p. 4), since embeddedness may appear at first a demonstration of how economic action and outcomes are affected by actors' dyadic relations, but actually and more holistically refers to structural aspects of the influence of overall networks of relations.

Embeddedness has been classified broadly on relational and structural terms (Zukin and DiMaggio, 1990; Gulati, 1998; Rowley *et al.*, 2000). Zukin and DiMaggio (1990), for instance, disentangle embeddedness into four forms:

1 *Structural*: concerning how the relational quality of information exchanges and network architecture of material exchange relationships influence eco-nomic activity.
2 *Cognitive*: concerning structured mental processes that direct economic logic.
3 *Cultural*: concerning shared beliefs and values that shape economic aims.
4 *Political*: concerning institutional limits on economic power and incentives.

There are also extremes: quite simply, 'under'- and 'over'-embeddedness. While 'under-embeddedness' characterises those agents failing to exploit their external networks into economic advantage, 'over-embeddedness' characterises those agents whose commitments to their associated community or social groups disallow them from accessing and exploiting opportunities in the external markets (Schnell and Sofer, 2002, p. 55). Grabher (1993a) is of the opinion that too little (i.e. under-embeddedness) may deprive an agent of the supportive tissue of social practices and institutions; while too much (over-embeddedness) may lead to a slow decay of this supportive tissue.

Discussion and empirical evidence

Embeddedness is prevalent at all technological levels, low-tech or high-tech, since exchange and other transactions take place across the entire firm, and at every level there are networks of personal relations (Granovetter, 1985). Embeddedness is prevalent in exchange relationships of information as well as of commodities, but as Masciarelli and colleagues (2010) empirically show, it persists more in the former: 'whereas for the internationalization of goods, firms that invest more in research and development (R&D) do not seem to suffer negative consequences of embeddedness, for the internationalization of knowledge, the negative effects of over-embeddedness tend to persist' (Masciarelli *et al.*, 2010, p. 3).

Firms often wish to be socially embedded to tap its many benefits. The logic of opportunism is shifted towards the logic of trustful cooperative behaviour (Uzzi and Lancaster, 2003), which reduces uncertainty and creates opportunities for exchange that price alone would not be able to enforce contractually (Uzzi, 1996). Since sourcing new information in most cases carries a cost, firms would not wish to spend resources in information search and building rapport but would rather spend money and time in repeated transactions with familiar partners. DiMaggio and Louch (1998) propose the hypotheses that the greater the uncertainty regarding the quality of a good or service, the greater the likelihood of within-network exchanges, and the greater the agent's preference for transacting with a socially connected partner. While this would result in fewer contacts, these contacts would be more worthwhile to maintain relationships with (Uzzi and Lancaster, 2003). When this behaviour is aggregated towards the network as a whole, decision making quickens, organisational learning enhances and monitoring costs reduce, offering economies of time (Uzzi, 1996, 1997). These and other findings on the manner in which social embeddedness favourably shapes economic outcomes and organisational behaviour are based on Uzzi's (1997) ethnographic work on the garment manufacturing industry in New York. His study proposes that the greater the level of embeddedness, the greater these economies of time. Search for information, while increasing with arm's length ties, also intensifies by depth in embedded ties (Uzzi, 1997, p. 51). In an industry such as apparel manufacturing where consumer preferences and competition experience frequent and erratic change, Uzzi shows how embeddedness offers many such advantages that price alone as an indicator would not, and how eventually an embedded network organisation would dominate a merely competition-based process. Burt (1992) also summarises the benefits of network embeddedness: namely access, timing and referrals. Access refers to information about current and potential partners regarding their assets, capabilities and trust-worthiness; timing refers to having the information at the right time; and refer-rals apply to information, passed through indirect links, about other organisations with which the firm has not had direct contact and about market or technological developments of interest (Vonortas, 2009). A study of embeddedness also allows us to distinguish between exploitative and explorative search among ties. It has been suggested that *explorative* learning is more likely through embedded ties, while arm's length ties may actually inhibit exploration and tend to transfer public knowledge by stimulating *exploitative* learning (Uzzi and Lancaster, 2003, pp. 393, 397).

Embeddedness generates a standard of expected behaviour that bypasses the need for policing (Granovetter, 1985), since unethical behaviour would result in one's reputation being tarnished among other close-knit members – information on bad behaviour passing rapidly through the network – and probably even result in ostracising of sorts where other firms may stop trusting the deviant firm and exclude it from exchange dyads.[25]

To study embeddedness and its effects, Uzzi (1996) suggests an ethnographic approach, since it is said to enable a researcher to understand in depth the causes, consequences and mechanisms, as well as to generate testable hypotheses. The emphasis by the literature on the importance of direct personal contact and per-sonalised ties among clustered agents, and the recognition that knowledge is embedded in people and that knowledge processes are 'people processes' (Dank-baar, 2004, p. 697) also prompts a qualitative enquiry on the nature of face-to-face encounters and collective experiences in knowledge processes in the same geographical environment. Ghezzi and Mingione (2007) advocate a network analysis approach complemented by a path-dependency analysis.

The concept of embeddedness has also been applied to the research on innovation and learning. For instance, Baba and Walsh (2010) have demon-strated the central role of embeddedness in their study of interactive learning between developer and evaluator in the context of performance in breakthrough innovations in the drug industry. They argue that the formation of embedded net-works leads members not only to share sophisticated scientific information and know-how, but also to form high degrees of mutual trust which makes it possible to assess the risks of applying new information to innovation. This, they argue, is especially the case for innovations that are (1) new to the world, (2) of uncer-tain benefit, and (3) with the potential for serious risks. Gebreyeesus and Mohnen (2013) have studied the characteristics of innovation in the Mercato footwear cluster in Ethiopia, looking at micro-level learning process, examining major channels through which small producers in these clusters obtain new knowledge, and the impact of network embeddedness on their innovation per-formance. In fact, they have found that the business networks in these clusters, founded to a large extent on social links, also double as knowledge networks.

Embeddedness hence emerges as an ideal framework for understanding information sharing and innovation, and is an important precondition for high-level performance (Andersen, 2013).

Ties that stifle and blind

As in the case of social capital, one of the most important findings in the embeddedness literature is that its advantages decrease over the long term. Khalaf and Shwayri (1966) argue that as community and family are often deeply rooted in individual behaviour, especially in developing regions, this has had a dramatic effect on economic life in these regions and, for the most part, with positive outcomes. But at the same time a whole body of studies, discussed below, argues that these benefits may hold only up to a certain limit, after which over-embeddedness backfires, as it cuts agents, or groups of agents, off from sources of information outside the established network which would in all probability offer fresh opportunities and innovations. Benefits through an agent's partners in an embedded network would over time appear redundant, since the group's resource pooling would begin to become obsolete, i.e. the same old ideas would float in the embedded network even when the rest of the industry outside the network has moved on to more profitable and advanced forms of organisation and production (Uzzi, 1996, 1997). Over-embeddedness prevents search outside the network, as reciprocal loyalties and obligations with local partners take precedence over 'looking at the larger picture', severely affecting the exchange of information (Masciarelli *et al.*, 2010). Ties that bind become 'ties that blind' (Grabher, 1993b, p. 24).

Agents become locked in due to over-dependence on a closed social system, affirmed by Duysters and Lemmens (2003) in their study of the global microelectronics industry from 1970 to 2000. They confirm the presence of 'relational inertia' and 'strategic gridlock', paralysing firms' abilities to move to new windows of opportunities, and decreasing their opportunities for learning and innovation. This has been found even in industries with ethnicity defined boundaries, such as the Israeli-Arab industries in Israel, where there is an over-embeddedness of Israeli-Arab firms in their local milieu due to kinship support structures taking primacy over innovation, and the obstruction of even minor organisational changes (Schnell and Sofer, 2002). Since most of these firms commenced with the support of kin, a culture of indebtedness set in, offering not only 'safety' and 'security' but also fuelling a political motivation to develop their autonomous economy.

Naturally, exogenous shocks destabilise industry performance when embeddedness acts beyond a threshold limit (Uzzi, 1997). Two studies that provide examples of industries falling behind on account of stifling ties and network rigidities are the watch industry in Switzerland in the 1970s (Glasmeier, 1991) and the Ruhr region in Germany in the early 1980s (Grabher, 1993b). Subsequent to the arrival of influential innovations in the watch industry (electronic, digital and quartz watches), the Swiss watch industry entered a dilemma, and the dominance of the Jura region in Switzerland foundered. Glasmeier focused specifically on the network production systems of this industry to explain the decline from its position in the early twentieth century. He observed that the coordinating organisations in this industry had become too absorbed into the regional fabric over time, and flexibility to industrial shocks had reduced:

> the tightly articulated network surrounding watch manufacturing strength-ened the status quo ... regional institutions [such as educational-, banking-, and machine-tool-making institutions] were interwoven into the fabric of the industry ... the complicated web of watch manufacturing permeated the core of the region's social, political and economic institutions.
>
> (Glasmeier, 1991, p. 478)

Cartels formed in the late 1920s to keep a check on the opportunistic behaviour of firms (though initially efficient and profitable) cultivated over-embeddedness and outlived their usefulness over time. In the case of the Ruhr region in Germany, specific interfirm linkages were found to be at the root of the low spell in the early 1980s:

> the close intraregional interdependence, which is what constituted the coal, iron, and steel complex, had disastrous consequences for the region's adapt-ability ... close intraregional relations embedded in long-standing personal connections resulted in serious shortcomings in so-called boundary span-ning functions, which are of utmost importance in scanning the economic environment and in making external information relevant for the firm.
>
> (Grabher, 1993b, p. 260)

Importantly, with this study, Grabher showed that the 'dependent supplier syn-drome' could not be solely blamed for such a decline (especially with regard to the medium- and high-tech firms he studied), since shortcomings in the boundary-spanning functions applied to almost all classes of industries at all levels of technology. He points out that it was personal cohesiveness and long-standing relations within the coal, iron and steel industries in the Ruhr that led itself into a trap.

It then follows that information-sharing networks must be composed not of entirely embedded or entirely arm's-length ties, but an integration of the two; there must exist a theoretic optimum between the countervailing effects of over- and under-embeddedness to facilitate a firm's adaptive capacity (Uzzi, 1996). At this optimum, while a firm's arm's-length ties can act as channels for gathering public information from diverse agents, embedded ties can extract from the experienced information pool to draw out novel and private information; i.e. learning capabilities of a firm can be expanded by combining both arm's-length and embedded ties for their exploratory and exploitative learning (Uzzi and Lan-caster, 2003). A firm's performance therefore peaks when it is linked by embed-ded ties to an integrated network or both embedded and arm's length ties (Uzzi,

1996). The policy implications of this are also significant. Uzzi (1997) advises that institutional arrangements must be crafted in a manner not disruptive to existing embedded relations, so as to avoid fracturing social ties and losing whatever gains embeddedness may bring; on the other hand, firms must also carefully build their competitive advantage using embedded and arm's-length ties so as not to be too vulnerable to policy and other exogenous shocks. The 'tightrope walker' (Gargiulo and Benassi, 2000, p. 194) analogy is recalled here, where firms must maintain a balance between nestling in the security of embedded networks and strategically creating new arm's length ties.

Woolcock (1998), analysing at a micro or individual level, labels an agent's extra-community network as a 'linkage' and an intra-community tie as 'integration'. When economic agents operate at different combinations of linkage and integration, different outcomes are experienced. According to Woolcock, the optimal combination of linkage and integration is when both are given high importance, as it is in this combination that social opportunity is the highest.

We began this discussion on embeddedness, like the discussion on social capital earlier, by asserting that the economic agent is not an atomised entity, and that one's identity drawn along social lines – and the social relations these identities entail – overlaps with purely 'economic' decisions of production and exchange. This overlap of business relations and social relations is neither necessarily disruptive nor frictional, but *inevitable*. It is advantageous but only to a point, and has immense implications for firm behaviour and government policy. Social capital and social embeddedness may end up being deployed for both developmental and destructive purposes, depending upon what combinations of ties characterise the networks; they augment physical and human capital, and hence are crucial elements in development processes (Woolcock, 1998).

We conclude this discussion by reiterating Granovetter's (1985) proposition that the general applicability of 'embeddedness' demonstrates that the place of sociology in economic life is not disruptive but required, and not independent but deeply intertwined.

Homophily

Drawing from the social capital and social embeddedness concepts is 'homophily', the tendency of agents to be linked to other agents with similar characteristics (Jackson, 2008, p. 1), i.e. the tendency of individuals to associate disproportionately with those similar to themselves (Golub and Jackson, 2009). It is the principle that similar people connect at a higher rate than dissimilar people (McPherson *et al.*, 2001, p. 416), or that the degree to which a pair of individuals who communicate are similar (Rogers, 2003, p. 135), the 'similarity' lying in attributes such as belief system, education, social status and so on. Although the adage 'birds of a feather flock together' has been familiar in common parlance for several centuries, the term 'homophily' itself has been concretised and conceptualised over the past sixty years.[26] Most studies point to Lazarsfeld and Merton (1954) as the first who employed the term, but there are differing opinions on this. Rogers (2003) points to Gabriel Tarde for offering one of the earliest suggestions (in 1903) to homophilous behaviour: 'social relations ... are much closer between individuals who resemble each other in occupation and education' (Rogers, 2003, p. 135), while Freeman (2004) points to Peter Blau for developing the notion of homophily in 1977 by arguing that interaction is more likely among individuals with similar characteristics. In any case, the concept eventually gained repute as one of the most pervasive and robust tendencies of social networks (Golub and Jackson, 2009), and has for long been studied as a statistical regularity in the structure of social interactions (Golub and Jackson, 2012).

Robinson and Aikens (2009, p. 404) dissect homophily into various types as follows. 'Induced homophily' refers to the tendency for interaction partners to be limited by social structure in ways that generate homogeneous groups and relations, while 'choice homophily' refers to the tendency of people to choose interaction partners who are similar to themselves. Robinson and Aikens argue that it is often difficult to dissect how much observed homogeneity occurs as a result of induced homophily and how much results from choice homophily, which is why studies often take into account what is known as 'baseline homophily' – the similarity among relationships that would be expected by chance, given the choices available. It tells us about the most basic, population-level constraints on our choices of interaction partners. Any amount of homophily over and above what probability would predict based on the relative sizes of the groups in the population is known as 'inbreeding homophily', which may also be induced by social structures.

Rogers (2003) explains that homophily and effective communication breed each other; individuals departing from homophily often facing obstacles due to differences in social status, beliefs, language and so on, which may distort the meanings of messages. Jackson and López-Pintado (2013) closely study homophily and diffusion, and propose that diffusion is favoured *within* a highly homophilous group that is heavily biased towards internal interaction, with a critical mass for diffusion being generated quickly; groups that exhibit less homophily may not be able to achieve this in the initial stages. On the contrary, Rogers (2003) proposes that heterophilous links cause agents to seek opinion leaders of higher status in terms of education, exposure, change-agent contact, technical competence and so on. Hence, like the balance between embedded and arm's length ties, or between cohesion and filling structural holes, agents must also balance homophilous and heterophilous links, especially to facilitate the diffusion of innovations and information.

Lazarsfeld and Merton distinguished homophily into status and value homophily; the former (based on ascribed status) including socio-demographic demarcations like race, ethnicity, religion, education and so on, and the latter (based on acquired status) including the variety of internal states shaping one's orientation towards future behaviour (McPherson *et al.*, 2001). An agent is drawn towards others of its own type, causing the average agent in a community to preserve a greater fraction of its links with other agents with similar characteristics, which then buttresses existing heterogeneities in the network, leading ultimately to locali-sation in the diffusion of any information that flows through the community (McPherson *et al.*, 2001; Golub and Jackson, 2009). Jackson (2008) compared net-works exhibiting homophily to networks without any such preferences, discovering that with increasing homophily, average distance and diameter of the network do not fall, but clustering shows increase. Golub and Jackson (2009) also show that homophily does not affect the average path length in the network, but communica-tion processes across the community slow down, even if only a small group in the network displays strong homophily.

On similar lines, Golub and Jackson (2012), on studying how the speed of learning and best-response processes depend on homophily, demonstrate that homophily slows down convergence, when agents' beliefs or behaviours are developed by averaging what is seen among neighbours. Jackson and López-Pintado (2013) study the effect of homophily on diffusion, and demonstrate that homophily can facilitate diffusion from a small initial seed; hence identifying the conditions under which a behaviour (or disease) diffuses and becomes per-sistent in a segregated population connected by a social network. Both Golub and Jackson (2012) and Jackson and López-Pintado (2013) point out that most of the literature on social network structure and diffusion has not focused on modelling the effect of homophily on learning and diffusion, a theme upon which this book reflects.

A threshold

Certain general observations have emerged.

1   The individual economic agent and his social-ethnic environment are inter-twined. Social identities have a bearing on the extent to which knowledge transactions are smoothly executed, or whether they are executed at all. This perspective offers a back seat to presumptions of rationality, self-interest and so on.
2   The network perspective is crucial to studying individual and aggregate behaviour.
3   Economic behaviour is driven by embedded social considerations (value intro-jections, bounded solidarity, reciprocity transactions and enforceable trust), as much as, and at times over and above, self-interest. This is often a survival strategy, especially when considerations of ethnicity and social community are as much a priority as maintaining quality of information shared.
4   Network links are preserved across generations; agents are locked in from birth, since inherited links are ingrained. Social and ethnic capital are real-ised by an individual's actions and strategic utilisation of his or her network.
5   Cohesiveness, exclusivity, embeddedness and homophily deliver numerous benefits that ordinary price-based market transactions cannot, by easing con-straints of uncertainty in cooperation and anti-defection, and reducing the costs involved in reliable information search and building rapport.

6   But the very tools that help buttress these uncertainties may backfire. There is a threshold beyond which cohesiveness and embeddedness are detrimental, and over-reliance on social capital can shut out necessary external links to an agent or a community, which may be beneficial over the long run.

7   Hence, highly dense networks, with a fair share of weak ties linking them with other networks, are generally the most efficient.

Summing up

Continuous processes of information exchange, among producers, among users, and between the two, are fundamental in the contemporary economy (Lundvall, 1993). The information exchanged, Lundvall continues, involves changing the knowledge base of the interacting parties, this process characterised as 'interactive learning'. Interactive learning, he explains, involves the learning of substance (technical learning), of communication (communicative learning) and of proper behaviour (social learning). We have seen across this chapter that this sort of learning is what pulls producers into clusters, emerging, as Breschi and Malerba (2005) propose, as the essential ingredient for the continued success of an innovative cluster.

   All clusters may not be able to undertake R&D or devote substantial financial and human resources for developing new information. In fact, a large number of clusters of small units undertake collective innovation and learning using defensive means such as observation, constant communication, interaction, informal information exchange, face-to-face exchange of information, reliance on social networks and so on. In addition, especially when these clusters are 'low-tech', defensive behaviour and collective invention become the first choice and not a last resort. Flexibility and geographical proximity are placed at the forefront, with local groups of producers and institutions agglomerating not simply for the convenience of production and for economies of scale, but to evolve a *knowledge system*, a learning region, or a localised system of innovation. Clusters support a milieu rich with the constant 'buzz' of new knowledge and information from local and internal sources, and, by means of cosmopolite agents in the cluster, from distant sources as well. Geography emerges as a powerful tool to exchange tacit knowledge, and in the long run to establish a local comparative advantage for a cluster. Networks within a cluster therefore become its principal component, and networking as a conscious endeavour progresses into becoming the vehicle through which learning is facilitated. 'Whom you know' becomes as important as 'what you know', and network analysis becomes the central instrument in investigating individual and aggregate behaviour in clusters. When this is the case, economic behaviour, especially in low-tech clusters of defensively behaving units, is intertwined in social relations and the social structure of the region; so much so that social identities even have a bearing on the nature of information sharing and learning. Economic relations become emergent properties of social relations, laced with reciprocity, value introjection and solidarity, over and above economic self-interest. Networks become emergent properties of the social structure in a region, acting as vehicles not only for learning but also for reinforcing social norms and values, which define the nature of the social capital of the region.

Varshney (2010) argues that in rural and semi-urban regions in the developing world, formal associations between people do not exist to the same extent as they do in larger cities or well-developed industrial districts. This, he argues, does not mean that civic interconnectedness or activities are absent. It only implies that informal networks between people are more prominent in these settings than are formal associations. The latter are only one form of social capital among socio-economic agents, while the former are often a more important form of social capital for sharing information of various kinds (Blomkvist, 2010).

With this background it becomes imperative, as Breschi and Malerba (2005) advise, to disentangle oversimplified notions of spillovers and proximity, and to investigate deeper into the underlying mechanics of informal interactive behaviour in clusters. This also calls for an expansion of the conceptual understanding of social embeddedness and social capital in terms of their implications for cohesiveness, in the study of such clusters.[27]

Outline of the book

A simulation model of informal know-how sharing among co-located agents in a rural low-tech cluster, coloured by various kinds of social relations, is taken up in Chapter 2. Through this exercise we see how boundedly rational agents in a simulated rural traditional technology cluster share information with other networked agents in the cluster purely through informal means. Many studies in know-how diffusion across social networks have dealt with the importance of network architecture in terms of the implications it has had for the equity and efficiency of information distribution. When we study rural traditional technology clusters whose only source of new information is through informal interaction and defensive innovation, enquiring about efficient network architecture is necessary, but the analysis needs to be coloured with the complex social relations that are inevitable in such clusters in real life. With this model, we test whether the small-world network structure is still the most efficient for information diffusion through informal information sharing in a cluster operating in a complex social relations environment. Second, we explore the effect of the intensity of social relations, and that of the influence of network distance as a concern among agents exchanging information, on the performance of the cluster. These enquiries are the contribution of this model to the existing series of studies on efficient network structures for information diffusion. Based on the findings of this model, we move on to the case studies that explore the nature of informal information sharing in real-life low-tech environments – two rural and traditional industrial clusters in the state of Kerala in southern India.

Chapter 4 presents the first empirical case study. This study is an exploration into the nature of informal technological information sharing within a low-tech cluster characterised by non-complicated social relations (what is referred to in this book as 'universal affinity', explained in further detail in Chapter 2). We reveal the role and significance of informal channels and mechanisms of technical information flow, taking the case of a rural coir (coconut fibre) yarn-producing cluster in Kerala which learned and adapted to a very simple exogenously introduced innovation – a mechanised spinning wheel. First, we get a brief idea of the technology prescription experiences from the state's point of view. The fieldwork component of the chapter then looks at the various dynamics of, and the environment for, informal learning and know-how sharing in a coir-producing cluster; the illustration of which has implications for our conceptual understanding of learning in low-tech, informal and interactive environments characterised by universal affinity among the cluster's agents. Lessons from this descriptive case study emerge as possible answers as to why some innovations, even with full financial and institutional backing, may or may not have diffused effectively across their target regions, or may or may not be completely learned and adapted to within a region.

While the coir-producing cluster was characterised by a 'clean' scenario with no turbulence in information-sharing activity by virtue of actors sharing 'universal affinity' with one another, the next cluster under study is characterised by informal information sharing heavily influenced by the social relations in the region. In Chapters 5 and 6, we study the case of the *Saliyar* community cluster in the town of Balaramapuram, Kerala state, India, producing handloom textile products. A unique characteristic of the Saliyar cluster is the unchanging nature of the technology. We see in this study that when information sharing through informal interaction in a cluster is demarcated by social groups and intensively involves social capital for an extended period, the emergent path that the cluster takes in terms of economic activity and in its dominance in the market is certainly noteworthy. The experience in Balaramapuram of the Saliyar cluster, populated almost entirely by members of the Saliyar community who were once the most successful community in this industry, is notable. Lessons drawn from this cluster's experience are worth investigating to witness the kind of effect that thickly homophilous social and production networks (resting on the Saliyars' historically rooted social and ethnic capital) can have on the long-standing dominance and eventual decline of this community, in the market for a product whose unchanging production technology is its forte.

By undertaking a network analysis of the Saliyar cluster in Chapter 5, we provide evidence that it is not just embeddedness alone, but in its *combination* with homophily in various intensities that is detrimental to clusters relying on information sharing chiefly through informal interaction. The study demonstrates how it is imperative to separate social embeddedness into homophilous and non-homophilous embeddedness. That is, the conceptual ambit of embeddedness has to broaden to recognise that social relations come in various 'homophilies'. In Chapter 6, we continue the issue of homophilous embeddedness to show how the example of the Saliyars is counter to the standard line in the literature on the adoption of innovations in handlooms. We see how the Saliyars' homophilous embeddedness was an attribute passed down over generations. While there are a multitude of cases in history demonstrating a healthy relationship between community cohesion and technological progress among handloom weaver communities in India, in the case of the Saliyars the relationship has been antagonistic and unhealthy. To understand why, we investigate the inherited nature of Saliyar networks, the centrality of community social capital among the Saliyars and, most importantly, the inherited homophilous embeddedness in their networks. This chapter argues that affiliation to a rigid network and homophilous embeddedness can weaken even a seemingly prosperous group, regardless of industry performance. On a broader plane, this chapter also allows for a study on complex social relations influencing economic relations and technological progress when these relations are relayed across generations.

Conclusions of the book are then laid out and summarised in Chapter 7, which also endorses an economic-sociology approach to study innovation and learning processes, especially in developing country clusters.

Notes

1 We define 'low-tech' according to the OECD's (ISIC Rev. 3) definition of technology intensity, which classifies those entities as low-tech, who dedicate less than 0.4 per cent of gross output on research and development (R&D) as low-tech.
2 Gomes (2001) points to a UNIDO study that reveals how, in India, the quantum of output of clusters is so big that they produce the bulk of the total volume of that particular product produced in India. For example, Panipat produces 75 per cent of the total blankets made, Tirupur contributes 80 per cent of India's cotton hosiery exports, Agra is virtually a footwear city where thousands of formal and informal small producers make millions of pairs of shoes per year, and Ludhiana produces 95 per cent of the country's woollen knitwear, and 85 per cent of the country's bicycles and bicycle parts.
3 Romijn (1999) explains that satisficing occurs, first, since it is less expensive to explore one's immediate neighbourhood, and second, since small producers cannot, sustainably and in the long term, rely on capability diffusion from large-scale and high-tech firms.
4 See Annex 1 in Hirsch-Kreinsen *et al.* (2003) for a compendium of literature on low-tech producer behaviour.
5 Tacit knowledge, according to Ernst and Kim (2002, p. 1423) refers to knowledge that can only be expressed through action, commitment and involvement in a specific context and locality. It is based on experience, and is acquired through observation, imitation and practice. Its diffusion requires face-to-face interaction. It may be embodied (as skills), embrained (as cognitive capacity), embedded (routinised as organisational practice) or encultured (as assumptions, beliefs and norms). Each type varies in ease of transfer. According to Foray (2004), tacit knowledge resides in people, institutions or routines, making it difficult to transport, memorise, recombine and learn. See also Howells (2002) for further discussion on the roles of tacit knowledge and geography on innovation.
6 Mani (2009), using data from the UN Comtrade database, has demonstrated how the technology content of India's manufactured exports in 2007 was 67.8 per cent (low-tech), 23.48 per cent (medium-tech) and 8.72 per cent (high-tech). In 1988, these proportions were 82.08 per cent, 12.96 per cent and 4.96 per cent, respectively. Although there has been a noticeable change in proportion, we can see that low-tech still dominates Indian manufactured exports.

7 Humphrey and Schmitz (1995) describe how there is a common misconception on collective efficiency, immediately implying a denial of competition. They explain that severe rivalry may exist among clustered producers, but they also often join forces to overcome common bottlenecks in infrastructure, input supply or access to distant markets. They explain that it is the combination of competition and cooperation which drives the search for improvement.

8 For a further detailed look at the literature on clusters and innovation, and their role in development at large, see Nadvi and Schmitz (1994), Nadvi (1995), Albu (1997), Bell and Albu (1999), Schmitz and Nadvi (1999), Breschi and Malerba (2005), Ketels and Memedovic (2008), and Parto (2008).

9 Much of the so-called 'local' or 'sticky' information that is 'in the air' in clusters is also termed 'practical knowledge'. This includes, according to Hirsch-Kreinsen and Jacobson (2008), explicit and formalised elements such as design drawing and requirement specifications, as well as implicit elements like accumulated experience and routines for problem solving (also everyday experiences and processes of learning by doing). Practical knowledge shows an individual and collective dimension, and a highly informal character; it is not easily documented or covered by operation plans or by an official organisation chart; it refers specifically to the informal side of a working process often marked by accepted working methods and cooperational and communication patterns (Hirsch-Kreinsen *et al.*, 2003).

10 In fact, Breschi and colleagues (2005) go so far as to propose that tacitness may not be an inherent property of knowledge; rather, it may be an explicit strategic choice of a firm (or group of firms) to exclude competitors from accessing strategic knowledge, and thereby creating a comparative advantage.

11 See Green and McNaughton (2000) for a compilation of studies on proximity dynamics. See Breschi and Malerba (2001), Howells (2002), and Morgan (2004), as well as Maskell (various), on the role of geography in clustering and innovation; also see Ceci and Iubatti (2012) for efficient coverage of the literature on geographical proximity as an enabler of personal relationships, which in turn allow for the development of other economic relationships. It should be evident from these studies that there is a wealth of research in the literature disentangling proximity and not oversimplifying it, especially in the context of medium-/high-tech industries in both developing and advanced economies.

12 This is also known in the literature on learning as 'observational learning'. Brenner (1999) describes how imitation is provoked by the reward another individual receives for certain behaviour, as agents who observe this behaviour and the resulting reward hope to gain the same reward. If the imitated behaviour is rewarded well, it is reinforced, and thus stabilises.

13 Knowledge located even in faraway regions may be accessed through observation by actually sending people to the location. Ernst and Kim (2002) describe an interesting strategy used and promoted in South Korea involving observation where the Small Industry Promotion Corporation and other small enterprises and associations organised observation tours of foreign firms to acquire new knowledge.

14 For example, as listed in Gault and von Hippel (2009, p. 10) on referring to other studies: medical equipment, semiconductor process equipment, library information systems and sporting equipment. Figueiredo (2001) illustrates the free revealing of information and sharing of technical experiences among Japanese and Brazilian engineers in the Brazilian steel firm USIMINAS in the 1970s.

15 Allen and colleagues (1983, p. 202) showed how documented information played a role only second to direct personal contact from 'particularly competitors and … international contact. … Nearly 60% of the messages came from other firms.'

16 See also Krackhardt and Hanson (1993) for the pivotal role of informal information sharing among employees within firms.

17 See Ceci and Iubatti (2012) for an excellent review of studies in the breadth and coverage of network analysis.

18 See fig. 1.4 in Esser (2008, p. 46) for a systematic representation of the different forms of social capital.

19 It must be clarified at this point that the concept of social capital in the empirical analyses in this book is understood in the manner by which it is held by individuals and communities, and not by regions or nations. This distinction is important because the public good nature of social capital may vary with the entity (individual, community or nation) with which it is associated.

20 An ethnic enclave is a spatially clustered network of businesses owned by members of the same minority, not dispersed among other populations, but emerging in close proximity to the areas settled by their own group (Portes, 1995, p. 27).

21 There is, however, a small body of literature on the strength of *strong* ties that stands in contrast with the argument here on the strength of weak ties. See, for instance, Bian (1997), Krackhardt (2003) and Rost (2011).

22 An interesting parallel to structural holes has been developed by Vedres and Stark (2010), which they term 'intercohesion', i.e. cohesive structures whose intersections are known as 'structural folds'. They describe its virtues as follows. Actors at the structural fold participate in dense cohesive ties that provide close familiarity with the operations of members in their group. Because these actors are members of more than one cohesive group, they gain access to diverse resources; this combination of familiarity and diversity facilitates the work of recombining resources. That is, through the overlapping of strong ties bonding to more than one group, structural folding provides opportunities for mixing or recombining knowledge practices. Intercohesion is the process through which new ideas are generated. An intercohesion thus becomes a closure *without* being closed off; i.e. cohesion without insularity.

23 For an excellent review of literature of the applications of social capital in research, see Portes (1998).

24 Krippner (2001) has in fact given a very elaborate and well-illustrated legacy of embeddedness, from Karl Polanyi, to Talcott Parsons, to its modern-day theoretical position.

25 Note that social influences and what is considered 'good' and 'bad' are never permanent, but constantly evolve and are reconstructed during interaction between agents (Grabher, 1993a).

26 According to McPherson and colleagues (2001), this adage was attributed by Lazarsfeld and Merton (1954) to Robert Burton, who in turn recognised its usage in Classical literature and thought. Diogeniasnus (again, cited by Burton) is said to have quoted 'jackdaw percheth beside jackdaw'.

27 Although the conceptual reach of social embeddedness and social capital span wider than the concept of 'cohesiveness'; in this book I focus mainly on their *implications* for cohesiveness.

References

Adam, F. and Westlund, H., 2012. *Innovation in Socio-Cultural Context.* New York and Oxon, UK: Routledge.

Akçomak, İ.S., 2009. *The Impact of Social Capital on Economic and Social Outcomes.* PhD UNU-MERIT and Universiteit Maastricht, The Netherlands.

Albu, M., 1997. Technological Learning and Innovation in Industrial Clusters in the South. Electronic Working Paper 7, University of Sussex.

Aldrich, H.E. and Waldinger, R., 1990. Ethnicity and Entrepreneurship. *Annual Review of Sociology*, 16, 111–135.

Allen, R.C., 1983. Collective Invention. *Journal of Economic Behavior and Organization*, 4, 1–24.

Allen, T.J., Hyman, D.B. and Pinckney, D.L., 1983. Transferring Technology to the Small Manufacturing Firm: A Study of Technology Transfer in Three Countries. *Research Policy*, 12(4), 199–211.

Andersen, K.V., 2013. The Problem of Embeddedness Revisited: Collaboration and Market Types. *Research Policy*, 42(1), 139–148.

Baba, Y. and Walsh, J.P., 2010. Embeddedness, Social Epistemology, and Breakthrough Innovation: The Case of the Development of Statins. *Research Policy*, 39(4), 511–522.

Bala Subrahmanya, M.H., Mathirajan, M., Balachandra, P., Srinivasan, M.N. and Prasad, L., 2002. *R&D and Technological Institutions in Small Scale Industries*. New Delhi: Allied Publishers.

Bala, V. and Goyal, S., 1998. Learning from Neighbours. *Review of Economic Studies*, 65, 595–621.

Basant, R., 2006. Bangalore Cluster: Evolution, Growth and Challenges. Working Paper 2 May 2006, Indian Institute of Management, Ahmedabad, India.

Bell, M. and Albu, M., 1999. Knowledge Systems and Technological Dynamism in Industrial Clusters in Developing Countries. *World Development*, 27(9), 1715–1734.

Bian, Y., 1997. Bringing Strong Ties Back In: Indirect Ties, Network Bridges, and Job Searches in China. *American Sociological Review*, 62(3), 366–385.

Blomkvist, H., 2010. Social Capital, Civil Society, and Degrees of Democracy in India. In C.M. Elliott (ed.) *Civil Society and Democracy: A Reader*. New Delhi: Oxford University Press.

Borjas, G.J., 1992. Ethnic Capital and Intergenerational Mobility. *The Quarterly Journal of Economics*, 107(1), 123–150.

Boschma, R., 2005. Proximity and Innovation: A Critical Assessment. *Regional Studies*, 39(1), 61–74.

Boschma, R. and ter Wal, L.J., 2007. Knowledge Networks and Innovative Performance in an Industrial District: The Case of a Footwear District in the South of Italy. *Industry and Innovation*, 14(2), 177–199.

Bougrain, F. and Haudeville, B., 2002. Innovation, Collaboration, and SMEs Internal Research Capacities. *Research Policy*, 31(5), 735–747.

Braguinsky, S. and Rose, D.C., 2009. Competition, Cooperation and the Neighboring Farmer Effect. *Journal of Economic Behavior and Organization*, 72, 361–376.

Brandes, U., Robins, G., McCranie, A. and Wasserman, S., 2013. What is Network Science? *Network Science*, 1(1), 1–15.

Brenner, T., 1999. *Modelling Learning in Economics*. Cheltenham, UK, and Northampton, USA: Edward Elgar.

Breschi, S. and Lissoni, F., 2001. Knowledge Spillovers and Local Innovation Systems: A Critical Survey. *Industrial and Corporate Change*, 10(4), 975–1005.

Breschi, S. and Malerba, F., 2001. The Geography of Innovation and Economic Clustering: Some Introductory Notes. *Industrial and Corporate Change*, 10(4), 817–833.

——, 2005. Clusters, Networks, and Innovation: Research Results and New Directions. In S. Breschi and F. Malerba (eds) *Clusters, Networks and Innovation*. Oxford: Oxford University Press.

Breschi, S., Lissoni, F. and Montobbio, F., 2005. The Geography of Knowledge Spillovers: Conceptual Issues and Measurement Problems. In S. Breschi and F. Malerba (eds) *Clusters, Networks and Innovation*. Oxford: Oxford University Press.

Burt, R.S., 1992. *Structural Holes*. Cambridge, MA: Harvard University Press.

——, 1997a. The Contingent Value of Social Capital. *Administrative Science Quarterly*, 42(2), 339–365.

——, 1997b. A Note on Social Capital and Network Content. *Social Networks*, 19, 355–373.

Cantner, U. and Graf, H., 2008. Interaction Structures in Local Innovation Systems. Jena Economic Research Papers 2008–40. Friedrich-Schiller University and Max Planck Institute of Economics.

Castiglione, D., van Deth, J.W. and Wolleb, G., 2008. Social Capitals Fortune: An Introduction. In D. Castiglione, J.W. van Deth and G. Wolleb (eds) *The Handbook of Social Capital*. Oxford: Oxford University Press.

Ceci, F. and Iubatti, D., 2012. Personal Relationships and Innovation Diffusion in SME Networks: A Content Analysis Approach. *Research Policy*, 41(3), 565–579.

Chamley, C.P., 2004. *Rational Herds: Economic Models of Social Learning*. Cambridge: Cambridge University Press.

Coleman, J.S., 1988. Social Capital in the Creation of Human Capital. *American Journal of Sociology*, 94, S95–S120.

Cooke, P., 2002. *Knowledge Economies: Clusters, Learning and Cooperative Advantage*. New York and London: Routledge.

Cowan, R., 2004. Network Models of Innovation and Knowledge Diffusion, MERIT-Infonomics Research Memorandum Series. MERIT, Universiteit Maastricht, The Netherlands.

Cowan, R. and Jonard, N., 2003. The Dynamics of Collective Invention. *Journal of Economic Behavior and Organization*, 52, 513–532.

——, 2004. Network Structure and the Diffusion of Knowledge. *Journal of Economic Dynamics and Control*, 28, 1557–1575.

Cowan, R. and Miller, J.H., 1998. Technological Standards with Local Externalities and Decentralised Behaviour. *Journal of Evolutionary Economics*, 8(3), 285–296.

Cowan, R., Jonard, N. and Özman, M., 2004. Knowledge Dynamics in a Network Industry. *Technological Forecasting and Social Change*, 71, 469–484.

Cross, R., Parker, A. and Sasson, L., 2003. Introduction. In R. Cross, A. Parker and L. Sasson (eds) *Networks in the Knowledge Economy*. Oxford and New York: Oxford University Press.

Dankbaar, B., 2004. Embeddedness, Context, Proximity and Control. *European Planning Studies*, 12(5), 691–701.

Das, K., 2005. *Indian Industrial Clusters*. Burlington and Aldershot, UK: Ashgate.

Dasgupta, P., 2005. Economics of Social Capital. *The Economic Record*, 81(255), S2–S21.

Dasgupta, S., 1989. *Diffusion of Agricultural Innovations in Village India*. New Delhi: Wiley Eastern.

DiMaggio, P. and Louch, H., 1998. Socially Embedded Consumer Transactions: For What Kind of Purchases Do People Most Often Use Networks. *American Sociological Review*, 63(5), 619–637.

Duysters, G. and Lemmens, C., 2003. Alliance Group Formation: Enabling and Constraining Effects of Embeddedness and Social Capital in Strategic Technology Alliance Networks. *International Studies of Management and Organisation*, 33(2), 49–68.

Dwivedi, M. and Varman, R., 2005. Industrial Clustering and Cooperation: The Kanpur Saddlery Cluster. In K. Das (ed.) *Indian Industrial Clusters*. Burlington and Aldershot, UK: Ashgate.

Ernst, D. and Kim, L., 2002. Global Production Networks, Knowledge Diffusion, and Local Capability Formation. *Research Policy*, 31(8–9), 1417–1429.

Esser, H., 2008. The Two Meanings of Social Capital. In D. Castiglione, J.W. van Deth and G. Wolleb (eds) *The Handbook of Social Capital*. Oxford: Oxford University Press.

Figueiredo, P.N., 2001. *Technological Learning and Competitive Performance*. Cheltenham, UK, and Northampton, USA: Edward Elgar.

Fong, E. and Isajiw, W.W., 2000. Determinants of Friendship Choices in Multiethnic Societies. *Sociological Forum*, 15(2), 249–271.

Foray, D., 2010. Knowledge Policy for Development. In E. Kramer-Mbula and W. Wamae (eds) *Innovation and the Development Agenda*. IRDC. Canada: Organization for Economic Cooperation and Development (OECD).

Foster, A.D. and Rosenzweig, M.R., 2000. Learning by Doing and Learning from Others: Human Capital and Technical Change in Agriculture. In P. Bardhan and C. Udry (eds) *Readings in Development Economics, Volume 2: Empirical Microeconomics*. Cambridge, MA, and London, UK: The MIT Press.

Freeman, C. and Soete, L., 1997. *The Economics of Industrial Innovation*. London, and Washington, DC: Pinter.

Freeman, L.C., 2004. *The Development of Social Network Analysis: A Study in the Sociology of Science*. Vancouver, Canada: Empirical Press.

García, M.S., 2006. *Social Capital, Networks and Economic Development*. Cheltenham, UK, and Northampton, USA: Edward Elgar.

Gargiulo, M. and Benassi, M., 2000. Trapped in your Own Net? Network Cohesion, Structural Holes, and the Adaptation of Social Capital. *Organization Science*, 11(2), 183–196.

Gault, F. and von Hippel, E., 2009. The Prevalence of User Innovation and Free Innovation Transfers: Implications for Statistical Indicators and Innovation Policy, 4722–09. MIT Sloan School Working Paper.

Gebreyeesus, M. and Mohnen, P., 2013. Innovation Performance and Embeddedness in Networks: Evidence from the Ethiopian Footwear Cluster. *World Development*, 41(c), 302–316.

Gertler, M.S., 2007. Tacit Knowledge in Production Systems: How Important is Geography? In K.R. Polenske (ed.) *The Economic Geography of Innovation*. Cambridge: Cambridge University Press.

Ghezzi, S. and Mingione, E., 2007. Embeddedness, Path Dependency and Social Institutions. *Current Sociology*, 55(1), 11–23.

Glasmeier, A., 1991. Technological Discontinuities and Flexible Production Networks: The Case of Switzerland the World Watch Industry. *Research Policy*, 20(5), 469–485.

Golub, B. and Jackson, M.O., 2009. How Homophily affects Learning and Diffusion in Networks. Working Paper 35, Fondazione Eni Enrico Mattei, Milan, Italy.

——, 2012. How Homophily Affects the Speed of Learning and Best Response Dynamics. *Quarterly Journal of Economics*, 127(3), 1287–1338.

Gomes, J., 2001. SMEs and Industrial Clusters: Lessons for India from Italian Experience. *Economic and Political Weekly*, 36(49), 4532–4533.

Goyal, S., 2007. *Connections: An Introduction to the Economics of Networks*. Princeton, NJ, and Oxford: Princeton University Press.

Grabher, G., 1993a. Rediscovering the Social in the Economics of Interfirm Relations. In G. Grabher (ed.) *The Embedded Firm: On the Socioeconomics of Industrial Networks*. London and New York: Routledge.

——, 1993b. The Weakness of Strong Ties: The Lock-in of Regional Development in the Ruhr Area. In G. Grabher (ed.) *The Embedded Firm: On the Socioeconomics of Industrial Networks*. London and New York: Routledge.

Graf, H., 2006. *Networks in the Innovation Process: Local and Regional Interactions.* Cheltenham, UK, and Northampton, USA: Edward Elgar.

Granovetter, M., 1973. The Strength of Weak Ties. *American Journal of Sociology*, 78(6), 1360–1380.

——, 1985. Economic Action and Social Structure: The Problem of Embeddedness. *American Journal of Sociology*, 91(3), 481–510.

Green, M.B. and McNaughton, R.B., 2000. *Industrial Networks and Proximity.* Aldershot, UK: Ashgate.

Griliches, Z., 1957. Hybrid Corn: An Exploration in the Economics of Technological Change. *Econometrica*, 25(4), 501–522.

Gulati, R., 1998. Alliances and Networks. *Strategic Management Journal*, 19(4), 293–317.

Hass, J.K., 2007. *Economic Sociology: An Introduction.* London and New York: Routledge.

Hassink, R., 2007. The Learning Region: A Constructive Critique. In R. Ruttan and F. Boekema (eds) *The Learning Region: Foundations, State of the Art, Future.* Cheltenham, UK and Northampton, USA: Edward Elgar.

Hirsch-Kreinsen, H. and Jacobson, D., 2008. The Low-tech Issue. In H. Hirsch-Kreinsen and D. Jacobson (eds) *Innovation in Low-tech Firms and Industries.* Cheltenham, UK: Edward Elgar, and Northampton, USA: Industrial Dynamics, Entrepreneurship and Innovation.

Hirsch-Kreinsen, H., Jacobson, D., Laestaduis, S. and Smith, K., 2003. Low-tech Industries and the Knowledge Economy: State of the Art and Research Challenges. STEP Report 16–2003. Paper written within the context of PILOT: Policy and Innovation in Low-Tech, Norway.

Howells, J.R.L., 2002. Tacit Knowledge, Innovation, and Economic Geography. *Urban Studies*, 39, 871–884.

Humphrey, J. and Schmitz, H., 1995. Principles for Promoting Clusters and Networks of SMEs. Paper Commissioned by the Small and Medium Industries Branch, UNIDO, Vienna.

Irawati, D. and Rutten, R., 2012. Learning in Regional Networks: The Role of Social Capital. In F. Adam and H. Westlund (eds) *Innovation in Socio-cultural Context.* New York and Oxon, UK: Routledge.

Jackson, M.O., 2008. Average Distance, Diameter and Clustering in Social Networks with Homophily. In C. Papadimitriou and S. Zhang (eds) *Internet and Network Economics.* Berlin, Heidelberg: Springer Verlag.

Jackson, M.O. and López-Pintado, D., 2013. Diffusion and Contagion in Networks with Heterogeneous Agents and Homophily. *Network Science*, 1(1), 49–67.

Jensen, M.B., Johnson, B., Lorenz, E. and Lundvall, B-Å., 2007. Forms of Knowledge and Modes of Innovation. *Research Policy*, 36(5), 680–693.

Kauffman, A. and Tödtling, F., 2003. Innovation Patterns of SMEs. In B.T. Asheim *et al.* (eds) *Regional Innovation Policy for Small–Medium Enterprises.* Cheltenham, UK: Edward Elgar.

Ketels, C.H.M. and Memedovic, O., 2008. From Clusters to Cluster-based Economic Development. *International Journal of Technological Learning, Innovation and Development*, 1(3), 375–392.

Khalaf, S. and Shwayri, E., 1966. Family Firms and Industrial Development. *Economic Development and Cultural Change*, 15(1), 59–69.

Krackhardt, D., 2003. The Strength of Strong Ties. In R. Cross *et al.* (eds) *Networks in the Knowledge Economy.* Oxford and New York: Oxford University Press.

Krackhardt, D. and Hanson, J.R., 1993. Informal Networks: The Company Behind the Chart. *Harvard Business Review*, July–August, pp. 104–111.

Krippner, G.R., 2001. The Elusive Market: Embeddedness and the Paradigm of Economic Sociology. *Theory and Society*, 30(6), 775–810.

Laumann, E.O., Galaskiewicz, J. and Marsden, P.V., 1978. Community Structure as Interorganizational Linkages. *Annual Review of Sociology*, 4, 455–484.

Lazarsfeld, P.F. and Merton R.K., 1954. Friendship as a Social Process: A Substantive and Methodological Analysis. In M. Berger (ed.) *Freedom and Control in Modern Society*. New York: Van Nostrand.

Lin, N., 2008. A Network Theory of Social Capital. In D. Castiglione, J.W. van Deth and G. Wolleb (eds) *The Handbook of Social Capital*. Oxford: Oxford University Press.

Lundvall, B-Å., 1993. Explaining Interfirm Cooperation and Innovation: Limits of the Transaction–Cost Approach. In G. Grabher (ed.) *The Embedded Firm: On the Socioeconomics of Industrial Networks*. London and New York: Routledge.

Lüthje, C., Herstatt, C. and von Hippel, E., 2005. User-innovators and Local Information: The Case of Mountain Biking. *Research Policy*, 34(6), 951–965.

Maharajh, R. and Kraemer-Mbula, E., 2010. Innovation Strategies in Developing Countries. In E. Kramer-Mbula and W. Wamae (eds) *Innovation and the Development Agenda*. Canada: IRDC, Organization for Economic Cooperation and Development (OECD).

Malecki, E.J. and Tootle, D.M., 1996. The Role of Networks in Small Firm Competitiveness. *International Journal of Technology Management*, 11, 43–57.

Malerba, F. and Vonortas, N.S., 2009. Innovation Networks in Industries with Sectoral Systems: An Introduction. In F. Malerba and N.S. Vonortas (eds) *Innovation Networks in Industries*. Cheltenham, UK, and Northampton, USA: Edward Elgar.

Malmberg, A. and Maskell, P., 1997. Towards an Explanation of Regional Specialization and Industrial Agglomeration. *European Planning Studies*, 5(1), 25–41.

Mani, S., 2009. Has India Become More Innovative since 1991? Analysis of the Evidence and Some Disquieting Features. Working Paper 415. Centre for Development Studies, Trivandrum, India.

——, 2011. Guide to Data on India's Industrial Sector. *International Journal of Development and Social Research*, 2(2), 81–88.

——, 2013. The Science, Technology and Innovation Policy 2013: An Evaluation. *Economic and Political Weekly*, 48(10), 16–19.

Mansfield, E., 1985. How Rapidly Does New Industrial Technology Leak Out? *Journal of Industrial Economics*, 34(2), 217–223.

Marshall, A., 1895. *Principles of Economics*, 3rd edn. London and New York: Macmillan.

Masciarelli, F., Laursen, K. and Prencipe, A., 2010. Trapped by Over-embeddedness: The Effects of Regional Social Capital on Internationalization. DRUID Working Paper 10–14.

Maskell, P., 2001a. Knowledge Creation and Diffusion in Geographic Clusters. *International Journal of Innovation Management*, 5(2), 213–237.

——, 2001b. Towards a Knowledge-based Theory of the Geographical Cluster. *Industrial and Corporate Change*, 10(4), 921–943.

Maskell, P. and Malmberg, A., 1999. Localised Learning and Industrial Competitiveness. *Cambridge Journal of Economics*, 23, 167–185.

Maskell, P., Eskelinen, H., Hannibalsson, I., Malmberg, A. and Vatne, E., 1998. *Competitiveness, Localised Learning and Regional Development: Specialisation and Prosperity in Small Open Economies*. Routledge Frontiers of Political Economy. London and New York: Routledge.

McCormick, D. and Oyelaran-Oyeyinka, B., 2007. Introduction: Clusters and Innovation Systems in Africa. In B. Oyelaran-Oyeyinka and D. McCormick (eds) *Industrial Clusters and Innovation Systems in Africa.* Tokyo: United Nations University Press.

McGaw, J.A., 1987. *Most Wonderful Machine: Mechanization and Social Change in Berkshire Paper Making.* Princeton, NJ: Princeton University Press.

McPherson, M., Smith-Lovin, L. and Cook, J.M., 2001. Birds of a Feather: Homophily in Social Networks. *Annual Review of Sociology*, 27, 415–444.

MoI, 1997. *Report of the Expert Committee on Small Enterprises.* Department of Small Scale Industries and Agro and Rural Industries, Ministry of Industry, Government of India.

Moody, J. and White, D.R., 2003. Structural Cohesion and Embeddedness: A Hierarchical Concept of Social Groups. *American Sociological Review*, 68(1), 103–127.

Morgan, K., 2004. The Exaggerated Death of Geography: Learning, Proximity and Territorial Innovation Systems. *Journal of Economic Geography*, 4(1), 3–21.

Mytelka, L.K., 2007. From Clusters to Innovation Systems in Traditional Industries. In D. Oyelaran-Oyeyinka and B. McCormick (eds) *Industrial Clusters and Innovation Systems in Africa.* Tokyo: United Nations University Press.

Nadvi, K., 1995. Industrial Clusters and Networks: Case Studies of SME Growth and Innovation. Paper Commissioned by the Small and Medium Industries Branch, UNIDO, Vienna.

Nadvi, K. and Schmitz, H., 1994. *Industrial Clusters in Less Developed Countries: Review of Experiences and Research Memoranda.* Discussion Paper 339, Institute of Development Studies, University of Sussex, Brighton.

Nelson, R.R. and Winter, S.G., 1982. *An Evolutionary Theory of Economic Change.* Cambridge, MA, and London: The Belknap Press of Harvard University Press.

Oakey, R., Rothwell, R. and Cooper, S., 1988. *The Management of Innovation in High-technology Small Firms: Innovation and Regional Development in Britain and the United States.* London: Pinter.

Padgett, J.F. and Powell, W.W., 2012. The Problem of Emergence. In J.F. Padgett and W.W. Powell (eds) *The Emergence of Organizations and Markets.* Princeton, NJ, and Oxford: Princeton University Press.

Parto, S., 2008. Innovation and Economic Activity: An Institutional Analysis of the Role of Clusters in Industrializing Economies. *Journal of Economic Issues*, 42(4), 1005–1030.

Pavitt, K., 2005. Innovation Processes. In J. Fagerberg *et al.* (eds) *The Oxford Handbook of Innovation.* Oxford: Oxford University Press.

Pedersen, P.O., Sverisson, A. and van Dijk, M.P., 1994. *Flexible Specialization: The Dynamics of Small Scale Industries in the South.* London: Intermediate Technology Publications.

Perry, M., 1999. *Small Firms and Network Economies.* Routledge Studies in Small Business. London and New York: Routledge.

Pillay, H., 2005. Knowledge and Social Capital. In D. Rooney *et al.* (eds) *Handbook on the Knowledge Economy.* Cheltenham, UK, and Northampton, MA: Edward Elgar.

Polanyi, K., 1944. *The Great Transformation.* Boston, MA: Beacon Press.

——, 1957. The Economy as an Instituted Process. In K. Polanyi *et al.* (eds) *Trade and Markets in the Early Empires.* Chicago, IL: Regnery.

Porter, K., Whittington, K.B. and Powell, W.W., 2005. The Institutional Embeddedness of High-tech Regions: Relational Foundations of the Boston Biotechnology Community. In S. Breschi and F. Malerba (eds) *Clusters, Networks and Innovation.* Oxford: Oxford University Press.

Porter, M.E., 1990. *The Competitive Advantage of Nations.* New York: Free Press.
——, 1998. Clusters and the New Economics of Competition. *Harvard Business Review*, November–December, pp. 77–90.
Portes, A., 1995. Economic Sociology and the Sociology of Immigration: A Conceptual Overview. In A. Portes (ed.) *The Economic Sociology of Immigration: Essays on Networks, Ethnicity, and Entrepreneurship.* New York: Russell Sage Foundation.
——, 1998. Social Capital: Its Origins and Applications in Modern Sociology. *Annual Review of Sociology*, 24, 1–24.
Portes, A. and Sensenbrenner, J., 1993. Embeddedness and Immigration: Notes on the Social Determinants of Economic Action. *American Journal of Sociology*, 98(6), 1320–1350.
Powell, W.W. and Grodal, S., 2005. Networks of Innovators. In J. Fagerberg *et al.* (eds) *The Oxford Handbook of Innovation.* Oxford: Oxford University Press.
Powell, W.W. and Smith-Doerr, L., 1994. Networks and Economic Life. In N.J. Smelser and R. Swedberg (eds) *The Handbook of Economic Sociology.* Princeton, NJ: Princeton University Press.
Robinson, D.T. and Aikens, L., 2009. Homophily. In *Encyclopedia of Group Processes and Intergroup Relations.* Thousand Oaks, CA.
Rogers, E.M., 1995. *Diffusion of Innovations.* New York: The Free Press.
——, 2003. Diffusion Networks. In R. Cross *et al.* (eds) *Networks in the Knowledge Economy.* Oxford and New York: Oxford University Press.
Romijn, H., 1999. *Acquisition of Technological Capability in Small Firms in Developing Countries.* Basingstoke, UK: Macmillan.
Rooney, D. and Schneider, U., 2005. The Material, Mental, Historical and Social Character of Knowledge. In D. Rooney *et al.* (eds) *Handbook on the Knowledge Economy.* Cheltenham, UK, and Northampton, USA: Edward Elgar.
Rost, K., 2011. The Strength of Strong Ties in the Creation of Innovation. *Research Policy*, 40(4), 588–604.
Rothwell, R., 1989. Small Firms, Innovation and Industrial Change. *Small Business Economics*, 1, 51–64.
Rothwell, R. and Zegveld, W., 1982. *Innovation and the Small and Medium Sized Firm.* London: Frances Pinter.
Rowley, T., Behrens, D. and Krackhardt, D., 2000. Redundant Governance Structures: An Analysis of Structural and Relational Embeddedness in the Steel and Semiconductor Industries. *Strategic Management Journal,* 21(3), 369–386.
Ruttan, R. and Boekema, F., 2007. The Learning Region: A Conceptual Anatomy. In R. Ruttan and F. Boekema (eds) *The Learning Region: Foundations, State of the Art, Future.* Cheltenham, UK, and Northampton, USA: Edward Elgar.
Ryan, B. and Gross, N.C., 1943. The Diffusion of Hybrid Seed Corn in Two Iowa Communities. *Rural Sociology,* 8, 15–24.
Saxenian, A., 1991. The Origins and Dynamics of Production Networks in Silicon Valley. *Research Policy,* 20(5), 423–437.
Schmitz, H. and Nadvi, K., 1999. Clustering and Industrialization: Introduction. *World Development*, 27(9), 1503–1514.
Schnell, I. and Sofer, M., 2002. Unbalanced Embeddedness of Ethnic Entrepreneurship: The Israeli Arab Case. *International Journal of Entrepreneurial Behaviour and Research*, 8(1/2), 54–68.
Sheffrin, S.M., 1996. *Rational Expectations*, 2nd edn. Cambridge: Cambridge University Press.

Smallbone, D., North, D. and Vickers, I., 2003. The Role and Characteristics of SMEs in Innovation. In B.T. Asheim *et al.* (eds) *Regional Innovation Policy for Small–Medium Enterprises.* Cheltenham, UK: Edward Elgar.

Sorenson, O., 2005. Social Networks and the Persistence of Clusters: Evidence from the Computer Workstation Industry. In S. Breschi and F. Malerba (eds) *Clusters, Networks and Innovation.* Oxford: Oxford University Press.

Storper, M. and Venables, A.J., 2004. Buzz: Face-to-face Contact and the Urban Economy. *Journal of Economic Geography*, 4(4), 351–370.

Swedberg, R., 2003. *Principles of Economic Sociology.* Princeton, NJ, and Oxford: Princeton University Press.

UNIDO, n.d., *General Review Study of Small and Medium Enterprise Clusters in India.* Vienna: United Nations Industrial Development Organisation.

Utterback, J.M., 1994. *Mastering the Dynamics of Innovation.* Boston, MA: Harvard Business School Press.

Uzzi, B., 1996. The Sources and Consequences of Embeddedness for the Economic Performance of Organizations: The Network Effect, *American Sociological Review*, 61(4), 674–698.

——, 1997. Social Structure and Competition in Interfirm Networks: The Paradox of Embeddedness. *Administrative Science Quarterly*, 42(1), 35–67.

Uzzi, B. and Lancaster, R., 2003. Relational Embeddedness and Learning: The Case of Bank Loan Managers and their Clients. *Management Science*, 49(4), 383–399.

van Dijk, M.P., 2005. 'Classifying Small Enterprise Clusters: A Conceptual Enquiry in Ahmedabad'. In K. Das (ed.) *Indian Industrial Clusters.* Burlington and Aldershot, UK: Ashgate.

van Dijk, M.P. and Rabellotti, R., 1997. *Enterprise Clusters and Networks in Developing Countries.* EADI Book Series 20. London: Frank Cass.

Varshney, A., 2010. Ethnic Conflict and Civil Society: India and Beyond. In C.M. Elliott (ed.) *Civil Society and Democracy: A Reader.* New Delhi: Oxford University Press.

Vedres, B. and Stark, D., 2010. Structural Folds: Generative Disruption in Overlapping Groups. *American Journal of Sociology*, 115(4), 1150–1190.

Vega-Redondo, F., 2007. *Complex Social Networks.* Cambridge: Cambridge University Press.

von Hippel, E., 1987. Cooperation between Rivals: Informal Know-how Trading. *Research Policy*, 16(6), 291–302.

——, 1988. *The Sources of Innovation.* Oxford and New York: Oxford University Press.

——, 1995. *Democratizing Innovation.* Cambridge, MA, and London: The MIT Press.

——, 2007. Horizontal Innovation Networks – By and For Users. *Industrial and Corporate Change*, 16(2), 293–315.

von Hippel, E. and Tyre, M.J. 2005. How Learning by Doing is Done: Problem Identification in Novel Process Equipment. *Research Policy*, 24(2), 1–12.

Vonortas, N.S., 2009. Innovation Networks in Industry. In F. Malerba and N.S. Vonortas (eds) *Innovation Networks in Industries.* Cheltenham, UK, and Northampton, USA: Edward Elgar.

Walker, G., Kogut, B. and Shan, W., 1997. Social Capital, Structural Holes and the Formation of the Industry Network. *Organization Science*, 8(2), 109–125.

Weber, M., 1978/1922. *Economy and Society: An Outline of Interpretive Sociology.* Los Angeles and London: University of California Press, Berkeley.

White, H.C., 1981. Where Do Markets Come From? *American Journal of Sociology*, 87, 517–547.

Wintrobe, R., 1995. Some Economics of Ethnic Capital Formation and Conflict. In A. Breton *et al.* (eds) *Nationalism and Rationality*. Cambridge: Cambridge University Press.

Woolcock, M., 1998. Social Capital and Economic Development: Toward a Theoretical Synthesis and Policy Framework. *Theory and Society*, 27(2), 151–208.

Woolcock, M. and Narayan, D., 2000. Social Capital: Implications for Development Theory, Research, and Policy. *The World Bank Research Observer*, 15(2), 225–249.

Young, H.P., 2009. Innovation Diffusion in Heterogeneous Populations: Contagion, Social Influence, and Social Learning. *American Economic Review*, 99(5), 1899–1924.

Zukin, S. and DiMaggio, P., 1990. *Structures of Capital: The Social Organisation of the Economy*. Cambridge, New York, and Melbourne: Cambridge University Press.

2 A simulation model of informal information sharing under complex social relations[1]

Introduction

This chapter presents a model of information sharing by means of informal interaction among agents in low-technology clusters. The appreciation of information sharing by means of informal interaction through social networks is not novel in the knowledge diffusion literature, and hence this model does not seek to reinvestigate simple barter-like information exchanges. Instead, it endeavours to understand these exchanges by placing them in environments of complex social relations, testing for whether the small-world network structure is the most favourable for information sharing in these environments, and exploring the influence of social relations and network distance on the magnitude and equity of information diffused.

Studies in the past on information diffusion across networks have dealt with the importance of the structure of the network for equity and efficiency of information distribution; an enquiry that still remains necessary when we deal with clusters whose only source of new information is informal interaction. But the analysis has to be extended by setting it in environments of complex social relations that are often inevitable in such clusters. On the one hand, informal information exchanges with co-located agents may be clean and untouched by any sort of social barrier among units (as in an environment of what is termed here a *universal affinity* between agents), while on the other hand these exchanges may arise as emergent properties of social differences that may exist in a more heterogeneous environment (as in a regime of complex social relations, or, at its extreme, of severe homophily). Community-based demarcations and long-existing social prejudices and affinities that arise as a result of these social boundaries would surely complicate social interactions and generate implications for vital knowledge flows. It might pay for agents to cross these long-existing social group demarcations to access new information, but at times it may not benefit, since reciprocity, value introjections and solidarity may take primacy over economic self-interest. It is in these environments that we question, in this chapter, the supremacy of the *small-world* network structure, which is often held by the literature as the most efficient network architecture for efficiency and equity in information diffusion.

Hence, this chapter has two objectives. First, it tests the hypothesis that the small-world network structure may *not* be the most efficient (in terms of magnitude and equity of knowledge diffused) for information diffusion through informal information sharing in a cluster set in a complex social relations environment. Second, it explores the effect of (a) the intensity of social relations in a cluster, and (b) the influence of network distance as a concern among information-exchanging agents on the performance of the cluster. These enquiries are the contribution of this model to the existing series of studies on efficient network structures for information diffusion. In the following section we review the background to this model by revisiting certain studies on informal information exchanges, network structure and the efficient diffusion of information.

Network structure and efficient knowledge diffusion

As we have seen in the previous chapter, exchanging new information on the latest and best production practices and technologies, on a continuous basis, free of monetary cost, even to rivals, is an oft invoked practice, since it is almost impossible and often expensive to keep information as a secret and it may sometimes work to the information giver's professional advantage to actually release the information (Allen, 1983). Most information flows through informal channels of word-of-mouth information exchanges and through social circles (Allen *et al.*, 1983). Networks gain prominence, serving as vehicles not only for learning but also for reinforcing social norms and values, defining the nature of the social capital of a region. They become a cluster's principal component and the vehicle through which learning is facilitated. Consequently, investigation into social networks is more than just an appealing metaphor or vocabulary; rather it is a precise way to test theories and propositions about social relationships (Wasserman and Faust, 1994).

In order to understand learning, diffusion and innovative performance, especially where tacit knowledge is freely shared or bartered to a subset of potentially interested agents, one is required to examine network dynamics and network structure, for which network models of diffusion have provided an ideal venue. A series of studies by Cowan and Jonard (2003, 2004, 2007) on information diffusion across networks provide the basis for the model and analysis in this chapter. In these models, the network structure is the pivotal element that decides the nature of information exchanges and long-run performance (in terms of mean knowledge level in the system, and speed and equity of knowledge distribution). They demonstrate that while short paths (and therefore a random network) diffuse information the fastest, and while cliquishness brings about advantages that provide the very basis for clusters, it is generally a *small-world network structure* – employing the advantages of both short path lengths and cliquishness – that reigns. Small-world networks enjoy the best of local cohesiveness with proximity (which provide rapid initial growth) as well as distant links (to access information beyond the immediate locale which provide for continued growth).[2] This rigorously demonstrates an established theme in the diffusion literature that while strong ties (and therefore strong cliques in networks) provide obvious benefits, it is weak ties (and therefore short path lengths) that provide the basis for continued progress and to source new ideas and know-how; this is based on the premise that with fewer indirect contacts an agent will be more restricted in terms of know-how (Granovetter, 1973). Small-world networks have been shown to arise in a wide variety of organised systems, from power grids to brain cells to scientific collaborations; which has led to the speculation that there is something fundamental and generalisable about their capacities to organise and govern success in social systems (Uzzi and Spiro, 2005).[3]

Cowan and Jonard (2003) study the importance of network architecture for collective invention and the rate of innovation, and find that network structure plays a fundamental role. They demonstrate the qualities of the small-world network as an efficient structure, especially when absorptive capacity is low.[4] Cowan and Jonard (2004) study diffusion, treating it as a process of barter and sharing, where the barter occurs when it is mutually profitable for the exchanging agents. Their results also demonstrate that the small-world network structure is the most efficient architecture where average knowledge reaches its highest steady state and coefficient of variation of knowledge diffused is lowest. Cowan and colleagues (2004) take it a step further and allow for the receiver of the new information to innovate and leap ahead of the broadcaster, a behaviour that is common among competing producers in an industry where becoming the innovation leader is a top priority. Cowan and Jonard (2007) also proceed further by analysing the relationship between network structure, population structure and scarcity of knowledge.

Hence, one of the most consistent findings in the series of papers by Cowan and Jonard is that network structure is pivotal for knowledge diffusion and, in the 2003 and 2004 studies, that the small-world network structure is generally the most effective in the progress and diffusion of information, barring exceptional circumstances. Of all the studies, Cowan and Jonard (2004) is the most influential for this chapter. In addition, as in that model, there is no innovation, only information sharing and learning.

The model

In this section, we begin with a description of the model's components: the cluster, its constituent agents, and their characteristics defined by their know-how and social group. We then introduce the affinity matrix characterising the social attributes of the agents and the cluster as a whole. This is followed by an illustration of interaction decisions on sharing information, and finally the mechanics of information sharing and learning. In this model, we simulate interactions for information sharing in the cluster across three kinds of network structure, each for four kinds of social relations in the cluster (represented by four types of affinity matrices). In the analysis, we test hypotheses that stem from the objectives of this chapter, and draw conclusions on the arguable superiority of the small-world network structure, the affinity regimes that perform best, and the effects of the model's parameters.

Model description

A cluster comprises N economic agents, with each agent i connected to n other agents. All agents can always observe everyone else's production. Each agent operates through a production function where output is determined only by an agent's efficiency, based on his or her knowledge level a_i. Hence, output Q_i takes the form:

$$Q_i = Ka_i \qquad\qquad [4.1]$$

The social network in the cluster is fixed, and generates an NxN social distance matrix $\mathbf{D}$, where

$$\mathbf{D} = [d_{ij}] \qquad\qquad [4.2]$$

Every agent can always observe every other agent's output and efficiency. An agent i is concerned about lagging behind the other $(N-1)$ agents in the cluster in terms of efficiency, which he or she attempts to overcome by learning through interacting from other agents. Decisions on whether to try to learn and from whom to learn are affected by a number of factors that have a bearing on both learners and teachers. An agent i becomes a 'learner' when he or she observes that his or her know-how a_i is less than the know-how a_j of another agent j.

The maximum information gain that i can aim for, on interacting with j and acquiring some extra know-how, is Δa_{ij}:

$$\Delta a_{ij} = \max (0, a_j - a_i) \qquad\qquad [4.3]$$

Agent j then appears as a potential 'teacher' from whom i can gain extra know-how. She remains only 'potential' until both teacher and learner actually agree to interact and share information.

Typically, a learner is unable to capture all of $\Delta a_{ij} = a_j - a_i$. Only a part of the know-how difference Δa_{ij} can actually be absorbed or learned by i, determined by an absorptive capacity parameter α that is set constant for all agents in the cluster. So while j may be willing to share Δa_{ij} in its entirety, the learner i can hope to gain only $\alpha \Delta a_{ij}$.

Network distance is an important determinant of whether or not i actually will approach the potential teacher j. A large network distance d_{ij} between the two will dissuade i from approaching j. The importance of network distance is captured in this model as parameter e_L, the 'strength of network distance'.

Now consider the potential teacher's point of view. There are two opposing effects of teaching that influence the potential teacher about whether or not to teach i the extra know-how. The first effect, a positive effect, is in the form of a 'reward' for teaching. The second effect is a 'teaching irritation' β, a negative effect on account of the time and effort he or she spends in teaching i. Understandably, β increases with Δa_{ij} as a bigger knowledge gap implies a greater effort for j, a potential teacher, to teach i.

Agents hold affinities or prejudices to one another, represented in an $N \times N$ affinity matrix **M**. Here, m_{ij} is a measure of the affinity between two agents i and j. Values of m range from 0 (complete prejudice) to 1 (complete affinity). Main diagonal elements are 1, out of each agent having perfect affinity towards oneself. For a cluster with N agents,

$$\mathbf{M} = \begin{bmatrix} 1 & m_{12} & m_{13} & m_{14} & \cdots & m_{1N} \\ m_{21} & 1 & m_{23} & m_{24} & \cdots & m_{2N} \\ m_{31} & m_{32} & 1 & m_{34} & \cdots & m_{3N} \\ \cdots & \cdots & \cdots & \cdots & \cdots & \cdots \\ m_{N1} & m_{N2} & m_{N3} & m_{N4} & \cdots & 1 \end{bmatrix} \qquad \begin{array}{l} 0 \leq m_{ij} \leq 1 \\ m_{ij} = m_{ji} \\ m_{ii} = 1 \end{array}$$

We examine four kinds of affinity matrices, one characterising 'simple' social relations and the other three 'complex' social relations.

1. **M1, Universal affinity:** an identity matrix, i.e. where all $m_{ij} = 1$, representing complete affinity between agents, and hence sense 'simple' social relations.
2. **M2, Group-level complex relations:** here, group level affinities appear. The N agents in the cluster are equally distributed across η social groups. In the affinity matrix, we carve out G_A, the entire set of agents (numbering N/η) in group A. G_{AB} in the affinity matrix **M2** shows affinity between two social groups A and B, where $0 \leq G_{AB} \leq 1$. Affinities between two agents depend on the affinities between the groups to which each is affiliated. That is, all agents in one group have equal affinity or prejudice towards all agents of another group. In addition, all agents within a group have, naturally, universal affinity to one another.

$$\mathbf{M2} = \begin{bmatrix} 1 & G_{12} & G_{13} & \cdots & G_{1\eta} \\ G_{21} & 1 & G_{23} & \cdots & G_{2\eta} \\ G_{31} & G_{32} & 1 & \cdots & G_{3\eta} \\ \cdots & \cdots & \cdots & \cdots & \cdots \\ G_{\eta 1} & G_{\eta 2} & G_{\eta 3} & \cdots & 1 \end{bmatrix} \qquad \begin{array}{l} 0 \leq G_{AB} \leq 1 \\ G_{AB} = G_{BA} \\ G_{AA} = 1 \end{array}$$

3. **M3, Perfect homophily:** here, **M3** is a block diagonal matrix, just as **M2**, where diagonal elements are 1 and all other G_{AB} are 0, due to homophily between social groups.
4. **M4, Individual-level complex relations:** where affinities and prejudices are between individuals, and **M4** is composed of entirely heterogeneous m_{ij} (except for $m_{ii} = 1$).

Agents receive social rewards and penalties upon interacting, which are based on affinities. A learner's rewards and penalties are denoted by Θ^L, and a teacher's by Θ^T. The importance of Θ^L and Θ^T in the interaction is controlled by a 'strength of affinity' effect γ, which acts like a cost affecting whether or not to approach a potential teacher, or for a teacher to teach a learner.

A learner's rewards Θ^L are the lowest when interacting with teachers with whom affinity is high. Θ^L increases for interacting with teachers that are increasingly prejudiced, at individual or group level, for the effort the learner has made in crossing a social barrier and accessing a more well-informed sub-network in the cluster.

That is,

$$\Theta^L = f\left(\frac{1}{m_{ij}}\right)$$

A teacher's rewards Θ^T, on the other hand, are zero for teaching a strongly prejudiced agent. His or her Θ^T increases when he or she teaches agents with increasing affinity, and Θ^T is the highest for teaching learners from the same social group, for helping reinforce group position in the cluster.

That is, $\Theta^T = f(m_{ij})$.

This is summarised in Table 2.1.

Hence, there are three impeding forces that bind learning: (1) absorptive capacity, (2) the effect of network distance, and (3) the effect of affinity.

Mechanics

Knowledge a_i is randomly assigned to all N agents, as are elements m_{ij} and G_{ab}, in each period. We randomly pick an agent i in the cluster and calculate Δa_{ij} with other $(N-1)$ agents in the cluster, to look for potential teachers. For a potential teacher j in the cluster, i.e. with whom $\Delta a_{ij} > 0$, the decision to actually approach the teacher is computed by Π^L_{ij}, known as the 'learner's payoff'. To recall, there are three elements for a learner that decide whether or not to actually approach a teacher: absorptive capacity α, a strength of network distance e_L, and the strength of affinity γ. These three parameters characterise the learner's payoff, as shown in [4.4].

$$\Pi^L_{ij} = (\alpha \Delta a_{ij}) - (e_L \cdot d_{ij}) - \gamma(\Theta^L) \qquad [4.4]$$

Note that the third element in the payoff, pertaining to the strength of affinity parameter, appears to act as a disincentive to approach a teacher j, on increasing affinity m_{ij}. From Table 2.1, we see that this is logical according to the rules of the model, with learners being incentivised to approach teachers from social groups that are prejudiced towards her own. That is, the payoff when affinity is low is greater than when affinity is high.

Table 2.1 Rewards for learners and teachers, based on affinities

Affinities	Learner	Teacher
1 (highest)	$\Theta^L = 0$	Θ^T is highest
Decreasing from 0.99	Θ^L increases	Θ^T decreases
0.01 (lowest)	Θ^L is highest	$\Theta^T = 0$

Source: author's own computations.

Learner i approaches $j*$ where:

$$j* = \frac{\max \Pi_{ij}^L}{j}$$ [4.5]

This potential teacher $j*$ then has to decide whether or not to teach i.

Now consider the potential teacher's decision making. For a potential teacher j to decide whether or not to teach agent i depends on his or her teaching payoff Π_{ji}^T. To recall, there are two elements influencing teaching: an irritation element β, and the strength of affinity parameter γ (whose magnitude determined the size of the effects of the different affinities). Hence, the teacher's payoff is:

$$\Pi_{ji}^T = \gamma(\Theta^T) - \beta ,$$ [4.6]

where β increases with Δa_{ij}.

The potential teacher $j*$ calculates [4.6], and teaches i only if the payoff is positive.

The direction of decision making is learner $\rightarrow$ teacher, i.e. first, a random learner i is picked, learner's payoffs Π_{ij}^L are computed, the potential teacher $j*$ who provides the highest Π_{ij}^L is selected, this teacher computes his or her Π_{ji}^T, and if $\Pi_{ji}^T > 0$, information sharing proceeds.

Only when *both* learner and teacher agree do interaction and information sharing proceed. If there is such an agreement, the learner i's know-how increases by $\alpha \Delta a_{ij}$; that is,

$$a_i + \alpha \Delta a_{ij}$$ [4.7]

In case $\Pi_{ij}^T \leq 0$, the teacher $j*$ declines to share information with i, and the learner's know-how remains the same at a_i. Note that there is no provision for the learner to pick the 'second-best' teacher and approach him or her. Once there is disagreement by the teacher $j*$, no information sharing proceeds, and we move on to the next period with the entire mechanics played out once again.

Network analysis and settings

Having constructed the decision-making rules of the model, we now proceed to enquire, for each **M**, the network structure fostering the highest and most equitable information diffusion in the cluster. We simulate interactions for information sharing in the cluster across three kinds of network structure (ordered, small-world and random network structures), for four kinds of social relations in the cluster. Many studies of know-how exchange and diffusion, reviewed in the discussion earlier, have convincingly shown that small worlds are the most efficient and equitable for information diffusion among agents engaging in barter and free broadcast of know-how when links are randomly generated. We follow an enquiry on network structure quite similar to the Cowan and Jonard series of studies, except that the model in this chapter is set in various social relations environments or regimes.

For simulation, we introduce a cluster with $N=300$ agents, divided into $\eta=10$ social groups, each agent possessing $n=4$ connections and an absorptive capacity $\alpha=0.80$. In each of the four social relations regimes we rewire the cluster's network in three arrangements corresponding to the Watts and Strogatz (1998) algorithm.[5] Using this algorithm permits us to construct three graphs: a circular n-nearest neighbour graph, an n-nearest neighbour graph in which we randomly rewrite 10 per cent of the connections, and a random graph. Randomness in the graph is therefore tuned to three levels: $p=0$ (ordered linear network), $p=0.10$ (small-world network) and $p=1$ (random network).

Hence, we have twelve sets of results: for three network structures in each of the four social relations regimes. We run the dynamics for 5,000 iterative 'periods' (each 'period' being the entire mechanics of interaction that occurs over section 3, from surveying potential teachers to actually absorbing the new information), and we calculate a number of measures over each network structure for each social relations regime (i.e. for each p value across each **M** regime). For each point in parameter space, we replicate 100 times (except for $p=0.10$ where we did 200 replications). For each (p, **M**) pair, we calculate average knowledge *AvgK* of the cluster (i.e. the average of all agents' a_i) and coefficient of variation[6] *CoeffVar* (of the entire cluster's a_i) in know-how in the cluster.

The hypotheses that stem from the two objectives of this study as mentioned at the outset of this chapter are as follows:

Hypothesis 1: The small-world network structure may not be the most efficient network structure for information diffusion, in terms of performance (*AvgK* and *CoeffVar*), in an environment coloured with complex social relations.

Hypothesis 2a: A regime with universal affinity, namely **M1**, is the regime that achieves highest performance in terms of both *AvgK* and *CoeffVar*.

Hypothesis 2b: A regime with perfect homophily, namely **M3**, is the regime that performs best among the complex social relations regimes **M2**, **M3** and **M4**.

Hypothesis 3a: Strong affinity effects (captured by the 'strength of affinity' parameter γ) and network distance effects (captured by the 'strength of network distance' parameter e_L) generally decrease *AvgK* in the cluster as a whole.

Hypothesis 3b: Strong affinity effects (captured by γ) and network distance effects (captured by e_L) generally decrease equity, i.e. increase *CoeffVar* in the cluster as a whole.

Results

The first part of this section looks at results compared across p for each **M**, while the second part looks at individual effects of γ and e_l. **M2** (Group Level Complex Relations) takes focus, as it is here where interactions occur in environments with complex social relations among social groups. We also see some interesting results in **M3**.

Performance across social relations regimes and across network structures

In this section, we compare results across the three network structures and four affinity regimes. We know from the literature that small-world networks allow for the most efficient and equitable knowledge distribution among network structures as they capture the benefits of both high cliquishness and short path lengths. In an ordered network, cliquishness is very high but path length is low, permitting the quick transfer of information among proximate nodes but slow diffusion to far-off nodes, which also means that they are inefficient in quickly tapping valuable information from distant nodes. Random networks on the other hand may surmount the network distance issue, but problems arise due to low cliquishness. Hence, small-world networks, which provide for the benefits of both short path length and high cliquishness, offer the most efficient and equitable information diffusion and distribution.

In our model, we complicate the case by demarcating the cluster by social group, and attach rewards and penalties for interactions between and within the groups. We test the supremacy of the small-world network structure for clusters with complex social relations. We realise that a small-world network structure *is indeed* more conducive for better performance in the cluster, but this is not the case for equity in knowledge distribution. Let us see the results for each type of network structure.

First, for each social arrangement (**M**) we ask at which network structure we observe highest *AvgK* and lowest *CoeffVar*. Second, at each network structure we find out which **M** scores the highest *AvgK* and the lowest *CoeffVar*. After this, we study the underlying dynamics of information sharing for each (p, **M**) pair.

Performance of network structures across social relations regimes

Tables 2.2 and 2.3 display at what network structure each **M** regime has its respective highest *AvgK* (Table 2.2) or lowest *CoeffVar* (Table 2.3).

We see that at a small-world network structure ($p=0.10$) all social relations regimes observe consistently higher performance in terms of *AvgK*, compared to other network structures. In addition, upon conducting a t-test for difference in means between $p=0.1$ and the other two p values, this result was found to be statistically significant in nearly all cases. However, the case is different for

Table 2.2 Network structure at which each regime scores highest AvgK

M1 Perfect affinity		M2 Group-level complex relations		M3 Perfect homophily		M4 Individual-level complex relations	
Network Structure	Highest AvgK	Network Structure	Highest AvgK	Network Structure	Highest AvgK	Network Structure	Highest AvgK
Ordered	0.982	Ordered	0.464	Ordered	0.430	Ordered	0.444
SW	0.986	SW	0.983	SW	0.847	SW	0.948
Random	0.908	Random	0.847	Random	0.309	Random	0.408

Source: author's own computations.

Note
SW = Small-world.

Table 2.3 Network structure at which each regime scores lowest *CoeffVar*

M1 Perfect affinity		M2 Group-level complex relations		M3 Perfect homophily		M4 Individual-level complex relations	
Network Structure	Lowest *CoeffVar*	Network Structure	Lowest *CoeffVar*	Network Structure	Lowest *CoeffVar*	Network Structure	Lowest *CoeffVar*
Ordered	0.001	Ordered	0.008	Ordered	0.166	Ordered	0.171
SW	0.001	SW	0.024	SW	0.179	SW	0.156
Random	0.026	Random	0.048	Random	0.132	Random	0.083

Source: author's own computations.

Note
SW = Small-world.

equity in knowledge distribution, *CoeffVar*. The regimes achieving their lowest *CoeffVar* are either ordered or random network structures; while **M2**, **M3** and **M4** achieve significantly lower *CoeffVar* at ordered (**M2**) and random (**M3** and **M4**) networks, **M1** achieves its lowest *CoeffVar* at both the ordered and small-world network. Hence, results are mixed for **M1** alone, but clear for the other regimes – small worlds do not provide significantly better equity in knowledge distribution in a cluster coloured by complex social relations.

Table 2.4 summarises the results of Tables 2.2 and 2.3. We can reinforce the superiority of small worlds for performance, but not for equity.

Hypothesis 1 proposed that the small-world network structure may not be the most favourable to interaction, learning and equity in clusters with complex social relations. The results here are mixed. Hypothesis 1 is partly rejected, and we state Proposition 1.

> **Proposition 1:** When information sharing is undertaken in environments of complex social relations among networked agents in a cluster, a small-world network structure may still be the best network structure facilitating the highest performance, but is not the best for most equitable knowledge distribution.

Performance of social relations regimes across network structures

We now address Hypotheses 2a and 2b. Hypothesis 2a proposes that **M1** (Universal Affinity), in any network structure, achieves the highest performance in terms of both *AvgK* and *CoeffVar*. Hypothesis 2b proposes that **M3** (Perfect Homophily) performs best among the three complex social relations regimes (**M2**, **M3**, **M4**). Hypothesis 2a is obvious, as information sharing is logically the easiest and smoothest where there are no complications in terms of affinities and prejudices among groups or individuals; as a result, knowledge is also most equitably distributed. Hypothesis 2b may appear odd at first, considering that performance and equity in a perfect homophilous regime would be very inferior

Table 2.4 Summary of results in Tables 2.2 and 2.3

Regime	Network structure at which highest AvgK is attained	Network structure at which lowest CoeffVar is attained
Universal affinity (**M1**)	Small-world	Ordered and small-world*
Group-level complex relations (**M2**)	Small-world*	Ordered*
Perfect homophily (**M3**)	Small-world*	Random*
Individual-level complex relations (**M4**)	Small-world*	Random*

Source: author's own computations.

Note

* Indicates significantly different, at a 10% level, from other network structures.

when social groups display the highest prejudices towards one another. However, we hypothesise thus because **M3** is nothing but a set of 10×10 unit matrices, which allows for a large majority of interactions within these blocks, therefore being ten versions of **M1**.[7] Results may be inferred from Table 2.5.

From Table 2.5 we see that **M1** clearly scores the highest *AvgK* and the lowest *CoeffVar* consistently across all network structures. In most cases, this result is also statistically significant. Hence, a cluster characterised by universal affinity is indeed the best-performing one. We therefore accept Hypothesis 2a, and state Proposition 2.

> **Proposition 2:** The best performance and most equitable knowledge distribution, with informal information sharing among networked agents in a cluster, are achieved when there is universal affinity among the agents.

But Hypothesis 2b can be rejected immediately. **M3** does not appear to perform better than **M2** (Group Level Complex Relations) or **M4** (Individual Level Complex Relations). In fact, **M2** shows a consistently (and, confirmed by a t-test, significantly) better performance compared to **M3** and **M4** in all networks. Hence, we reject Hypothesis 2b.

We also observe the extent of cross-group interactions in each social relations regime across network structure. Interestingly, the regime that hosts the highest cross-group interactions is **M3** (Perfect Homophily), where inter-group prejudices are the *highest*.

As observed in Table 2.6, the cross-group interactions in **M3** are *double* in ordered and small-world networks, compared to the respective regime in second position. **M1** (Universal Affinity) seems to have the lowest inter-group interaction in two out of three network structures. This may be because, in this model, learners are rewarded the highest when prejudices are highest (see Table 2.1). Hence, in a perfect homophily regime they strive to tap information from out-of-group teachers. But it may be argued, conversely, that teachers are severely penalised when prejudices are highest, and must hence refuse to teach. The reason why this result here comes about may simply be because the difference in knowledge Δa_{ij} between teachers and learners may be low enough to allow the teachers' payoff [4.6] to remain positive, to coax teachers to agree to impart information. A point to note, and the reason why we do not frame a generalisable proposition here, is that this result may have stemmed from the way in which the rewards and penalties in this model have been constructed.[8]

Individual effects of strength of affinity (γ) and strength of network distance (e_L) on performance

For this section we refer to Figures 2.1 and 2.2. The results are represented by contour plots of *AvgK* (Figure 2.1) and *CoeffVar* (Figure 2.2) across a $\gamma - e_L$ space. Again, the perfect homophily regime **M3** displays some interesting results.

Table 2.5 For each network structure, which social relations regime performs best

Ordered network (p = 0)

Regime	Max AvgK	Regime	Min CoeffVar
M1	0.982	M1	0.001
M2	0.464	M2	0.008
M3	0.430	M3	0.066
M4	0.444	M4	0.171

Random network (p = 1)

Regime	Max AvgK	Regime	Min CoeffVar
M1	0.908	M1	0.026
M2	0.424	M2	0.048
M3	0.309	M3	0.132
M4	0.408	M4	0.083

Small-world network (p = 0.10)

Regime	Max AvgK	Regime	Min CoeffVar
M1	0.986	M1	0.001
M2	0.983	M2	0.024
M3	0.847	M3	0.179
M4	0.948	M4	0.156

Source: author's own computations.

Table 2.6 Proportion of cross-group interactions (as percentage of all learner–teacher interactions) across *p* and **M**

Ordered network (p = 0)		Small-world network (p = 0.10)		Random network (p = 1)	
Regime	Cross-group interaction (%)	Regime	Cross-group interaction (%)	Regime	Cross-group interaction (%)
M1	3.25	**M1**	19.00	**M1**	49.25
M2	5.50	**M2**	16.75	**M2**	54.00
M3	10.50	**M3**	37.25	**M3**	71.50

Source: author's own computations.

Individual effects of γ and e_L on AvgK

The discussion below relates to Figure 2.1. What is interesting is that high *AvgK* is consistently achieved at high *γ* levels. Let us discuss these results.

In all regimes, and at all network structures, we observe that the effect of *γ* (affinity effect) appears very strong at low e_L (network distance effect) levels. This strong effect diminishes at higher e_L levels (especially in **M1**, **M2** and **M3** at ordered network *p*=0), at which e_L exerts its influence. This result suggests that when network distance is an unimportant factor, learners in an ordered network are willing to contact well-endowed out-of-group teachers located even

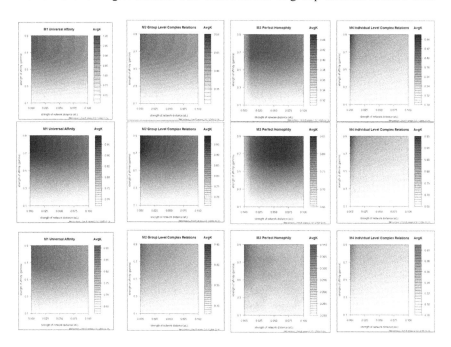

Figure 2.1 Effect of e_L (strength of network distance) and *γ* (strength of affinity) on *AvgK* (source: author's own computation).

at far network distances. But when network distance steadily increases in importance, seeking out-of-group teachers (which in an ordered network are relatively further away) becomes less of a possibility.

In a small-world network, however, strong affinity effects (γ) last slightly longer. The reason, based on the constraint of network distance of cross-group teachers, is as follows. While in an ordered network, for a learner, teachers of other groups are on average very distant in the network, the learner therefore faces high network distance costs in approaching knowledgeable teachers of other social groups in an ordered network. In a small-world network, cross-group teachers can be closer in terms of network distance (due to the presence of long-distance links in the network), and consequently a learner faces lower network distance costs in approaching them. Hence, learners enjoy the strong positive effects of γ for slightly longer in a small-world network.

According to Table 2.1, learners are incentivised to approach accessing out-of-group teachers, since learners are given high rewards as prejudices increase. This incentive is compounded when γ is strengthened.In addition, as long as a very low teaching irritation or very low Δa_{ij} offsets the teacher's penalty for teaching an out-of-group learner, teaching will proceed. This is one reason why high $AvgK$ is achieved at high γ levels. Thus, the part of Hypothesis 3a which states that strong affinity effects would decrease $AvgK$ is rejected.

Hence, as we see, the effect of e_L gets stronger from middle levels of γ onwards, and it decreases $AvgK$ as expected. Hence, the part of Hypothesis 3a which states that strong network distance effects decrease $AvgK$ is not rejected.

Individual effects of γ and e_L on CoeffVar

We now turn to the individual effects of γ and e_L on *CoeffVar*. The discussion below relates to Figure 2.2. Hypothesis 3b proposed that strong affinity effects (γ) and strong network distance effects (e_L) would generally decrease equity (increase *CoeffVar*).

In addition, it was expected that at higher γ, agents would learn only from own-group teachers, which would result in improvements only in those groups with more knowledgeable teachers, with the cluster ultimately ending up unequally knowledge endowed.

It was conjectured that at higher e_L, learners who were proximate in network distance to very knowledgeable teachers would learn more and those who were proximate to not-so-knowledgeable teachers would learn comparatively less, due to which *CoeffVar* would increase.

The results, as we see, are mixed.

At low network distance effect (e_L), a higher affinity effect (γ) appears to strongly stimulate *higher* equity (lower *CoeffVar*). At higher e_L, however, just as for $AvgK$, this strong effect of γ on *CoeffVar* diminishes. The only exception for this is in a perfect homophily regime **M3** (note particularly $p=0.10$), where an increasing e_L begins to exert its influence in increasing equity, especially at a higher γ level.

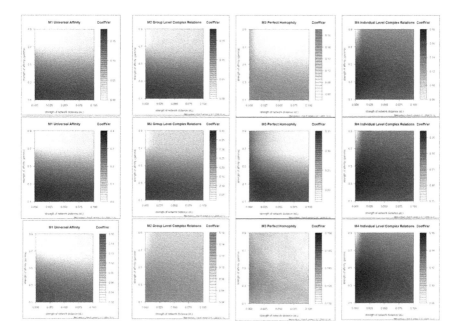

Figure 2.2 Effect of e_L (strength of network distance) and γ (strength of affinity) on *Coef-fVar* (source: author's own computation).

The reason for this may be that for learners in a perfect homophily regime **M3**, which out-of-group teacher they approach is irrelevant, since all out-of-group learners are perceived equally, and incentive to approach them is equally high. For teachers too, the incentive to teach is also equal, since all out-of-group learners are at par, and, as long as knowledge gaps are small, they are indifferent to teaching anyone outside of their group. In such a situation, despite a high network distance bringing in a relatively higher cost in approaching out-of-group teachers, the effects of affinity are stronger. Especially in a small-world network, where out-of-group teachers are more proximate, a higher e_L does not pose as much a constraint, and interaction occurs across groups.

The lighter patches signifying lower *CoeffVar* and therefore greater equity are generally concentrated in the higher γ regions. The highest equity is in most cases reached at high-γ-low-e_L values, nearly in correspondence with the area at which highest *AvgK* is also reached. And consistently, the lowest equity (highest *CoeffVar*) is reached at low-γ-low-e_L values in most cases. Hence, the part of Hypothesis 3b that strong affinity effects (through γ) generally decrease equity (increase *CoeffVar*) is rejected, while the part that states that network distance effects (through e_L) generally decrease equity (increase *CoeffVar*) is not rejected.

Summing up results, and lessons

Results of this simulation are summed up in Table 2.7.

Two propositions have emerged out of these results.

1   **Proposition 1:** When information sharing is undertaken in environments of complex social relations among networked agents in a cluster, a small-world network structure may still be the best network structure facilitating the highest performance, but is not the best for most equitable knowledge distribution.

2   **Proposition 2:** The best performance and most equitable knowledge distribution, with informal information sharing among networked agents in a cluster, is achieved when there is universal affinity among the agents.

In addition, we have observed that the perfect homophily regime **M3** has unexpected and often contrasting results compared to the other regimes. **M3** emerges as the regime with the most cross-group interactions, with even **M1** (Universal Affinity) generally experiencing much less cross-group interaction. In addition, the effects of network distance are generally positive with regard to performance and equity, only in **M3** in a small-world network structure.

As we discussed earlier in this chapter, a broad stream of the literature in know-how diffusion across social networks in clusters deals with the importance of network architecture and the equity and efficiency of knowledge distribution. Vega-Redondo (2007) and Vedres and Stark (2010) have explained how network architecture is the key issue while studying diffusion, embeddedness, structural holes and so on. In this stream of literature, small-world networks have received a large proportion of the attention, due to their proven effects on system dynamics (Uzzi and Spiro, 2005).

When we deal with clusters inhabited by economic agents whose only source of new information is informal interaction and defensive innovation, enquiring into efficient network structure is necessary, as Vega-Redondo explained, but the analysis has to also be coloured with complex social relations that are inevitable in such clusters. This is the contribution of this model to the existing series of studies on efficient network structures for knowledge diffusion around a new technology. In addition, as Golub and Jackson (2012) and Jackson and López-Pintado (2013) point out, much of the literature on the impact of social network structure on learning and diffusion has not focused on the effect of homophily on diffusion, emerging as a theme that requires more attention in the diffusion literature.

In recent times when production demands and learning take priority among agents even in traditional technology clusters, long-existing complex social relations may still hold sway in economic decision making; but they may not be able to take complete control of agents' behaviour at an individual level while calculating information-sharing decisions. Agents may cross these social groups to share know-how. Even for information providers (depicted as 'teachers' in this

Table 2.7 Summary of results

Objective	Hypothesis	Result
Whether a small-world network structure is most efficient in a complex social relations environment	Hypothesis 1: The small-world network structure may not be the most efficient network structure for knowledge diffusion, in terms of performance (*AvgK* and *CoeffVar*), in an environment coloured with complex social relations.	A small-world network structure is significantly better for high performance, but not superior in equitable knowledge diffusion, in complex social relations environments. Hypothesis 1 is partly rejected.
Which social relations regime generally performs the best	Hypothesis 2a: A regime with universal affinity and no complexity in social relations, **M1**, is the regime that achieves highest performance in terms of both *AvgK* and *CoeffVar*.	**M1** (universal affinity) does turn out to be the best-performing regime in achieving both highest *AvgK* as well as lowest *CoeffVar*. Hypothesis 2a is accepted.
	Hypothesis 2b: A regime with perfect homophily, **M3**, is the regime that performs best among the complex social relations regimes **M2**, **M3** and **M4**.	The second-best performing regime is **M2**. Hypothesis 2b is rejected.
Individual effects of strength-of-affinity and strength-of-network distance on performance and equity	Hypothesis 3a: Strong affinity effects (captured by the 'strength of affinity' parameter γ) and network distance effects (captured by the 'strength of network distance' parameter e_L) generally decrease *AvgK* in the cluster as a whole.	*AvgK* generally reaches its peak at lower e_L levels. The only exception is for **M3** in a small-world network. But, contrary to expectation, *AvgK* always reaches its peak at higher γ levels. Hypothesis 3a can be completely rejected for γ, but generally not rejected for e_L.
	Hypothesis 3b: Strong affinity effects (captured by γ) and network distance effects (captured by e_L) generally decrease equity, i.e. increase *CoeffVar* in the cluster as a whole.	*CoeffVar* seems to increase in e_L, except in the **M3** case, but consistently decreases in γ. Hypothesis 3b can be completely rejected for γ, but generally not rejected for e_L.

Source: author's own computations.

model) who share their new know-how, old inclinations to retain group dominance may fall flat. We end the study on this positive note: demarcations erected
by prejudices between social groups can be overcome, permitting information
sharing and learning, and allowing for the aggregate progress of a low-tech
cluster in an environment of complex social relations.

Notes

1 A modified version of this chapter has appeared in Kamath (2013).
2 While Watts and Strogatz (1998) and Watts (1999) are popular citations for the small-
world network structure, Freeman (2004) points out that it was Ithiel de Sola Pool and
Manfred Kochen who introduced the term 'small world' in the network context,
through a 1958 manuscript, which was republished as De Sola Pool and Kochen (1978)
twenty years later. A 1967 article by Stanley Milgram drew from the 1958 manuscript,
and it was only subsequent to this that Watts and Strogatz (apparently unaware of the
de Sola Pool and Kochen study) based their popular 1998 work on the small-world
structure (Freeman, 2004, p. 164).
3 However, Uzzi and Spiro (2005) have shown that even when agents in social networks
are connected as a small world, there is a high probability of cohesion stemming from
this. They demonstrate that the relationship between a small world and performance
follows an inverted U-shaped curve. They describe how when separate clusters of
agents become more interlinked, cohesion in turn increases, reducing the probability of
innovativeness, of fresh ideas, and consequently of high performance. Uzzi and Spiro
construct and employ what is termed a 'small-world quotient' Q, which indicates how
connected and cohesive agents in the network are, and consequently how productive or
unproductive performance and creativity can become. Using the example of Broadway
musicals, they find out that the financial and artistic success of a production increases
at medium levels of Q and decreases at either low or high levels of Q. That is, the
positive effects of connectivity backfire by homogenising the pool of creative material,
and rendering agents incapable of breaking out of conventional ideas and styles.
4 The only situation where the small-world network structure does not rule in this model
is when knowledge is easy to transmit and absorb. A random network is most efficient
in this case.
5 The Watts–Strogatz algorithm permits us to construct a spectrum of graphs, which, at
one end represents an 'ordered' or 'regular' graph, and on the other end a 'random'
graph with uniform degree. From the ordered graph, with the probability p, we may
disconnect one vertex and reconnect it to another vertex at random, as long as there are
no duplications. The graph is varied in structure from completely regular, with a $p=0$,
to a completely disordered and random graph of $p=1$. Randomness in the graph is
therefore tuned to three levels: $p=0$ (ordered linear network), $p=0.10$ (small-world
network) and $p=1$ (random network).
6 We use coefficient of variation instead of a simple measure of variance, since results
shown by a measure of variance can be misleading when the mean increases through
scaling effects.
7 Following this, we may also assume that in **M3**, cross-group interactions may only be
occasional. We will be shortly verifying this by looking at the extent of cross-group
interactions among regimes across network structures.
8 This is not to say that this model has been 'engineered' for this result – in fact, we
assumed earlier on the contrary, and for good reason, that **M3** would most likely have
the *lowest* cross-group interactions.

References

Allen, R.C., 1983. Collective Invention. *Journal of Economic Behavior and Organization*, 4, 1–24.

Allen, T.J., Hyman, D.B. and Pinckney, D.L., 1983. Transferring Technology to the Small Manufacturing Firm: A Study of Technology Transfer in Three Countries. *Research Policy*, 12(4), 199–211.

Cowan, R. and Jonard, N., 2003. The Dynamics of Collective Invention. *Journal of Economic Behavior and Organization*, 52, 513–532.

——, 2004. Network Structure and the Diffusion of Knowledge. *Journal of Economic Dynamics and Control*, 28, 1557–1575.

——, 2007. Structural Holes, Innovation and the Distribution of Ideas. *Journal of Economic Interaction and Coordination*, 2, 93–110.

Cowan, R., Jonard, N. and Özman, M., 2004. Knowledge Dynamics in a Network Industry. *Technological Forecasting and Social Change*, 71, 469–484.

De Sola Pool, I. and Kochen, M., 1978. Contacts and Influence. *Social Networks*, 1(1), 5–51.

Freeman, L.C., 2004. *The Development of Social Network Analysis: A Study in the Sociology of Science.* Vancouver: Empirical Press.

Golub, B. and Jackson, M.O., 2012. How Homophily affects the Speed of Learning and Best Response Dynamics. *Quarterly Journal of Economics*, 127(3), 1287–1338.

Granovetter, M., 1973. The Strength of Weak Ties. *American Journal of Sociology*, 78(6), 1360–1380.

Jackson, M.O. and López-Pintado, D., 2013. Diffusion and Contagion in Networks with Heterogeneous Agents and Homophily. *Network Science*, 1(1), 49–67.

Kamath, A., 2013. Interactive Knowledge Exchanges under Complex Social Relations: A Simulation Model of a Developing Country Cluster. *Technology in Society*, 35(4), 294–305, Elsevier.

Uzzi, B. and Spiro, J., 2005. Collaboration and Creativity: The Small World Problem. *American Journal of Sociology*, 111(2), 447–504.

Vedres, B. and Stark, D., 2010. Structural Folds: Generative Disruption in Overlapping Groups. *American Journal of Sociology*, 115(4), 1150–1190.

Vega-Redondo, F., 2007. *Complex Social Networks.* Cambridge: Cambridge University Press.

Wasserman, S. and Faust, K., 1994. *Social Network Analysis: Methods and Applications.* Cambridge: Cambridge University Press.

Watts, D.J., 1999. *Small Worlds: The Dynamics of Networks between Order and Randomness.* Princeton, NJ, and Oxford: Princeton University Press.

Watts, D.J. and Strogatz, S.H., 1998. Collective Dynamics of Small-world Networks. *Nature*, 393, 440–442.

3 From modelling to empirical study

There were four social relations regimes in the model in Chapter 2: universal affinity, group-level complex relations, perfect homophily and individual-level complex relations. This categorising was convenient for the model but it is stark, and clusters in the real world fall mostly within the range of group-level and individual-level complex relations. Perfect homophily is virtually non-existent, though there are a few examples of clusters whose members hold universal affinity with one another.

We had, in the model, observed that a cluster with universal affinity among its social groups would show the most seamless information sharing and display the best performance in terms of both average level of knowledge in the cluster as well as equity in the distribution of knowledge among the cluster's agents. For the first empirical study in this book, we go deeper into a universal affinity regime, undertaking the study of an actual case of such a cluster and its attempt to adapt to an innovation purely through informal information sharing between the cluster's members, who shared universal affinity with one another. The reason we do so is to study what the characteristics of such an environment are, to explore interaction mechanisms and channels within and around the cluster, to investigate the importance of information flows and learning processes within such clusters in their attempt to learn and adapt to technological change, and the institutional terrain within which these mechanisms and dynamics operate.

But clusters with universal affinity are in a minority. The majority of clusters display complex social relations, often at the group level. In India, these 'groups' are often divided on the basis of community (which could be delineated by caste, religion, and other such social attributes), which often bring along with them centuries of prejudices and affinities. To study information sharing in these environments becomes only imperative, as many clusters in the low-tech end of the spectrum in India are rural and traditional technology clusters, and many of these, such as traditional artisan clusters and even some industrial and manufacturing clusters, are heavily caste- and community-based. We had observed from the model that high performance results when the strength of social group relations is the strongest, i.e. when prejudices and affinities among social groups matter significantly to the agents exchanging information. However, the social capital and social embeddedness literature discussed in Chapter 1 had at its core the fact that social relations steer production relations, often with favourable results in the short term, but in the long term with unfavourable consequences. We need to examine the actual nature of information sharing in group-level complex social relations environments to ascertain both what the model has shown us as well as what the literature has propositioned.

Hence, there are two empirical tasks ahead of us, addressing questions for which the simulation model in Chapter 2 has given us the basis: (1) to study the nature and characteristics of informal information sharing in a low-tech cluster with universal affinity among its agents; and (2) to study the effect of social capital, and especially social embeddedness and homophily, on informal information sharing between agents in a traditional technology cluster where social groups and the divisions among them matter significantly and influence their information-sharing interaction decisions over the long term. For the first task we choose a coir (coconut fibre)-producing cluster, and for the second task an ethnic handloom weavers' cluster. The second exercise is composed of two parts: a network study and a historical study.

The entire empirical part of this book is set in Kerala state in south India, a state where low-tech industries form the backbone of its industry.

4 Informal information sharing in a universal affinity setting

Empirical study of a coir cluster[1]

Introduction

This chapter is a descriptive case study of a cluster in a low-tech traditional industry – the coir[2] industry – in Kerala, southern India. The aim of this chapter is to examine the nature of informal information sharing in a low-tech cluster characterised by universal affinity among its agents, using the case of a coir cluster as an illustration of the consequences of universal affinity on various dimensions of interaction in the cluster, and its role in allowing for smooth information diffusion.

South India, particularly Kerala state, has long been the world's principal coir-producing and processing region with tens of thousands of units ranging from large exporting firms to households producing and processing coir. Some have fully (and easily) mechanised, but many units at cottage and household levels still operate with traditional production methods, or intermediate technologies at best. There are several studies devoted to the study of the technologies operated in this industry, but they have given little attention to the informal learning sources, methods and practices that are vibrant in the clusters that constitute this industry. Early as well as contemporary studies on the coir industry (Isaac *et al.*, 1992; Rammohan, 1999; Rammohan and Sundaresan, 2003; CSES, 2008) may be very comprehensive, but evidently lack investigation into learning and information-gathering capabilities of clusters. Even a detailed ground-level study like CSES (2008) is deficient in this regard.

This chapter therefore has two aims. First, it examines the intricacies around information diffusion through informal information sharing in a universal affinity setting. Second, it aims to supplement the literature on the technology development and diffusion experiences in the coir industry by illustrating characteristics of learning experiences at the cluster level. These concerns are addressed by means of an empirical study of one coir yarn-producing cluster in the village of Manappuram in the district of Aleppey in Kerala, in its experiences in learning and adapting to an exogenously introduced innovation – a ½ horse-power (HP) motorised spinning wheel (or *ratt*) to spin the coir fibre into yarn. We provide evidence that an environment of affinity was the chief factor behind the cluster's smooth information diffusion experience around this innovation, ultimately leading to an improvement in the cluster's daily spinning output.

We first look at some essentials on technological modernisation in coir, to get a picture of what the industry has gone through so far. Following this, we examine what the Information Base has had to say about prescribing technological change in coir, and details on field procedures. We then move on to the findings of the field study, followed by lessons.

Technological modernisation in coir

The term 'traditional industry' refers not only to an industry's historical traditions, but also to its continuous and living traditional technology (Rajan and Kumar, 2004). 'Traditional technology' implies that labour processes are essentially manual and less dependent upon machine power (Isaac *et al.*, 1992). The coir industry in Kerala was (and for the most part still is) largely a traditional industry characterised by traditional technology. It is the second largest employer and source of livelihood in Kerala after agriculture, employing around 350,000 people (GoK, 2009). One-third of villages in the state are 'coir villages' and one-third of the land in Kerala is used for coconut cultivation (Coir Board, 2001; GoK, 2009). This industry attracts considerable budgetary support each year from the central and state governments, and is also a large export revenue generator. It holds global significance, since around half of the world's coir comes from India, particularly from the coir industry in Kerala. Almost 98 per cent of the coir industry in Kerala consists of units in the household sector (Table 4.1), a feature that has changed little over the past three decades (SPB, 1973; CSES, 2008).

These household units engage mostly in spinning, weaving and fibre extraction work; spinning alone accounts for 75 per cent of household employment in the industry. Three-quarters of coir workers are unskilled women (GoK, 2009; Rajan and Kumar, 2004). Historically, too, coir and Kerala have been synonymous.[3]

Table 4.1 Distribution of units across eleven districts in Kerala state (as of 2007)

District	Coir units	Household units (% of total coir units)		Cooperatives (active and functioning)	Other units (exporters, merchants, manufacturers, etc.)
Aleppey	62,549	11,724	*(98.68)*	152	673
Calicut	3,627	3,468	*(95.61)*	59	106
Kottayam	3,313	3,241	*(97.82)*	26	46
Kollam	1,744	1,612	*(92.43)*	54	78
Trivandrum	1,562	1,443	*(92.38)*	50	69
Malappuram	1,004	974	*(97.01)*	12	18
Thrissur	808	757	*(93.68)*	12	39
Kasargod	320	307	*(95.93)*	7	6
Ernakulam	253	209	*(82.60)*	21	23
Kannur	248	213	*(85.88)*	20	15
Palakkad	43	25	*(58.13)*	4	14
Total	75,471	73,973	*(98.01)*	411	1,087

Source: own computations from data in CSES (2008).

In the past, many minor incremental inventions were said to have developed in coir-producing clusters as a result of day-to-day experiments and on-the-spot solutions to immediate problems. One such innovation was the use of a bicycle wheel as a spinning wheel, and another was the introduction of a polythene thread at the commencement of the yarn while spinning to facilitate effective bonding of the yarn. All these innovations were locally created inventions that incrementally improved intermediate stages of the production process. Diffusion of these inventions in the immediate surroundings was relatively easy, since production knowledge in coir was freely accessible for decades. Minor incremental inventions in the local neighbourhood were easily perceptible and replicable. But invention has not always been in the sole purview of local actors. Across the last century, the state and other agents often stepped in and introduced crucial innovations that furthered the mechanisation of this industry. However, the response to mechanisation has been negative for most of these decades, Rammohan (1999) even likening the resistance to a Luddite kind.[4] The resistance to mechanisation and large-firm entrepreneurship was at its height from the 1950s to the 1980s, a trend that threatened to propel the industry into a long-term technological lock-in and a slow death. So strong was the trade union movement in this industry that most of the literature on the coir industry in Kerala has found it hard to separate the analysis of technological change in coir from the saga of trade union movements and cooperative movements in the state.

But by the mid-1980s, the coir industry in Kerala slowly began weakening its bond with the trade unions out of a sense of urgency that had arisen in the industry at the time. The rise of synthetic substitutes, more attractive in appearance and less expensive in cost, gestured towards an eventual replacement of coir fibre. Severe shortages of coconut husk (the chief source of the fibre) and a general disinterest among young workers to participate in this industry also added to the industry's difficulties. Due to these two factors, the coir industry had slowly become a 'sick' traditional industry by the 1990s. The industry that hitherto vociferously resisted technical change and prided itself on traditional technological practices was now in crucial need of mechanisation and modernisation for survival. By the end of the 1990s, the only path to survival appeared to lie in technological innovation.

Despite all of this, advanced technology has only superficially reached the household sector, the broadest part of the industry. In fact, a comprehensive survey of the coir industry by CSES (2008) shows that the majority of households in the state use mostly intermediate technologies, in spite of the highly subsidised and vigorous promotion of innovations across all stages of coir fibre and yarn production. Traditional methods are preferred over intermediate technologies, and fully mechanised production technologies are utilised the least. Table 4.2 shows this divide, taking as an example the use of the motorised ratt which is considered by many as a simple but significant innovation in this industry.

However, the unpopularity of advanced mechanisation is distinctive to Kerala state, and is not a feature of other coir-producing regions such as the neighbouring state of Tamil Nadu.

Table 4.2 Usage of technology in ratt spinning (as of 2007)

Type of ratt	Household units (% of total coir units)		Cooperatives (% of total coir units)		Other units (% of total coir units)	
Traditional ratt	9,823	(23.8)	946	(35.02)	992	(38.10)
Ratt with ¼ HP motor	31,423	(76.10)	1,263	(46.76)	1,591	(61.10)
Fully mechanised ratt	44	(0.11)	492	(18.22)	21	(0.81)
Total	41,290	(100)	2,701	(100)	2,604	(100)

Source: own computations from data in CSES (2008).

Note
These data are based on the sample taken by CSES, and not the whole state of Kerala.

In the decade beginning in 2001, it was discovered that the solution for the survival and prosperity of coir in Kerala lay not only in process innovations, but also in product innovations around the domestic and industrial applications of coir fibre and its by-products.[5] While earlier studies (e.g. Isaac *et al.*, 1992; Rammohan, 1999) focused on the economics of process innovations in coir fibre production, later studies and policy documents (e.g. Coir Board, 2001; Rajan and Kumar, 2004; GoK, 2009) highlighted the product innovations in the fibre itself. In addition, technology adapted from the textile industry created opportunities for further product innovations such as jute-coir textiles. But the old problems have not disappeared. Although campaigns promoting the new product innovations appear to overshadow the old process innovations, institutions such as the NCRMI (National Coir Research and Management Institute) at Trivandrum and the CCRI (Central Coir Research Institute) at Aleppey – two government research institutes at the forefront of a whole host of other interlinked public and private institutions undertaking research on coir production and marketing – continuously undertake R&D on fundamental processes in coir production and processing. With this short introduction and overview of the industry, we move on to the empirical study.

The information base and pilot field visits

In addition to Yin's (2003) detailed methodological guidelines on the case study method, guidelines for empirical enquiry as also set down in Rea and Parker (2005) and Fowler (2002) were consulted. Rea and Parker's stages in survey research, modified to the requirements of this case study, are: establishing an information base, determining the sample and refining the instrument of enquiry, implementing the empirical enquiry, and codifying and analysing information received.

Information base

The first stage of empirical study is the establishment of an information base. An information base was set up for this study comprising those individuals at the state level, in academia and among other organisations actively in charge of the economic and technological development of the coir industry. From these, we get a broad idea of what the technology prescription experience has been so far in this industry. The information base in this study consisted of eight individuals – two from academia, three from government departments, one from a government research institute, one involved in skill development and one exporter. The government organisations included the CCRI, NCRMI, NCT&DC (National Coir Training and Design Centre), the Directorate of Coir Development and the Coir Board. Interviews with these members were undertaken in April and May 2009 at policy and management institutions in Aleppey district in south-central Kerala, the principal coir-producing region. The support of an interpreter was sought for some interviews, since they were required to be interviewed in the native language Malayalam.[6]

It was reported by the information base that the state heavily subsidises innovation and diffusion of technology in this industry, and claims to approach cooperative societies to serve as information nodes for details on technological necessities and issues at the ground level in these small household clusters. The Directorate of Coir Development reportedly refers to coir cooperatives regularly for this information while crafting prescriptions, on the grounds that this source of information keeps the state in touch with the technological needs of even the most unsophisticated units. Many members of the information base claimed that one of the fallouts of prescribing and subsidising new technologies and their diffusion was the drastic reduction in day-to-day experimenting and household-level incremental innovation that characterised the coir industry, since mechanisation brought in standardisation and therefore uniformity in production. In addition, while spinning and weaving were activities that were formerly carried out in the open and new improvements were easily replicable by anyone in the vicinity, machine spinning and weaving was now done indoors in state-funded work-sheds, threatening to rule out any interaction. Technological progress, however miniscule, was no longer in the hands of the units and the individuals working in them, but according to what the market and trade demanded, and according to what the government R&D institutions prescribed. The various government departments claimed to have appreciated the gravity of this particular problem that they had visualised, and, rather than standardising the dozens of coir fibre varieties to just a few, it began training coir workers to produce fibre varieties besides those with which they were familiar.[7]

One of the most important processes that the state has had to undertake, while prescribing innovations to low-technology and traditional industries, is skill development. Since the majority of workers cannot immediately cope with new technologies, the state has had to intervene in order to ensure effective dispersion of information and awareness of product and process innovations. Training and skill development is given to a few individuals in a coir-producing region or cluster to ensure that new information invested in these people would spread to other workers through informal communication channels. Training centres were thus established at various spots in the state for skill development and dissemination of new information in the local coir-producing communities.

Pilot visit and subsequent field procedures

Information base members were instrumental in helping gain access to the field site and providing rapport with the coir-spinning households.[8] Initial visits to Manappuram village near Chertala town in Aleppey district, as well as to Chirayinkeezh town in Trivandrum district, were undertaken in August and September 2009 to shortlist a cluster for study and to refine the preliminary questionnaire. Chirayinkeezh was not conducive to this research, since households were in a minority and most units found in the area were cottage and large manufacturers who were relatively well mechanised, but more importantly that respondents here answered in the negative on enquiring whether their main sources of new information for technological or production-related issues were informal links with other units in the vicinity. They reported to have obtained information from more formal sources, such as government nodal agencies and large manufacturers. In fact, producers at Chirayinkeezh also revealed that the production structure and functioning in their town was not typical of the industry. Manappuram, on the other hand, on first sight appeared the archetypical coir-producing and spinning cluster, and respondents were more affirmative in acknowledging the prevalence of interactions between units on a day-to-day basis for technological issues. The coir-producing cluster of households at Manappuram was therefore chosen as the target for this empirical study. The information collection source was selected as the household unit, and the targeted interviewees were the women in these households who performed the task of coir yarn spinning.

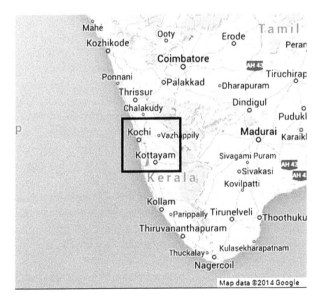

Figure 4.1 Kerala state and location of major coir-producing region near Chertala (source: map data ©2014 Google).

Figure 4.2 Location of Manappuram village (source: map data ©2014 Google).

Access to the units was possible only through assistance from a cottage-unit entrepreneur and a large manufacturer located in this village, who were instrumental in providing the list of coir-spinning households in the cluster. Following pilot visits to Manappuram in September and October 2009, interviews of household units for exploration of informal information sharing and interaction were conducted from November to January 2010. Initially, a list of twelve households was provided by the above two individuals, but on snowballing, fourteen more were discovered through the field stay, totalling the survey households to twenty-six. There was no necessity for sampling, given that the population of this cluster was well within manageable limits for full coverage, and that this study's purpose was an empirically supported conceptual exploration of informal information sharing in a universal affinity setting, and not a statistical generalisation of the industry as such (Yin, 2003).

Coir-producing and spinning households units in the Manappuram cluster literally spilled into one another. Often only a thin woven fence separated one unit from another, and at most a small patch of marsh or a grove of trees provided a short separation of distance between two units. The terrain is marshy and weather perennially humid, with fresh water and canals aplenty (which is what, for centuries, facilitated Aleppey district to remain the hub of coir production and trade).

One characteristic feature of all household units is that they each owned and operated two motorised spinning-wheels and one cleaning machine. Production was undertaken in households by women individually (only three households employed two assistants), blurring the distinction between 'home' and 'production unit'. Spinning, the main source of household income, commenced every morning, when husk and electric power were available, and concluded when the daily requirement of coir yarn was spun. Spinning is not a perennial activity and fluctuates throughout the year based on availability of husk. Sale of produce by the household, predominantly *Vaikom* variety coir yarn, was mainly to the large manufacturer in the vicinity of this cluster, who then wove the yarn into matting and other commercial products.

Manappuram as a coir-producing cluster has emerged only since the late 1980s. Before this period it was engaged in agriculture and fisheries, and constituted only a few coir-spinning households; but through the late 1990s more households in the vicinity joined in the activity and Manappuram grew into a twenty-six-household coir-spinning cluster. This was also reported by the respondents to be the average size of household coir clusters in the region.

The respondents were aged between thirty-five and seventy years, with the oldest two – both women – having spun coir all their lives. A high degree of economic homogeneity among households is a pivotal characteristic of the cluster. The cluster is characterised by a complete network (a network where *all* individuals are connected to one another) with perfect affinity among the women. All the women in the cluster know one another very personally, and hence no individual needed a mediator to meet any other individual in the cluster to seek advice or to share information.

Interviews with all twenty-six households were essentially in the manner of conversation. Schmitz's advice on freely held interviews rather than sectioned questionnaires was followed, to allow respondents to be much more relaxed and forthcoming, adding that this was 'of particular relevance in research on small-scale producers who are often not registered and therefore needed to be reassured that the information was not to be used for purposes of government inspection' (Schmitz, 1982, p. 443). Interviews were hence open-ended and conversational, and audio-recorded to avoid some expected problems of the interview method – inaccurate rendition of information due to poor recall, and reflexivity, i.e. the interviewee providing what the interviewer wants to hear (Yin, 2003, p. 86).

The innovation in focus: the ½ HP motorised ratt

Another important reason for choosing Manappuram was that it was one of the first regions to be prescribed, in about the year 2001 from the Coir Board, a ½ HP motorised ratt or spinning-wheel. This innovation was introduced by the state with the help of a few prominent private actors in the industry, with ample subsidy (to the tune of 75 per cent of the retail price), and meticulously positioned state-sponsored nodal points across districts for dissemination of the machine. This extremely simple innovation, basically a manually run spinning-wheel appended by a motor, revolutionised the coir industry.

This motorised ratt is the technological reference point of this study, since the adaptation to this machine at Manappuram was done mostly through informal face-to-face interaction among spinners with very little teaching or training from either the Coir Board or the large coir manufacturer in the vicinity. According to the members of the Manappuram cluster, the arrival of this innovation was said to have set off a flurry of interactive activity among spinners who resorted to discussing with one another the best ways to use this machine, troubleshooting, possibilities of incremental alterations and so on. Whereas with the traditional hand-operated manual ratt the women reported to have spun a daily output of only about twenty to twenty-five standardised lengths (known in common parlance as 'hanks') of coir yarn, with this machine they reported to have all spun almost *seventy lengths* a day, inching from twenty to twenty-five to seventy hanks within two months on average, through the cooperative process of sharing information at various forums and through various channels. In fact, as the surveys revealed, universal affinity is what allowed households to interact easily, given that there was almost no effort required in establishing familiarity with one another.[9]

Findings

Before 2001, when spinning was entirely manual, the respondents claimed to have had 'complete knowledge' of spinning and the very objective for keeping in constant contact with one's neighbour was to maintain general interpersonal relations and occasionally to discuss industry issues. But upon the arrival of the ½ HP motorised ratt in 2001, there arose, almost immediately, a multitude of problems and uncertainties in operation, and adaptation to the machine was a pressing requirement for survival given the sudden and sharp rise in output demand on the spinners. The pressure to increase efficiency of production was said to have called for greater interaction with, and observation of, proximate coir-spinning households in a frantic search for any 'uncomplicated ways' anyone might have found in operating this new machine. Hence, injecting an innovation into this low-tech cluster seems to have actually accentuated inter-active behaviour, contrary to a claim by some of the information base members, mentioned earlier in this chapter, that one of the fallouts of prescribing and sub-sidising new technologies and their diffusion was the drastic reduction in informal and day-to-day experimenting, on the grounds that mechanisation brought in standardisation and uniformity in production.

Almost every respondent in the cluster affirmed to interact by means of informal conversation with other household units for technical matters and to source new information on production, marketing, or on any incremental innova-tions around the motorised ratt. Information being free and production activity being easily observable, any new development in one household was reported to be easily perceptible to other households in the vicinity. Devoid of R&D in the conventional sense, defensive behaviour such as constantly watching one another, discussing and comparing everyday practices were mentioned by the respondents as the only channels to be well informed about incremental innovations and possible problems around adapting to the innovation. Any obstacles while learning and adapting to the innovation experienced by one household, and experiments leading to solutions, were said to be immediately noticeable by neighbouring households and the experiences were shared. Hence, for almost all households in the cluster, *neighbours* were reported to be the first to be approached during troubleshooting or for any other technical and production issues, and the most likely agents to be constantly observed for new updates on technical matters.

Sharing of know-how and information on dealing with day-to-day problems in the operation of the mechanised ratt were undertaken in the full awareness of the non-vitality of information, a characteristic feature of knowledge in these low-tech settings. Von Hippel (1988) had indicated that non-vitality of newly innovated processes, offering no great comparative advantage to the inventor, would permit its free informal sharing even with competitors. In the Manappuram cluster, too, it was argued by the respondents that there was little incentive in keeping to oneself any solutions or new methods to operate the motorised ratt.

This increased interaction among neighbours and friends, and a complete lack of 'secrecy' among households, was effortlessly possible on account of the *universal affinity* shared among these households in this cluster. This also enabled a general agreement among the women on a disavowal of secrecy among themselves. Households reported that it was mutual affinity, above all, that induced them to freely and willingly share information about the operation of the innovation. Respondents suggested that secrecy by one household might have provoked unnecessary interpersonal differences between that uncooperative household and the rest of the women in the cluster, given the fact that each of one's neighbours were constantly on the watch on how one was dealing with the machine, given that there were literally no other sources of new information on this machine, and given that all the households were facing similar initial difficulties in learning the operation of the machine. Respondents were well aware that unhesitatingly sharing and exchanging know-how with other producers, by maintaining interpersonal affinity, would bring reciprocation in the future in the form of further information sharing. Hence, free sharing of information was fuelled by, as well as contributed to fuelling, the interpersonal affinity among the twenty-four or so households in the cluster. That is, in some sense the universal affinity in the cluster was the motive *precluding* any sort of secrecy among households, which allowed for free information sharing.

There was said to be considerable disparity among units on being net-providers or net-receivers of information/queries from neighbours. Two older units in the cluster, who had spent many decades operating under the older technological regime of the traditional manually operated ratt, reported to be net-receivers of technical queries primarily due to their experience and consequently faster adaptive capabilities compared to the rest of the households in the cluster. These two older units in the cluster, who did not cite neighbours as first sources of information, were also the only units who reported to have taken only a few *days* to adapt fully to this machine (while others reported to have taken many weeks, or even months in the case of women who had commenced spinning in 2001). One household member reported to have had a large number of queries regarding the motorised ratt by virtue of the fact that she had experience in coir spinning not even by the traditional ratt, but *by hand* (a technology even older than the manual spinning-wheel) since childhood at her maternal home near Manappuram.[10] These teachers evidently had little disincentive to teach the women who had approached them for help, given the fact that there was little interpersonal animosity in the cluster based on any social demarcation. In addition, from the learners' side there was no evidence that any of these teachers ever hesitated to interrupt production to teach and share even the smallest piece of information. This again points to the affinity that prevailed in the cluster among the women, which laid the foundation for smooth sharing of information among the more experienced teachers and the many novices at the time.

Interaction was not only within the confines of their homes and work areas, but interestingly also at the weekly 'Kudumbasree' (a state-supported women's self-help group) meetings. Thus, while everyday interaction was only with immediate neighbours, this was one forum within which all the women reported to have met regularly and shared their experiences in adapting to this motorised ratt. An institutional environment with platforms such as these for collective interaction for solutions was therefore highly conducive to information sharing among the household units. Institutional environments such as Kudumbasree in this region were (and still are) characterised by very little socioeconomic differences among their members. Since they are forums for addressing common concerns of livelihood and employment, inter-social group prejudices are usually kept at bay.[11] This again demonstrates that a setting of universal affinity, through the community self-help organisation, served as a foundation for easy information sharing.

But there was one unexpected finding. Surprisingly, the entire cluster claimed to maintain minimal interaction with the large manufacturer located in the cluster for technological and information purposes. However, it was the efforts of this large manufacturer that had resulted in the organisation of Coir Board training sessions.[12] The large manufacturer and the cottage unit were therefore valued in this cluster not as opinion makers but only as intermediate links to government R&D and skill development institutions. The households' success was therefore purely on account of smooth interpersonal interaction among the women, with very little assistance from more formal sources.

Hence, it was by virtue of a complete lack of any inter-community and little interpersonal animosity in their cluster that information sharing was smooth, which nurtured a comprehensive understanding of the motorised ratt, and which facilitated a progressive transition of the entire cluster in a very short period (under a year) from spinning, on average, twenty to twenty-five hanks of rope a day to seventy hanks a day.

To robustly establish this, one would have to undertake a comparative study of performance between this cluster at Manappuram, and another cluster in the vicinity with a similar socioeconomic make-up but with some degree of animosity among communities. Such a comparative study would ideally provide evidence for the claim by the Manappuram respondents that the lack of any prejudice whatsoever among households in their cluster was the catalyst for easy sharing of information on efficient operation of the motorised ratt. But finding a comparable cluster with the above-mentioned characteristics is tricky, and the lack of such a comparative study poses a significant limitation of this study. For this study, one has to read the findings and the lessons that follow in the next section by accepting the emphasis by the respondents: had it not been for the universal affinity their success story would not have been possible.

Lessons

In traditional industries such as coir, technological know-how on prescribed innovations would be seemingly difficult to diffuse, if not for the informal information sharing among proximate producers in an environment of universal affinity. In his prominent work *Diffusion of Innovations*, Rogers described how some innovations have two components: a 'hardware' component, consisting of the tool that embodies the technology as a material or physical object, and a 'software' component, consisting of the information on operation of the tool (Rogers, 1995, p. 12). He continued to describe how, in horizontal interaction networks for diffusion of the software component of the innovation, a decentralised diffusion system was at the centre where participants shared information and at times even created incremental modifications to the original innovation.

During the introduction of the motorised ratt in Manappuram, the 'hardware' of the motorised ratt was designed and delivered in a top-down approach, supported by a large subsidy and a vast distribution system to help diffuse the machine. But the diffusion of the 'software' of its operation and best-practice methods – to reach the highest production possibility of seventy lengths of yarn a day – was left to the horizontal interactions and the informal communication channels in the cluster, which depended heavily on the social relations between the agents. The story at Manappuram is also in concordance with of the work of Maskell – in our coir cluster at Manappuram, each unit saw itself, in Maskell's words, 'in a situation where every difference in the solutions chosen, however small, can be observed and compared' (Maskell, 2001, p. 928), and that even the most 'subtle, elusive and complex information of possible relevance' (Maskell, 2001, p. 929) developed in the cluster was watched, discussed and compared, by which small low-tech units became engaged in the process of continuous learning and innovation.

We can see how relevant it is for policy to take advantage of the knowledge of information sharing as it happens on the ground. From the findings of this case study, we may be able to imagine why some simple innovations, even with full financial backing and uncomplicated functioning, may or may not diffuse effectively across target regions, and may or may not be completely learned and adapted to, causing regional and intra-industry disparities. The answer may lie in the nature of interpersonal affinity within the social environment for information sharing at the grassroots level, which may support or hinder easy information sharing. Especially for the coir sector, we intend these findings on the presence of rich information-sharing practices and mechanisms to be useful in supplementing the literature on the technological modernisation of the industry.

Thus, we have seen an empirical case wherein universal affinity was the basis for smooth information sharing and improved performance. But for the most part, information sharing occurs in environments quite unlike those we saw in the Manappuram coir cluster here. We need to study information sharing in environments where social relations extensively affect and steer production relations – an environment that is far more common in a country like India. We therefore move to the second and more detailed empirical study in this book.

Notes

1 An earlier version of this chapter has appeared in Kamath (2012).
2 'Coir', from the Malayalam root *kayar* (cord), is the stiff coarse fibre obtained from the husk (outer shell) of the coconut after a long process of extraction. The fibre is used to make ropes, mats and related products.
3 For a good historical account of the industry, see Rammohan (1999) and Rammohan and Sundaresan (2003).
4 Although not a contemporary work, Isaac *et al.* (1992) is a useful reference for a detailed description and a critique of the evolution of technologies for the production of coir fibre and further products.
5 Two product innovations come to the forefront – pith and geo-textiles. 'Pith', a semi-solid black material that exudes while beating the husk, considered hitherto as waste, was now being treated, processed and sold in brick form as a fertiliser. 'Geo-textiles', large matted sheets made from coir rope and yarn, were being applied in erosion control, soil conservation and road construction.
6 Thanks are due to Neethi for interpretation.
7 There exist many different varieties of coir yarn exclusive to each region in Kerala, a diversity which brings with it tacit knowledge, incremental and region-specific innovations, and local diffusion of new knowledge.
8 Mr Saikumar (at Chirayinkeezh) and Mr V.R. Prasad of TMMC (at Chertala) along with Mr Shaji and Mr Paul (both at Manappuram) deserve special mention and thanks for this. Rapport with household-level respondents would have been impossible without the guidance of these individuals.
9 This brings to mind Storper and Venables (2004) on face-to-face (F2F) contact, who credited F2F as efficient but entailing heavy opportunity costs in spending time in establishing partners – these costs in building relationships and rapport among units having been negligible in the Manappuram cluster. Households in this cluster spoke the same socioeconomic language, shared conventions and norms, and had personal experience of benefiting from interacting; in other words, proximation in social space as much as in geographical space (Cowan, 2004; Malmberg and Maskell, 1997).
10 This prompts the proposition that those units which had longer experience in the traditional technology seemed to adapt to the new technology faster.
11 Thanks are due to Dr J. Devika for discussions on this point.
12 A venue that was intended as a formal training session, as a forum for discussion and collective learning on the mechanised ratt, and for providing information on updates in the market was the Coir Board-sponsored training session. Although there have been many programmes on the part of the state in training and skill development, the actual experiences in many areas were not as successful as planned. The Manappuram cluster reported that this training exercise had utterly failed there due to irregularity in

stipends to the women, and little in the way of technological learning. But the households reported that despite this, they would welcome future training sessions, as it was their only intermediate link to the Coir Board for monetary benefits and subsidies for machinery.

References

Coir Board, 2001. *Souvenir.* Indian International Coir Fair and Seminar on Coir, October. Ministry of Small and Medium Enterprises, Government of India.

Cowan, R., 2004. Network Models of Innovation and Knowledge Diffusion. MERIT-Infonomics Research Memorandum Series, MERIT, Universiteit Maastricht, The Netherlands.

CSES, 2008. *Report on the Census of Coir Units and Sample Survey of Coir Workers in Kerala.* Cochin, India: Centre for Studies in Environmental Sciences (CSES).

Fowler, F.J. Jr., 2002. *Survey Research Methods.* Applied Social Research Methods Series, 3rd edn, Volume 1. Thousand Oaks, CA, London, and New Delhi: Sage.

GoK, 2009. *Kerala Economic Review 2008.* Planning Board, Government of Kerala.

Isaac, T.M.T., van Stuijvenberg, P.A. and Nair, K.N., 1992. *Modernisation and Employment: The Coir Industry in Kerala.* Indo-Dutch Studies on Development Alternatives – 10. Thousand Oaks, CA, London, and New Delhi: Sage.

Kamath, A., 2012. Enabling Inclusive Innovation: The Role of Informal Knowledge Exchanges through Interaction in Rural Low-tech Clusters. Working Paper 13/2009. Centre for Policy Research, New Delhi, and IDRC, Canada.

Malmberg, A. and Maskell, P., 1997. Towards an Explanation of Regional Specialization and Industrial Agglomeration. *European Planning Studies*, 5(1), 25–41.

Maskell, P., 2001. Towards a Knowledge-based Theory of the Geographical Cluster. *Industrial and Corporate Change*, 10(4), 921–943.

Rajan, A.C. and Kumar, M.T.B., 2004. *Report of the Sectoral Study on the Coir Industry.* Kerala State Industrial Development Corporation, Government of Kerala.

Rammohan, K.T., 1999. Technological Change in Kerala Industry: Lessons from Coir Yarn Spinning. Discussion Paper 4. Kerala Research Programme on Local Level Development (KRPLLD), Centre for Development Studies, Trivandrum, India.

Rammohan, K.T. and Sundaresan, R., 2003. Socially Embedding the Commodity Chain: An Exercise in Relation to Coir Yarn Spinning in Southern India. *World Development*, 31(5), 903–923.

Rea, L.M. and Parker, R.A., 2005. *Designing and Conducting Survey Research: A Comprehensive Guide*, 3rd edn. San Francisco, CA: Jossey-Bass.

Rogers, E.M., 1995. *Diffusion of Innovations.* New York: The Free Press.

Schmitz, H., 1982. Growth Constraints on Small-scale Manufacturing in Developing Countries: A Critical Review. *World Development*, 10(6), 429–450.

SPB, 1973. *Report of the Study Group on Mechanisation in the Coir Industry in Kerala.* State Planning Board, Government of Kerala.

Storper, M. and Venables, A.J., 2004. Buzz: Face-to-face Contact and the Urban Economy. *Journal of Economic Geography*, 4(4), 351–370.

von Hippel, E., 1988. *The Sources of Innovation.* Oxford and New York: Oxford University Press.

Yin, R.K., 2003. *Case Study Research: Design and Methods*, 3rd edn. Applied Social Research Methods Series Volume 5. Thousand Oaks, CA, London, and New Delhi: Sage.

5 A network study of two handloom weavers' clusters[1]

Introduction

This chapter drives the trajectory of this book towards studying informal information sharing in environments where complex social relations affect and steer production relations. We commence with a network study of two handloom weaving clusters in Kerala, focusing on one community – the Saliyar community constituting one of these two clusters – which was once the predominant handloom textile weaving community, but which eventually declined and now occupies a marginal position in the region. The analysis in this chapter intends to demonstrate that the decline of this community was fuelled by significantly higher social cohesion in its networks, compared to the other handloom-engaged communities in these two clusters.

When information sharing through informal interaction in a cluster is influenced by complex social relations for an extended period of time, the emergent path that the cluster takes in terms of economic activity, and in its position in the market, is noteworthy. The experience of the Saliyar community cluster in Balaramapuram town (in Trivandrum District in the southernmost tip of Kerala state), whose hereditary occupation is handloom textile production, is notable in this regard. While even thirty years ago every Saliyar household was a weaving and producing unit, today there are fewer than a handful of Saliyar weavers in this cluster. We attribute this to a heavy involvement of social relations in business and production relations; such a setting would not be unfamiliar given the discussion in Chapter 1 on the vast literature that has extensively studied the economic implications of business networks and production relations among actors who have been deeply influenced and overlapped by their social structures and community relations.

Social relationships are known to enter economic relations at almost every stage of economic activity, from the selection of economic goals to the organisation of relevant resources (Portes, 1995, p. 3). The nature of information sharing is often contingent upon the social identities of the economic agents providing or receiving it (as work by Uzzi and others has illustrated), to the extent that social identities and affinities among social groups may even decide whether the information is shared at all. Production, exchange and business relations are not peripheral to – and may develop as emergent properties of – complex social relations in the region, and may be characterised by homophily.

The main proposition in this chapter is that high homophily, high insularity and excessive involvement of social relations in business relations led the Saliyars' networks to be too cohesive, compared to the networks of the other communities in the region, and restricted the Saliyars' participation in information exchanges regarding new and valuable information. We study production, information and social networks of the Saliyar community cluster at Balaramapuram and compare them to the networks of various other communities in a socially heterogeneous cluster called Payattuvila, near Balaramapuram, producing exactly the same product, but occupying a more dominant position in the industry. Through a comprehensive study of these networks, we provide evidence that it is not just social embeddedness alone, but in its *combination* with homophily in various intensities that is detrimental. In other words, this study demonstrates how merely evading over-embeddedness does not divert an actor or a group from decay and technological obsolescence, if its production and information networks are still homophilous; on the other hand, over-embeddedness may still not be as detrimental if a unit's or a group's networks are non-homophilous. That is, we show how the conceptual ambit of embeddedness must broaden, recognising that social embeddedness comes in various 'homophilies'.

This study is placed in an interesting technological setting characterised by technological *constancy*. Weavers in the numerous handloom clusters across Balaramapuram town specialise in the weaving of cotton textiles in a style unique to Kerala, where the antiquity of handloom technology and product design are the very *basis* of its consumer demand and its niche in domestic and international markets. Upgrading the technology to electric 'powerlooms', and changes in design deviating from a traditional standard would in fact *endanger* the industry and consumer demand. However, this constraint does not imply that there are no avenues for the creation and diffusion of new information. On the contrary, it may be even more imperative to share new information given this atypical situation of knowledge improvements constrained by unchanging production technology.

The chapter first introduces the handloom industry in Balaramapuram and the Saliyars. It then moves to explaining the field procedures and survey methods. In the next stage, we begin comparing the networks of the Saliyar community cluster and the networks of the other communities in terms of their homophily and embeddedness. The chapter then moves on to illustrating the relevance of a joint measure of cohesion in such a study, and draws conclusions.

Overview of handlooms at Balaramapuram, and the Saliyar cluster

The Indian textile industry as a whole contributes around 20 per cent of rural industrial production, around one-third of total exports, has a low import intensity of around 2 to 3 per cent and is the single largest foreign exchange earner (Niranjana and Vinayan, 2001; Soundarapandian, 2002). Within textiles, handloom textile production – constituting 20 per cent of total textile production – is the second largest employer in India, employing some 6.5 million people (60 per cent of whom are women) on 3.8 million looms (Hanveev, 2006; MoT, 2010). In Kerala state, handloom employs around 100,000 people, concentrated in Trivandrum district in the south (with 42 per cent of total weavers), and Kannur district in the north (GoK, 2009, 2010). Many operate under a cooperative system, while the rest operate either independently or under master-weavers.[2] Procurement and marketing are undertaken primarily by state agencies such as Hantex (Kerala State Handloom Weaver's Co-operative Society) and Hanveev (Kerala State Handloom Development Corporation). While handloom in most of Kerala concentrates on household products, clusters in Trivandrum district (including in Balaramapuram) have always had a niche in traditional clothing for many decades (Rajagopalan, 1986). The Geographical Indication Tag with Intellectual Property protection for ten years was granted to the 'Balaramapuram *sari*' in January 2010 by the Government of India (MoT, 2010).[3] In this region, the Fly-Shuttle loom and the Pit loom are the most popular technologies preferred over other weaving technologies such as the Dobby or Jacquard looms (Hanveev, 2006). Yet the unchanging nature of production technology appearing as a constraint has not deterred weavers in this region, who have displayed remarkable resilience, having adjusted to changing market requirements with low energy-intensive and low capital-cost production methods (Niranjana and Vinayan, 2001).

Cooperative organisation in production was promoted throughout India, and especially in Kerala given its long communist rule. Cooperative societies dominate 94 per cent of the handloom industry in Kerala, with the largest number of cooperatives in Trivandrum district (GoK, 2010; Oommen, 2010). But in reality, most registered cooperatives are said to exist only on paper; even in 2001, at least 250 out of the 366 listed cooperative societies in Trivandrum district were said to be either non-existent or non-functional (Niranjana and Vinayan, 2001). Weaving in this district, including in Balaramapuram town, is hence mostly at the weaver's residence, or under a master-weaver's unit (in Kannur district, however, cooperatives are still dominant). Across most of India too, handloom is generally household based, with production shared by the whole family and not only the weaver at the loom (Raman, 2010). According to the Kanago Committee report, on average around 55 per cent of a weaver's family are gainfully employed at various stages of production (Niranjana and Vinayan, 2001; Soundarapandian, 2002). Besides household units, there are also a small but significant number of factories and large units in Kerala.

Handloom weaving in Trivandrum district is centuries old. The early 1800s were a turning point when the Maharaja of erstwhile Travancore built up a weavers' cluster of various communities at Balaramapuram town (Hanveev, 2006).[4] The late 1800s saw another significant turning point when the then Maharaja brought in, from the neighbouring state, weaver families belonging to five particular weaving communities, the most prominent among these being the Tamil-speaking Saliyars, all settled as a cluster on one set of streets in central

Balaramapuram (Niranjana and Vinayan, 2001).[5] The Saliyar community cluster of weavers in Balaramapuram town in Trivandrum district was, and still is, surrounded by socially heterogeneous (and predominantly Malayalam-speaking) clusters of other weaving communities. The Saliyars were for long the dominant weaving community in the region, catering to orders from the royal family and reportedly intermingling mostly within for business and social relations, but not out of any animosity towards other communities. Over time, the dominance of the Saliyars as handloom producers began to decay, gradually reducing into a rather marginal role. There is no single dominant weaver community in Balaramapuram today, but the position of the Saliyars in weaving has eroded; this community is now involved in activities at other stages of handloom clothing production from the same location.

The population of the Saliyar community in Balaramapuram today, according to local government sources, is almost 1,000, residing in over 300 households in Wards 7 and 8 in south-central Balaramapuram town. But the number of Saliyar households in this cluster who deal with handloom production today is just under thirty, and most households are now involved in pre-weaving activities such as plying and yarn supply. A few members of the oldest generation, above seventy-five years of age, have recently retired altogether. A temple is centrally located in the community region, neighboured by a community hall, as well as a now-defunct Saliyar community welfare organisation and cooperative society. The Saliyar Cluster is composed of four main roads (Single Street, Double Street, New Street and Vinayagar Street) about thirty feet wide and each 500 feet long, radiating out from the four walls of the temple, with numerous small alleys in between. While until even forty years ago the Saliyar cluster had a pit loom at each house, there are today barely any households with regularly functioning looms, undertaking weaving as a professional activity. In the past, every family member was involved in some stage of production – women in weaving while men worked in the many other activities or weaving only large textiles; but today this handful of households are operated mostly by male weavers, including two master-weavers under whom a few looms are operated by employees from other communities. Old business and family links with Valliyur near Nagercoil town (a town in southern Tamil Nadu state around fifty kilometres from Balaramapuram from where most Saliyars in Balaramapuram trace their ancestry) are still maintained by the Saliyars, as are links with small producers in Surat (a major town in Maharashtra state in western India, hundreds of kilometres away from Balaramapuram) for gold thread, and with Muslim beamers in Trivandrum district for ordinary yarn. It may be noted that there are a few agents (mainly shop owners) who operate within the Saliyar community cluster, but who do not belong to the Saliyar community.

Field procedures and questionnaire

To study the cohesiveness and eventual decline of this community, we focus on the networks of Saliyar community members who are engaged in any stage of handloom production (not the entire community residing in the Saliyar neighbourhood). Following Arora (2009), we map out the *social, production* and *information* networks of the Saliyars, paying close attention to the expected homophily and cohesiveness of the community. We compare these networks to the expected non-homophilous and non-cohesive links of a similar handloom textile-producing cluster of a similar (though socially heterogeneous) population, covering a similar geographic area as the Saliyar community, in a village called Payattuvila in the vicinity of Balaramapuram. Networks in both cases extend outside the cluster, and to suppliers and procurers besides Hanveev and Hantex. Figures 5.1 and 5.2 show the location of the two clusters.

As with the empirical study of the coir cluster in the previous chapter, an information base was set up for this study too. This case study engaged seven information base members – three in government, one large retailer in Balaramapuram, one prominent (non-Saliyar) master-weaver in Balaramapuram town under whom almost twenty-five looms operate, one elderly Saliyar weaver, and another elderly master-weaver at Payattuvila. Sessions with the information base in May and September 2010 gave a broad picture of the Saliyar community and social relations in general in the region's handloom clusters.

The unit of analysis within the community was the household unit engaged in handloom production activity, and the targeted interviewee in each household was that member of the family currently engaged in handloom textile production at any stage.

Two community elders in the Saliyar community and one elder at Payattuvila served as key informants in the respective clusters, and who provided us access to the households. An interpreter's support was inevitable for the entire study,

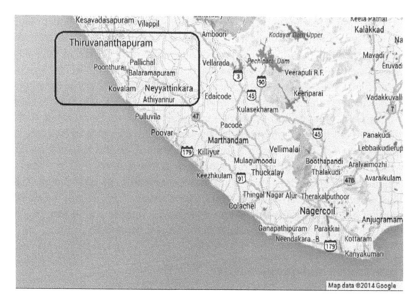

Figure 5.1 Kerala state and the location of Trivandrum (Thiruvananthapuram) (source: map data ©2014 Google).

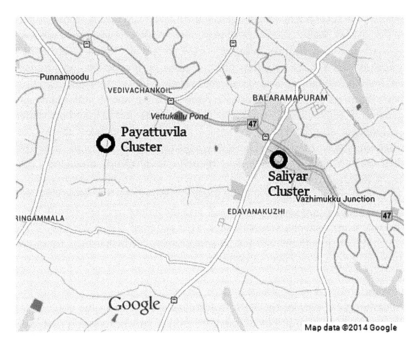

Figure 5.2 Location of the Saliyar and Payattuvila clusters (source: map data ©2014
       Google).

since all enquiries, even in the information base, had to be undertaken in Malayalam.[6] Following a pilot visit in early September 2010, interviews of households
units in the Saliyar community at Balaramapuram were conducted across late
September, October and November 2010; and at the Payattuvila cluster in
November and December 2010. This study, like the coir cluster study, conducted
interviews with all households in the manner of conversation, but also relied on
a sectioned questionnaire. The questionnaire for network structure survey,
inspired in structure by Arora (2009), was divided into five modules: basic
information on household and production activity, professional network, social
network, information network, and miscellaneous information.

1   The basic information section elicited the main activity of the household,
    members involved in the main activity and whether this was the only
    income-generating activity, as well as the capital employed, and the techno-
    logy used for the respective production activity.
2   The professional network section elicited lists of main providers of input/
    raw material, consumers and financiers.
3   The social network section elicited lists of relatives and friends who were *very*
    close, such that they met the respondent at least once a day, and whom the
    respondent approached first in the event of domestic and family emergencies.

4   The information network section elicited lists of the first individuals or agencies the respondent would approach if there were any business or production issues, such as new consumers, new market trends, new technologies (in activities besides weaving, such as plying, dyeing, etc.), new designs, tastes, etc., i.e. any new piece of news on production and commercial know-how and on tastes and preferences. The section also enquired about the method of communication used with the above individuals and agencies. When naming individuals or other agents, it was asked not whom a respondent simply 'knew' as, say, a provider of the latest know-how, rather who the *first* few individuals or agents the respondent would approach when curious as to the latest developments in products, production processes, designs, trends, etc.

5   The miscellaneous section enquired about whether there is anyone such as a 'most influential' person in the cluster, and the nature of relations and reputation kept up with the respondent. It also enquired about the role of the state and local handloom and textile cooperatives – whether they are of any use at all for providing new information.

It was essential for the respondent to name his or her social group, activity and exact location, as a part of the basic information section. In the case of the Saliyars, no restriction was placed on the respondent to preferably list individuals in the same community; on the contrary, enquiries were also specifically made as to whether there were non-Saliyar actors in their networks. Data collection for the network questions was based on guidelines in Wasserman and Faust (1994). It was not possible to acquire a complete list of actors in the Saliyar community cluster or Payattuvila cluster networks; hence a snowballing listing of respondents for interview was relied upon. Free choice was adopted (as opposed to fixed choice, where respondents are told how many individuals to list in their network). Ranking of individuals in terms of importance, in a respondent's list, was originally attempted in the pilot interviews and the first few household interviews, but was eventually abandoned. Given the fact that the handloom textile profession at the household level requires meeting clients and suppliers on an everyday basis, this survey's enquiry on strength of ties was limited.

There is little distinction between 'home' and 'production area' in households in both the Saliyar and Payattuvila clusters since a major part of the house, sometimes the very entrance, is used for production along with other domestic purposes. In almost all the households surveyed, handloom production is undertaken nearly every day and intensifies during seasons such as weddings when custom-made orders are in high demand. There are no definite 'work-days' (almost every day is a work-day), no rigid work routines except at the master-weavers' units, and production at almost all stages uses traditional technologies – hand-plied yarn for plying, pit looms and fly-shuttle looms for weaving, and so on – except at the spinning stage where electrically operated spinning machines are employed, located inside the house.

Network analysis

Besides the Saliyars, there are three other communities (categorised along lines of caste) in the network, denoted here as Community II, Community III and Community IV. Actors in the network who could not be categorised by community – including state agencies, showrooms, shops, financiers and media sources – are categorised as Community NIL. Many actors operate in locations beyond the two clusters, spread across Kerala state and India. Table 5.1 summarises the community and regional distribution of the sixty-two actors in this network.

The networks

UCINET (Borgatti *et al.*, 2011) was used to generate the network diagrams. In all three networks, actors have been grouped by location and their community has been differentiated by shape. Hence, for example, node 42 in the network diagrams that follow is a square (Community II member) operating in the Payattuvila cluster; node 47 is a down-triangle (Community IV member) operating in Kerala; node 14 is a circle (Saliyar community member) operating in the Saliyar cluster, and so on. Occupations – weavers, yarn sellers, plyers, etc. – are not assigned attributes since it might result in some confusion in the diagrams to have nodes classified into a large number of occupational categories. Table 5.2 shows the occupational distribution of actors in each cluster.

'Raw input supplier', 'Miscellaneous customer', 'Media sources' and 'Others' have been excluded from Table 5.2 as they operate beyond the two clusters. In the course of the sections that follow, occupations of some noteworthy nodes will be revealed.

In the professional network (Figure 5.3), nodes in the Saliyar cluster and Payattuvila cluster may be heavily connected within, but there are also a number of dyads that span the two clusters: (13,33), (13,43), (13,41), (15,41), (17,33), (17,41), (17,43). Besides these dyads, there are a few nodes that bridge both clusters, including twenty-one (retail shops), fifty-three (plyers), fifty-four (yarn sellers) and fifty-five (yarn spinners), all in Balaramapuram.

Table 5.1 Distribution of actors by community and region

	Saliyar cluster	Payattuvila cluster	Balaramapuram	Kerala state	Tamil Nadu	Rest of India	Total
Saliyar	17	0	0	0	2	0	19
Community II	0	7	0	0	0	0	7
Community III	0	3	0	2	0	0	5
Community IV	2	4	0	0	0	0	6
Community NIL	0	3	9	5	2	6	25
Total	19	17	9	7	4	6	62

Source: fieldwork.

Table 5.2 Occupational distribution of actors in each cluster

	Weaver	Retail and wholesale shop	Plyer	Yarn shop	Spinner	Master-weaver	Financier	Cooperative	Total
Saliyar cluster	3	8	4	2	1	1	0	0	19
Payattuvila cluster	10	0	0	0	0	4	1	2	17

Source: fieldwork.

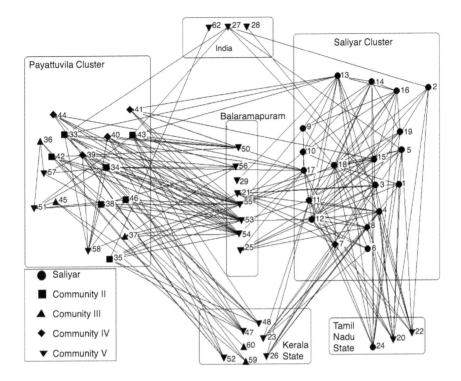

Figure 5.3 Professional network (source: author's own computation).

In the Information Network (Figure 5.4), too, a number of dyads span the two clusters: (11,46), (13,41), (17,33), (17,38), (17,39), (17,40), (17,42). Besides these dyads, nodes that bridge both clusters include thirty-one, forty-seven and forty-eight (large retail sellers that operate across various districts in Kerala and India). Actors 47 and 48 will be revisited in a later section.

The social network (Figure 5.5) is completely polarised along cluster lines. Here, the Payattuvila cluster's community heterogeneity is noticeable. Node 22 in the Saliyars' social network stands out, this node referring to a few families in Nagercoil town whose inhabitants are Tamil-speaking and some of whom are even distantly related to the Saliyars. Members of the two clusters know each other by name, but, as explained earlier, the questionnaire requested names of relatives and friends who were *very* close.

Descriptive observations on homophily and links across regions

This section serves to describe homophily of the four communities, in order to demonstrate the nature of affinities of actors to other actors in their own community, in each of their networks. We also look at the geographic spread of each community's links.

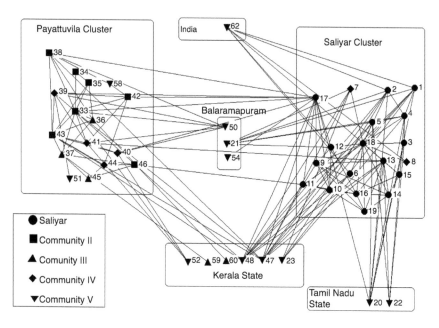

Figure 5.4 Information network (source: author's own computation).

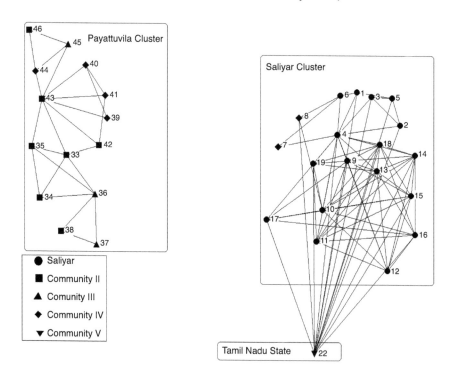

Figure 5.5 Social network (source: author's own computation).

Most measures of homophily are closely related to the in-group/out-group ratio by Duysters and Lemmens (2003) based on Wasserman and Faust (1994).[7] Generally homophily H_i of an actor i can be measured as the ratio of the number of links of actor i to the community to which he or she belongs (s_i), to the total number of links he or she possesses ($s_i + d_i$), which includes links with other communities (d_i).

$$H_i = \frac{s_i}{s_i + d_i} \qquad [5.1]$$

This measure, cautioned by Coleman (1958) and Currarini *et al.* (2009), fails to account for group size. Instead, we use inbreeding homophily (*IH*) in Currarini *et al.* (2009), which normalises to control for the sizes of the different groups in the network.

$$IH_i = \frac{H_i W_i}{1 + W_i} \qquad [5.2]$$

H_i is the basic homophily measure in [5.2], while W_i is the size of the group to which actor i belongs. An average of the *IH* of all members in the group A to which actor i belongs gives the homophily of the whole group IH_A. Group A is said to display complete inbreeding when $IH_A = 1$, pure baseline homophily when $IH_A = 0$, inbreeding homophily when $IH_A > 0$, and inbreeding heterophily when $IH_A < 0$. We measure homophily using *IH* for each community (except Community NIL, of course), and across professional, information and social networks. The descriptive results provide evidence on the relatively high community cohesion of the Saliyars. Table 5.3 shows the homophily of each community across networks.

It can easily be seen that the Saliyars are highly homophilous in all three networks. Only the Saliyars and Community III show professional network homophily; the other two communities display heterophily in this network. In the information network, the Saliyars show much higher homophily than do Communities-II and -III (but not Community IV, which has a very small population). The Saliyars also show the highest homophily in their social network, by virtue of its members residing in a socially homogeneous cluster. A Welch t-test

Table 5.3 Homophily across communities

	Professional network	*Information network*	*Social network*
Saliyars	0.500	0.526	0.930
Community I	−0.145	0.310	0.388
Community III	0.178	0.330	0.057
Community IV	−0.120	−0.009	0.160

Source: author's own computation.

to assess differences between means among the Saliyars and the other three communities with respect to these results found that while differences were mostly significant in the professional and social networks, they were very insignificant in the *information networks* (except between the Saliyars and Community IV).

We should draw the reader's attention to the non-significance of differences in information network homophily; in this chapter and in the next, a central idea is that access to *information* has always been vital to prosperity in this industry. Thus, the lack of significant differences in information network homophily creates a problem for the core argument in this chapter that rests deeply on homophily.

Let us also study how each community differs in the geographical spread of their professional and information links (Tables 5.4 and 5.5).

It may be seen in Table 5.4 that the Saliyars are the only community maintaining more within-cluster professional links compared to out-of-cluster links. Disaggregating the out-of-cluster professional links, we see that the Saliyars keep around 42 per cent of their out-of-cluster professional links with Tamil Nadu (particularly with Nagercoil town), i.e. with their own community members living there. Saliyars appear to prefer homophilous connections even in their out-of-cluster links.

In their information links, all communities maintain more within-cluster than out-of-cluster links, as seen in Table 5.5, of which Community IV maintains the highest out-of-cluster information links. Interestingly, the Saliyars seem to maintain the lowest within-cluster information links. This is not surprising however, since on disaggregating the out-of-cluster information links we observe that around one-fifth of the Saliyars' out-of-cluster information links are with Tamil Nadu – once again, with their own community members living in Nagercoil town.

To sum up, we have seen that Saliyars are significantly more homophilous than the other communities in terms of professional and social networks, but not in terms of the information network. Their homophily is also evident in the geographical spread of their links. We turn now to the issue of embeddedness.

Embeddedness and path lengths to influential information actors

We are interested in the extent to which a community's production and information networks are embedded in its social network. This, along with the previous section on homophily, addresses the social cohesion of the Saliyars. To anticipate the results, the Saliyars appear to be much more cohesive than other groups, prompting the argument that their excessive social cohesion caused their decline.

Before enquiring about the magnitude of embeddedness of each community, we must perform a correlation to test the association of the social network with the professional and information networks individually. The test of the extent to which one network resembles another is a correlation between the adjacency matrices of these networks. This test is required because calculating confidence bounds on a correlation of adjacency matrices is not straightforward due to the interdependence

Table 5.4 Geographical distribution of professional links

Community	Proportion of links within cluster (%)	Proportion of links outside cluster (%)	Disaggregated out-of-cluster professional links (% of professional links outside cluster)			
			Balaramapuram town	Kerala state	Tamil Nadu	Rest of India
Saliyars	61	39	30.70	20.85	42.54	5.91
Community II	16	83	67.28	28.14	0	4.58
Community III	33	67	33.33	66.67	0	0
Community IV	19	81	64.19	30.24	5.57	0

Source: fieldwork.

Table 5.5 Geographical distribution of information links

Community	Proportion of links within cluster (%)	Proportion of links outside cluster (%)	Disaggregated out-of-cluster information links (% of professional links outside cluster)			
			Balaramapuram town	Kerala state	Tamil Nadu	Rest of India
Saliyars	56.1	43.9	13.11	40.22	21.76	24.91
Community II	79.3	20.7	32.17	61.72	0	6.11
Community III	61.9	38.1	49.99	49.99	0	0
Community IV	91.7	8.3	0	66.65	0	33.35

Source: fieldwork.

both among cells of the matrix and among different properties of the nodes (Krack-hardt, 1987; Arora, 2009). A standard technique in network analysis for generating confidence intervals is the Quadratic Assignment Procedure (QAP). QAP is a permutation text which in essence generates the distribution of a statistic according to some null hypothesis, by permuting rows and columns (simultaneously) of one of the matrices, consistent with the null hypothesis. This creates a frequency distribution of the test statistic, which is taken as an estimate of the true underlying distribution. This permits estimation of confidence intervals around the observed statistic. Results of the QAP test on the correlations of the social network with the professional and business networks are given in Table 5.6.[8]

Table 5.6 indicating the Pearson correlation shows the observed value of correlation between the social network matrix and the other two network matrices individually, namely 0.195 and 0.397. The Average random correlation is simply the mean value of the correlations between the professional (information) network and each of the permuted social networks. The number of random correlations that were larger than 0.195 and 0.397 was zero, as shown in the 'Percentage (larger)' column, i.e. none of the 5,000 random permutations produced a correlation higher than 0.195 or 0.397 for the respective matrices. With these results, we can say that the correlation between the social network matrix and the professional and information network matrices, respectively, is statistically significant, and the correlations between these matrices are unlikely to have occurred by chance.

Let us now define embeddedness directly. Here we follow Arora (2009, p. 154).

$$\textit{Social embeddedness of production network} = \frac{\Sigma_{ij} P_{ij} S_{ij}}{\Sigma_{ij} P_{ij}} \qquad [5.3]$$

$$\textit{Social embeddedness of information network} = \frac{\Sigma_{ij} K_{ij} S_{ij}}{\Sigma_{ij} K_{ij}} \qquad [5.4]$$

P_{ij}, K_{ij} and S_{ij} are the adjacency matrices of the production network, information network and social network respectively. An element in P_{ij} (equivalently K_{ij} and S_{ij}) takes the value 1 if i and j are professionally (or for information or socially)

Table 5.6 QAP correlation results

	Pearson correlation	Significance	Average random correlation	s.d.	Percentage (larger)
Professional network matrix	0.195	0.000	0.000	0.025	0.000
Information network matrix	0.397	0.000	0.000	0.026	0.000

Source: author's own computations.

connected and 0 otherwise. If two actors are connected both by a production link as well as a social link, their professional connection is said to be socially embedded, and likewise for their information network link. Table 5.7 shows these measures of embeddedness for the different communities.

What is striking, and apparently discordant with the observations on homophily, is that the Saliyars are relatively *less* information network embedded. In addition, the differences are not statistically significant. These results are discordant with our initial conjecture that community cohesiveness is an intrinsic characteristic of the Saliyars, which is at the root of their decline. The embeddedness statistics give a mixed message: professionally the Saliyars seem to operate within their social network, but when it comes to accessing information they appear less embedded than the two other communities. The measure may be too crude.

Information flows between randomly selected pairs of agents may be much less important than flows from particular agents, as short path lengths to more well-informed actors or groups are known to be conducive to fast and effective diffusion of information in a network (Cowan, 2004). We can estimate this for a group by the proximity of each community to nodes in the network that are influential trendsetters in the industry.

There are two major Influential Information Actors (IIA) in this network: two successful upmarket retail showrooms, actors 47 and 48, recognised by industry and the state government as being at the forefront and cutting edge of design and innovation in the handloom industry in Kerala (GoK, 2007, p. 21). These were also mentioned by the respondents (recorded in the Miscellaneous section of the questionnaire) as influential trendsetters on design and market information on handloom in Kerala. To calculate path length, we may rely on a simple measure of geodesic distance, in this case the distance from an actor to nodes 47 and 48. We can compute a simple mean of the distance to both of these nodes for each actor in a group. This individual actor measure may be averaged across all actors in the group to obtain the mean path length of the group to the IIA (Table 5.8).

According to these results, the Saliyars on average appear relatively closer to the IIA and should therefore have had easier access to new information, providing a competitive advantage and supporting their long-term viability. The impression conveyed by these results is puzzling, as the story has been different. We should also observe, however, that differences in means between communities with respect to these results were found to be not significant.

Table 5.7 Social embeddedness of each community

	Professional network	*Information network*
Saliyars	0.379	0.456
Community II	0	0.544
Community III	0	0.500
Community IV	0.456	0.278

Source: author's own computations.

Table 5.8 Mean path length to Influential Information Actors (IIA) of each community

	Mean path length to IIA
Saliyars	1.68
Community II	1.71
Community III	2.33
Community IV	2.08

Source: author's own computations.

Neither homophily nor embeddedness

The literature makes a strong case that any group exhibiting either strong homophily or strong embeddedness, and especially if both, would, in time, find itself at a competitive disadvantage. The networks of the Saliyar community show homophily, but their professional and information networks are not strongly embedded in their social network. At least they are not too significantly different in terms of embeddedness, compared to those groups whose presence in weaving has not declined. Further, the Saliyars in general are closer, in network terms, to the most important information actors than are the other groups. Thus the Saliyars have networks that are not particularly socially embedded, are close to the important information sources, but show some homophily. The simple conclusion to draw would be that only homophily matters. But this seems too quick, particularly since information about technologies and markets must surely be central for survival in any business. In the sections that follow we argue that treating homophily and embeddedness jointly leads to a more satisfactory explanation of the gradual decline of the Saliyar position.

A measure of joint cohesion

The Saliyars have networks that are not particularly embedded, are close to important information sources, but show some homophily. None of these differences between groups is statistically significant, however, and further, the suggested differences do not sit well with the theory of cohesion reviewed in Chapter 1. Neither of the conventional indicators of cohesion shows results indicating significant differences between the Saliyars' networks and the others', which is not consistent with the fact that the historical trajectories of the different groups are very different. The statistics even seemed to suggest that the Saliyars had more open information networks. This suggests that the simple measures are too crude, and that a joint measure may lead to an improvement in the way we think of or measure cohesion.

We argue that treating homophily and embeddedness *jointly* brings out deep-seated differences between the Saliyars and the others. An agent's production (or information) link may be overlapped by his or her social link (i.e. it may be embedded), but this need not be homophilous. Similarly, his or her homophilous

Table 5.9 Proportion of cohesive links in professional network (in %)

	Non-embedded and non-homophilous	Non-embedded but homophilous	Embedded but non-homophilous	Homophilous-embedded
Saliyars	30.10	31.67	0.66	37.24
Community II	100	0	0	0
Community III	51.67	48.33	0	0
Community IV	97.90	0	2.08	0

Source: author's own computations.

Table 5.10 Proportion of cohesive links in information network (in %)

	Non-embedded and non-homophilous	Non-embedded but homophilous	Embedded but non-homophilous	Homophilous-embedded
Saliyars	23.68	30.25	0	46.07
Community II	39.35	6.22	20.85	33.57
Community III	22.22	27.78	38.89	11.11
Community IV	67.74	4.46	22.38	5.42

Source: author's own computations.

production (or information) link may not be socially embedded. We therefore have four kinds of links in the cohesion spectrum:

1   **Non-homophilous and non-embedded**, when an agent's link is neither homophilous nor socially embedded.
2   **Embedded but non-homophilous**, when an agent's socially embedded link is non-homophilous.
3   **Homophilous but non-embedded**, when an agent's homophilous link is not socially embedded.
4   **Homophilous-embedded**, when an agent's socially embedded link is also homophilous.

We would expect that homophilous-embedded links are more detrimental in the long run than the other three types, since they draw the combined deteriorative effects of both embeddedness and homophily, while the others may bring in deteriorative effects of only embeddedness or only homophily. It follows that one must beware not only of over-embeddedness, but also of its *combined effect* with homophily. The literature on embeddedness has not entirely ignored the fact that it is not monolithic, but has not articulated it very clearly either. This study contributes to the disentangling of social embeddedness by demonstrating, through the case of the Saliyars, the vastly different effects of homophilous-embeddedness and non-homophilous-embeddedness, from merely 'embeddedness' or 'homophily'. The Saliyars may have declined not simply because they possessed homophilous links or embedded links, but due to the effect of their predominantly homophilous-embeddedness networks. We measure this cohesion. We calculate an actor's homophilous-embedded links as a proportion of his or her total links to calculate the extent of his or her homophilous-embeddedness.

Tables 5.9 and 5.10 show a different picture of each community's cohesion, and, compared with Table 5.7, there is significant change. In their professional and information networks, the Saliyars show a high proportion of links of the most cohesive type: homophilous-embedded. They show essentially no embedded non-homophilous links, but a relatively high proportion of non-embedded homophilous links, in both networks. The strongest pattern in these tables is that the Saliyars have (statistically) significantly more links of the most cohesive type, in both their professional and their information networks. For the Saliyars, the most common type of link they display is the most cohesive, and, compared to the other groups, Saliyars have the most strongly cohesive links. These results are concordant with our initial proposition that the Saliyars' networks, particularly their information networks, are very cohesive.

The new measures provide a better way of distinguishing between the different communities in terms of how and why social relations affect economic outcomes. Whereas theoretical arguments seemed to suggest strong differences between the communities' networks, neither of the conventional indicators of cohesion – homophily and embeddedness – found strong differences between the communities' networks. In fact, results computed using the conventional embeddedness and homophily measures were, by and large, statistically insignificant regarding the differences between the Saliyars' networks and the others'. Hence, though the Saliyars had a very different history than the other communities, traditional measures of cohesion conveyed the impression that there was little difference between the Saliyars' links and the others'. We see nothing in the results generated from these conventional measures that would explain the difference in experiences and histories of the different groups. By contrast, Tables 5.9 and 5.10 show results from using more sophisticated measures of cohesion that capture both embeddedness and homophily. The new joint measures identify statistically significant differences between the Saliyars and other communities, which are consistent with the proposition that the Saliyars' heavily cohesive networks – particularly their information network – are connected to their eventual decline.[9]

The conventional measures of cohesion may therefore have been crude, as they find no differences between the Saliyars' networks and the others'. Both embeddedness and homophily matter, and the new measures indicate the substance of this joint effect as they bring out significant differences among the communities' networks. The dominance of the Saliyars' homophilous-embedded links, significantly different when compared to the others, indicates the kinds of network characteristics that would explain the different histories. Socially cohesive links are detrimental under certain conditions, a position that applies well to the Saliyars.

The final task is to test whether there is a significant difference in the proportion of homophilous-embedded links between weavers and non-weavers, in these clusters, in their professional and information networks. For this, one needs to group actors, across all communities in the two clusters, into weavers and non-weavers. The homophilous-embeddedness in each group's professional and information network links needs to be computed. It was expected that, in general, weavers in these handloom clusters would have *lower* homophilous-embeddedness in their networks than non-weavers, as weaving is an activity that intensively involves information gathering from various sources, sustainable only by those actors who are less cohesive. Non-weavers on the other hand can afford to be more homophilous-embedded in their professional and information networks.

These expectations were affirmed with the results in Table 5.11. Weavers appear to be significantly less homophilous-embedded in their professional and information networks compared to non-weavers. And as Saliyars comprise

Table 5.11 Proportion of homophilous-embedded links between weavers and non-weavers (in %)

	Professional network	Information network
Weavers	11.43	25.09
Non-weavers	24.82	37.50

Source: author's own computations.

mostly non-weavers (while the other communities in general and Payattuvila cluster as a whole comprise mostly weavers), this result stands in concordance with the results in Tables 5.9 and 5.10.

With these results, we can ascertain that it is indeed predominantly their homophilous-embedded networks, not just their embeddedness or homophily alone, that captures the Saliyars' cohesion. Homophily and embeddedness do matter, but the combination effect brings out the true differences among the communities.

Conclusions

The idea of complex social relations shaping business and production relations among economic agents is not new, and these relations are often characterised by embeddedness and homophily. In this chapter, we have studied the Saliyars of Balaramapuram who exhibited cohesion to such an extent that it has marginalised their community cluster in the overall scheme of production and information-sharing relations in the Balaramapuram handloom clusters. Lessons drawn from this cluster's experience show social embeddedness in combination with thick homophily in production and information networks can fuel the decline of a community. Through this network analysis we have seen evidence that it is not just embeddedness or homophily alone, but cohesion in its broader sense that is detrimental. The Saliyars are, as they have been for a long time, over-embedded in a sense broader than the traditional definition of the term.

The conceptual ambit of embeddedness has to broaden in order to recognise that embedded economic relations are influenced by homophily. While assessing their business and information networks, agents must be cautious about being not only over-embedded but also whether their embedded links are homophilous.

In India, community relations are the driving force in many industries – especially in traditional technology industries – and social capital drawn on the lines of caste and community still prevail. Monetary schemes and packages, export-oriented incentives and so on are vital to the handloom industry. But region-specific network studies, especially of small pockets like the Saliyar cluster, would provide new revelations at the micro and meso level of the industry that would assist in region-specific policies.

Notes

1 An abbreviated version of this chapter, and the next, has appeared as Kamath and Cowan (2014), and appear here by permission of Oxford University Press. Full publication details are below.
2 A master-weaver is an entrepreneur of sorts who manages (often owns) a handloom textile manufacturing unit. A number of looms (ranging from just three or four to almost a hundred) are operated under one roof, employing labour and producing on a large scale.
3 A Geographical Indications (GI) Tag and its associated Geographical Indications of Goods (Registration & Protection) Act 1999, which India enacted as part of the WTO's TRIPS agreement, ensures that a product originating in and associated with a certain geographical region (such as 'Bordeaux wine' to the Bordeaux region in France, or 'Darjeeling Tea' to Darjeeling in India) is not produced elsewhere outside the region.

4 The princely state of Travancore occupied most of southern modern-day Kerala and a few regions in modern-day Tamil Nadu state. Travancore merged with the neighbouring princely state of Cochin and a former British province Malabar to form Kerala in 1949, the entire combination eventually merging with the Republic of India by 1956. Travancore had Trivandrum as its capital (also the capital of Kerala), 20 kilometres from which is Balaramapuram town.
5 See also the Appendix to this book on 'The Saliyars of Balaramapuram'.
6 Thanks are due to Neethi, again, for interpretation.
7 The ratio assesses degree of replication of ties in alliance groups and assesses in-group strength. A value greater than 1 shows that firms engage in more ties within the core group compared to outside it (Duysters and Lemmens, 2003, p. 60).
8 The correlation between two matrices is simply the correlation between elements of the adjacencies matrices. The element ij of an adjacency matrix takes the value 1 if i and j are linked in that network, 0 otherwise.
9 An interesting pattern in the significance tests is present. Differences in means between communities (in both networks) with regard to non-homophilous embeddedness were consistently non-significant, while differences in means with regard to non-homophilous embeddedness and homophilous-embeddedness consistently showed significance. The cohesion category in focus – homophilous-embeddedness – always showed strong significant differences between the Saliyars and others.

References

Arora, S., 2009. *Knowledge Flows and Social Capital: A Network Perspective on Rural Innovation.* PhD. UNU-MERIT and Universiteit Maastricht, The Netherlands.
Borgatti, S.P., Everett, M.G. and Freeman, L.C., 2011. UCINET 6 for Windows: Software for Social Network Analysis. Analytic Technologies, Harvard, MA.
Coleman, J.S., 1958. Relational Analysis: The Study of Social Organizations with Survey Methods. *Human Organization*, 17, 28–36.
Cowan, R., 2004. Network Models of Innovation and Knowledge Diffusion. MERIT-Infonomics Research Memorandum Series, MERIT, Universiteit Maastricht, The Netherlands.
Currarini, S., Jackson, M.O. and Pin, P., 2009. An Econometric Model of Friendship: Homophily, Minorities, and Segregation. *Econometrica*, 77(4), 1003–1045.
Duysters, G. and Lemmens, C., 2003. Alliance Group Formation: Enabling and Constraining Effects of Embeddedness and Social Capital in Strategic Technology Alliance Networks. *International Studies of Management and Organisation*, 33(2), 49–68.
GoK, 2007. Karalkada: Elegance Manifested. *Kerala Calling*, February, 27(4), 20–21, Government of Kerala.
——, 2009. *Kerala Economic Review 2008*. Planning Board, Government of Kerala.
——, 2010. *Kerala Economic Review 2009*. Planning Board, Government of Kerala.
Hanveev, 2006. *Diagnostic Study of Thiruvananthapuram Handloom Cluster.* Report submitted to the Development Commissioner (Handlooms), Ministry of Textiles, Government of India, by P.S. Mani, Kerala State Handloom Development Corporation Ltd (Hanveev), Kannur, Kerala, India.
Kamath, A. and Cowan, R., 2014. Social Cohesion and Knowledge Diffusion: Understanding the Embeddedness–Homophily Association. *Socio-Economic Review*, Oxford Journals.
Krackhardt, D., 1987. QAP Partialling as a Test of Spuriousness. *Social Networks*, 9, 171–186.

MoT, 2010. *Annual Report 2009–2010*. Ministry of Textiles, Government of India.

Niranjana, S. and Vinayan, S., 2001. *Report on Growth and Prospects of Handloom Industry*. Study Commission by the Planning Commission, India.

Oommen, M.A., 2010. *The Economy of Thiruvananthapuram*. CPBS Monograph. Bangalore, India: Centre for Budget and Policy Studies.

Portes, A., 1995. Economic Sociology and the Sociology of Immigration: A Conceptual Overview. In A. Portes (ed.) *The Economic Sociology of Immigration: Essays on Networks, Ethnicity, and Entrepreneurship*. New York: Russell Sage Foundation.

Rajagopalan, V., 1986. *The Handloom Industry in North and South Kerala: A Study of Production and Marketing Structures*. MPhil. Centre for Development Studies, Trivandrum, India.

Raman, V., 2010. *The Warp and the Weft: Community and Gender Identities among Banaras Weavers*. New Delhi and Abingdon, UK: Routledge.

Soundarapandian, M., 2002. Growth and Prospects of Handloom Sector in India. Occasional Paper 22, National Bank for Agricultural and Rural Development (NABARD), Mumbai, India.

Wasserman, S. and Faust, K., 1994. *Social Network Analysis: Methods and Applications*. Cambridge: Cambridge University Press.

6 Community social capital and inherited cohesive networks

The previous chapter argued for expanding the conceptual understanding of social embeddedness. In this chapter, we continue the study of informal information sharing where complex social relations affect and steer production relations in low-tech clusters, by examining how the homophilous-embeddedness in the Balaramapuram Saliyars' networks and an extreme sense of community cohesion worked its way across generations, influencing a variety of economic and cultural factors, eventually driving the Saliyars into decline. We see in this chapter how homophilous-embeddedness among the Saliyars was a deep-seated attribute and not simply a characteristic of their modern-day professional and information networks. We also see the mechanisms through which the absence of homophilous-embeddedness among the many other socially heterogeneous clusters of weavers in this town stimulated their rise. We realise that affiliation to a rigid network and traits of homophilous-embeddedness can weaken even a seemingly prosperous group, regardless of industry performance.

At a broader level, this chapter also studies how complex social relations influence economic relations and technological progress, when these relations are relayed across generations in low-tech clusters. We begin by asking the seemingly simple question of why the Balaramapuram Saliyars cannot simply amend their links.

Background

What is it that hinders an individual in the Saliyar community at Balaramapuram from amending his or her links, especially when there is no animosity among communities? The answer lies in the community's perception of its social capital. The Saliyars treat their social capital almost as 'ethnic' capital; many in this community strongly believe that weaving is 'in their genes' and a matter of 'community pride'. We know from the literature that social obligations are deep-seated elements in the everyday economic functioning of communities. Networks may be, to reiterate, the results of gradually solidified historical processes, iterated production rules, and communication protocols in interactions (Padgett and Powell, 2012, p. 3). Inherited production links cannot be amended easily and attempts to do so may be socially expensive, since it may involve tampering with community relations and with investments made in the past by the community to maintain social ties and obligations specifically for economic purposes (Coleman, 1988; Borjas, 1992, 1995). 'Cultural values', which often materialise in economic links, are often transferred across generations purely for their survival and preservation (Wintrobe, 1995; Dasgupta, 2005). Many Saliyars who were interviewed for this study reported that links were ingrained into them as they grew up familiarising with suppliers and consumers (essentially members of their own community) arriving at home everyday, since childhood. The baggage of loyalty and communal obligation was relayed generation after generation, 'locking them in' from birth (Dasgupta, 2005). Information on links was directed by tradition, just as in a network 'clan', where transmission of orders is not based on market signals such as price or on account of hierarchical commands, but due to traditions or informal regulations (Bianchi and Bellini, 1991). The Saliyars recognised all this and it is based on this recognition that they have encouraged their children to quit the profession.

The expected problems with cohesive communities and ethnic enclaves – such as free riding associated with the public goods nature of social capital, or isolation due to a different language – were bypassed in the case of the Saliyars. Free riding associated with the public good nature of social capital was averted due to a strong presence of numerous closed networks within the community (note the many triangles in the Saliyars' networks displayed in the earlier chapter), and consequently the inescapable monitoring of each individual by the community. In addition, both Malayalam and Tamil languages are freely spoken by the majority of the population in an inter-state border region such as Balaramapuram town, which is populated by many native (non-Saliyar) Tamil speakers. This surmounted any sense of cultural isolation from outside the Saliyar community.

In addition, it is not the case that handloom was an unprofitable industry. The ongoing sustenance of the Payattuvila cluster and many other such small clusters in Balaramapuram town and Trivandrum district show that handloom (though plagued with numerous other problems such as fluctuations, competition from powerloom, unorganised production, defunct cooperatives, etc.) has enjoyed a modest level of success, having also acquired a Geographical Indication tag for the Balaramapuram sari and for four other textile products, and catering to a strong product demand state-wide and in upmarket showrooms across India. In fact the literature has demonstrated that a unit's failings may not be on account of organisational issues or due to shortcomings in the industry, but due to its position and affiliation to a cohesive and rigid network (Walker *et al.*, 1997) – this seems to apply well to the Saliyars in the handloom industry, as has been revealed in the previous chapter, and as we will disentangle in detail in this chapter.

The ultimate solution among the Saliyars to escape their inherited lock-in and eventual decline was to abandon weaving and, in the long run, move away from the handloom industry altogether. But one must bear in mind throughout that this analysis of the Saliyars is not about why they moved from weaving to other professions; it is about the cause of their decline in the handloom industry at Balaramapuram, the root of which is found to be community cohesion and homophilous-embeddedness in their networks. This is not so much about why other professions appeared more promising, but how the Saliyars reached a dead-end in weaving – their hereditary profession – due to rigidity and excessive cohesion in their networks, which was relayed across generations.

We organise and unpack these arguments by first presenting the proposition that *community social capital has been central and congruent to technological progress in the handloom industry in India throughout the centuries. One consequence of this argument or claim is that the Saliyars, the exemplar in community bondage among weaving communities in Balaramapuram, should have actually progressed.* This is backed by the evidence supporting the fact that since weaving as a full-time activity in handloom-engaged households in Kerala is pursued with an intensity no lesser (and at times greater) than in India as a whole, the Saliyars are not specially disadvantaged either in the industry or in the region from which they are operating, and should not outmigrate for good but rather exercise a flexibility to exit and re-enter as other communities have done in other states in India (see Mamidipudi *et al.*, 2012):

> jumping off a home ship that is carrying too much load in bad weather, and swimming alongside on their own steam, till fair weather allows [weavers] to hop back on. There are casualties, of course, but the ship continues its journey, ferrying people from subsistence to sustainability.
>
> (Mamidipudi *et al.*, 2012, p. 47)

While there are a multitude of cases in history demonstrating healthy relationships between community cohesion and technological progress among handloom weaver communities in India, in the case of the Saliyars the relationship over time became antagonistic and unhealthy. The Saliyar outmigration from the industry in Balaramapuram has been permanent, quite unlike the analogy given by Mamidipudi *et al.* (2012) above. To understand why the Saliyars are a counter-example to the standard line in the literature (proposing harmony between community social capital and technological progress in handloom) in more ways than one, we are compelled to investigate the centrality of community social capital among the Saliyars and inherited homophilous-embeddedness in their networks.

In this chapter, we first unpack the standard line mentioned above. This is done by first adopting a perception of handloom as a 'socio-technology' and the weaver as a 'socio-technologist', as well as by reviewing the evidence in the literature on the congruent relationship between family/community centrality and technological progress in the handloom industry. This is then followed by a discussion based on data from NCAER (2010) and MoT (2012) that compel us to believe that since participation in weaving in Kerala has fared quite similarly to India in general, the Saliyars operate in an environment that is no more disadvantaged than the rest of India, and hence need not really permanently exit from the industry. The chapter then moves on to investigate what roles the centrality of community social capital and homophilous-embeddedness have played in the Saliyars' decline. In order to investigate this, we first survey the plethora of schemes and programmes that the central as well as state governments provided to the handloom industry in order to stimulate its progress and growth. We then witness how the Saliyars did not participate in these, partly by excluding themselves from organisational innovations, and how this led to their design information entering into a long-term phase of redundancy, and how issues of land subdivision plagued the sustenance of their functioning. As a parallel, we see how the absence of the possibility of community cohesion, and flexibility in networks, fuelled the rise of the other socially heterogeneous clusters in Balaramapuram.

The standard line: the centrality of community in technological progress in handloom

The literature on historical trends in the Indian handloom weaving industry has shown that community cohesion and the adoption of innovations have often played a *symbiotic* and not an antagonistic role. To better understand this, we must first adopt the perception of handloom as a 'socio-technology' and the weaver as a 'socio-technologist' – a view expanded upon by Mamidipudi *et al.* (2012) in their analysis of weaver mobility in Andhra Pradesh state in India.

The handloom industry: a family/community-based socio-technological system

Mamidipudi *et al.* (2012) allege that there has been some unfairness in characterising handloom in India as static, traditional and outdated. Their recent study on handloom weavers in Andhra Pradesh has challenged this notion and it convinces us to appreciate the argument that the handloom industry must be studied as an elastic and evolving *socio-technological system*. Technical functions in the industry are well rooted within the structure and functioning of community, and the coexistence of the two is inevitable.

> Each weaving family … is linked to another five families through the auxiliary activities of dyeing, warping, sizing and winding. The weaving system is further linked to dyeing, credit and marketing through hybrid institutions that link rural and urban environments. This builds a complex socio-technical and economic network that weaver households maintain and by which they are maintained.
>
> (Mamidipudi *et al.*, 2012, p. 50)

Weavers are aware, according to Mamidipudi *et al.* (2012), that their performance and technical expertise at almost every stage of production is correlated with their investments in social relations and in building social networks. The recognition that they speak a common technical and social vernacular has prompted weavers to mobilise knowledge within their social networks. By virtue of this, the weaver becomes a socio-technologist. This is demonstrated with the evidence from the literature on the history of technological progress in the hand-loom industry which gives a sense of how innovation and information diffusion in handloom has always revolved around community, and has for the most part been positively stimulated by community social capital. We term this the 'standard line' in the literature and build on it by reviewing the historical experi-ence drawn from works primarily by Tirthankar Roy (1987, 1993, 1996, 1999, 2002) and Douglas Haynes (1996, 2001, 2012). It is against this standard line that the experiences of the Saliyars of Balaramapuram are examined in this chapter.

There is a common misconception on handloom in India, which bestows a pastoral notion on handloom textile production, with rural or small-town weavers operating in a rustic (and somewhat static) setting. Haynes (2001, 2012) argues that handloom has, on the contrary, always been a dynamic industry, character-ised by frequent innovation and weaver mobility; it has also always been a community-based industry, with entire communities engaging in it as their tradi-tional profession. In other words, handloom in India has been characterised by the household-based weaving family working not alone but embedded in community-based clusters that consider weaving (and generally handloom textile production from start to finish) as their community heritage and not simply as a family's source of income, the community being the agency through which innovations have filtered into the industry.

The weaver or weaver family historically has rarely existed outside of com-munity, a fact valid even to this day, where weaving in many regions in India is still community and caste based at the core (Mamidipudi *et al.*, 2012). Familiar labour was always the basic unit of production in nearly all processes of hand-loom textile production (Haynes, 2012). In addition, in terms of the adoption of weaving innovation, the first adopters of innovations (such as electrification and modernisation of weaving, pre-loom and post-loom processes) were com-munities drawn from hereditary 'weaving castes' such as the migrant *Padmasa-lis* and the Muslim *Momins* or *Julahas* (Haynes, 2001, 2012; Roy, 2002). What makes this fact more interesting is that even ancillary activities were community-based, distributed across different communities. Haynes (2012) provides a number of examples: dyeing communities regularly developed new knowledge of preparing fast dyes; different communities processed different kinds of col-oured thread or cloth; gold-thread manufacturers (of a particular caste) also developed incremental innovations on their machines in the early 1900s; carpen-ters (again, of the carpenter castes) were making improved dobbies, English healds and other weaving accessories; and yarn preparation also saw incremental innovations.

The central place of caste and community in handloom has, according to Roy (2002), long been recognised in Indian policy, even during the British Raj. Roy explains that many innovations were intended to be introduced top-down by

British administrators in the Indian subcontinent who were interested in population estimates of craftsmen in handloom regions – estimates that could be
unearthed only through regular *caste* censuses (and not industry surveys, as
would be the case in most other sectors).[1] These administrators had also dis-
cerned the fact that caste-based professions shared one (and probably the only)
feature of the European guild: that of exclusive unity, which had connotations of
collective information sharing and hence encouragement of absorption and diffusion of new information (Roy, 2002).

Let us look at Roy's development of this argument in more detail. The
nuances of production in handloom were known only within certain castes, and
the communities and clusters that were based on these castes. These provided
(and still do provide, though in a reduced capacity) a social bond and distinct
identity that influenced its members to channel profit to the common good by
building community centres, temples and so on. But they often also obliged
members to share technical information and teach their progeny the profession
with which the caste was associated, assist others in the community with production and technical problems, and at the same time restrict outsiders from all this.
Learning in handloom had a 'strong apparent correlation with collective social
identity' (Roy, 2002, p. 527). Cooperation, trust, assistance and learning were,
hence, through informal channels of communication in the community clusters,
demarcated by social boundaries of caste and community.

In fact, the centrality of the family and community in weaving was always
resilient, evident in English records dating to very early periods such as the late
1700s, which detailed meticulously how tedious it was in the beginning to pene-
trate long-existing community networks and caste hierarchies and enter into
direct relationships with weavers (Arasaratnam, 1980). It took much longer than
the British had expected to gain direct access to (and therefore control of) the
weavers. The sense of community was so strong that weavers were known to
simply evacuate entire villages and migrate to other towns to set up production
whenever their community structure and relations were under threat from the
new systems that the British had introduced.[2] Arasaratnam (1980) also provides
a detailed account with case studies of a total embeddedness of production relations in caste relations, in weaving clusters in villages on the Coromandel Coast
(southwestern coast of India), and how, at times, social heads of communities,
who had absolutely no role in pre- or post-loom activity, administered the community's production activities simply because they were heads of the weaver
caste.

The emergence of caste associations and community clusters was the direct
consequence of weavers migrating from the villages in the southern part of the
subcontinent to larger towns such as Sholapur and Bombay in present-day
Maharashtra state, which, Roy (1999) explains, served as an important feature of
the strategy of migrant weavers to 'establish themselves economically and rede-
fine themselves socially' (p. 72). Even within cities, caste groupings were so
strong that their agglomerations assisted in promoting and maintaining their
traditional lifestyle (Haynes, 2012). Re-creation of community and regeneration

of roots characterised these migrant weaver communities, who faced a need to collaborate and create a 'common good', but at the same time compete (Roy, 1999).[3]

> The very maintenance of a history of having moved from another place, often under conditions of duress, served to demarcate them from others around and to sustain their sense of distinctiveness.
>
> (Haynes and Roy, 1999, p. 66)

Often, these migrations, and the final destinations of these migrant weavers, were assisted and directed by well-to-do patrons with political acquaintances. Weaver communities would have only welcomed this, according to Haynes and Roy (1999), since patronage by nobility and migrations of weaver communities were symbiotic: clothing was a means of defining social status, and association with the aristocracy brought the weavers social and ritual privileges over and above what had been endowed to them by the caste system.[4] It should be noted that, through all the migrations, the organisational structure of these weaving communities changed only very slowly, with community identity at the centre at all times.

When things slowly began to change in the Indian subcontinent after the 1860s with the introduction of organisational innovations in the handloom industry such as workshops (the *karkhanas*) consisting of dozens of looms with paid labour and formal systems of production of handloom cloth and delivery for export markets (primarily Britain), the family/community-based economy still stood strong and resilient. Haynes (1996), who has studied this in detail, says that the reason for this was the initial fear among weaver communities of the disruption of traditional production and delivery systems, and a fear that the new system might hinder surplus creation. Venkataraman (1935) explains that the introduction of the workshops also confronted the traditional family/community system with an unfamiliar work environment that involved specific work hours, punctuality in arriving at work every morning, wages on a monthly basis for senior workers and on a piece-rate basis for weavers, and so on. This may have caused workshops to appear, at first, unattractive to caste-weavers (i.e. those weavers for whom it was a hereditary community profession) and attractive only to those who belonged to non-weaver castes. This was the case, Venkataraman documents, in the northern part of present-day Kerala state in the early decades of the twentieth century. In the Madras Presidency (comprising most of the southern peninsula) too, attempts by the British-run Industries Department to set up government-sponsored handloom factories were not successful at their introduction, as caste-weavers would not accept a workday governed by a clock (Haynes, 2012).

But the initial resilience was overcome and the workshop form of organisation was eventually absorbed; not displacing the family/community system but rather growing alongside it (Haynes, 2001). According to Haynes, who has documented in detail the entry of workshops in the industry in western India, the family slowly began to incorporate the management of the workshop and marketing of produce into its existing division of labour. In regions such as central Tamil Nadu state (which was, like western India, a thriving textile centre in the subcontinent) caste-weavers were still dominant by virtue of comprising most of the workforce in the workshops that developed there. Caste and community monopolies in various artisan and other occupations in India, which underwent an eventual breakdown during the British Raj, did not seem to affect the handloom industry very much, as seen in the Madras Presidency where, for over two-thirds of weavers, handloom textile production continued to be an entirely hereditary and community-centred activity (Venkataraman, 1935).[5]

Haynes (2012) describes how *karkhandars*, the chief operators of these *karkhanas* or workshops, were essentially people from weaving communities, who happened to be wealthier than the average household weaver and more enterprising in terms of diversifying their clientele. His meticulous analysis of the workshops as essentially family- and community-based is presented as follows. As families with strong pre-existing craft skills, *karkhandars* and their families were able to seamlessly adapt their products and practices to demand shifts, by building on personal and community relationships to develop more reliable workforces. By patronising community causes and by creating cooperative societies, they established themselves strongly, and invested enormous efforts to prevent the skills of weaving from leaking out of their community. The labour for these workshops was, hence, sourced from existing weaving communities, and there was little possibility of developing a 'free' labour market without caste affiliations. In smaller workshops, the owners, their wives and their children continued to weave and perform other tasks alongside hired labour. Employing 'outside' labour often involved hiring entire families, employing the female workers within hired families in preliminary processes and the men for weaving. Haynes (2012) provides numerous examples of this, including the case of the *Vakharias* in Surat who built a workshop of about thirty looms, involving the members of a large joint family; in another instance, different brothers performed different management, production and technical functions. Thus, though the wage labour was supposedly from outside the 'family' in the workshop system, it was actually sourced largely from within the community through informal networks of kinship, friendship and neighbourhood (Haynes, 2001). There was little evidence of public joint-stock offerings or partnerships between unrelated individuals (Haynes, 2012).

All this evidence might prompt the argument that workshops were units that fostered an extreme sense of community cohesion. This is not entirely incorrect, but the reason for their success was simply that despite being very cohesive, they were not opposed to experimenting with new machines, designs from outside of the workshop and community cluster, or expanding their client base and networks well outside of the community. In fact, the very fact that the workshop coexisted alongside the family/community system is what laid the path to the adoption of one of the most significant innovations in the textile industry in the Indian subcontinent – the fly-shuttle loom – in the late 1800s and early 1900s.

Innovations such as the fly-shuttle loom found favour, gradually, among weavers in regions such as the western part of the Indian subcontinent, since they did not appear to disrupt the division of labour in weavers' families. The *Padmasali* community weavers (also the *Momins)*, for example, were said to be exemplars in introducing the fly-shuttle, even bringing in migrant labour from their home region of Telengana (present-day northwestern Andhra Pradesh state) to operate the new looms. It is of interest to note that this innovation was adopted by many well-off weavers' households in the western Indian subcontinent well before the formal top-down introduction by the British (Haynes, 1996); only later did it eventually move into the workshops on a much larger scale.

> We must be careful about attributing too much of the credit for change to the impetus of government. At the time Bombay began to introduce new kinds of loom, processes of ethnological transformation were already under way in many centres where the *karkhanas* predominated. We have already seen how ... several workshop owners in Sholapur had adopted the fly-shuttle loom before the government had decided to disseminate it. In Surat, local weavers largely abandoned the traditional throw-shuttle loom for the Hattersley loom ... without any encouragement from the state.
>
> (Haynes, 2012, pp. 215–216)

The workshops adopted these new technologies into their scheme of activities slowly and carefully, testing out their impact not only on fluctuating market conditions but also, importantly, on existing family and community relations. The progress from pit- to fly-shuttle, and in some cases even to powerloom, was by means of using this cautious and meticulous approach, attempting to maintain the long-existing division of labour based on family and community. The *karkhandars* who graduated to electric-powered powerlooms in the 1920s and 1930s were hereditary caste-weavers, once again relying on their own social groups. Haynes (2012) proposes that their decision to use power-driven machinery was often 'just one step in a series of technological changes, not a unique moment in history that departed from all others before' (p. 247). Similar to the workers in the coir cluster in an earlier chapter, these *karkhandars* and their staff relied on trial and error to learn the new machines, and called upon relatives or neighbours who often helped them to solve mechanical difficulties; for example, aged *Momin* workers were seen to move from Bombay to a town called Bhiwandi to work as mechanics in powerloom workshops (Haynes, 2012, p. 251).

According to Haynes' (1996) assessment, the division of labour in 1940 (when the workshop form of production was strongly developing and operating almost entirely by fly-shuttle loom) was in fact not very different to that which existed in about 1900 (when these large process and organisational innovations were just being introduced). In addition, despite the workshops being very successful in the production and adoption of innovations, they never entirely displaced small family-based household units, even by the mid-twentieth century (Haynes, 2012). In fact, even in Independent India, by the 1960s it was found by surveys and policy reports such as one by the Planning Commission (GoI, 1967) that the principal establishment in the handloom industry in India was still the weaver household and the principal workers of the industry were still weaver families. Thus handloom remained for the large part, in the late 1960s, still a hereditary and community-based industry:[6]

> handloom weaving is a hereditary industry where the son learns from the father the techniques of weaving.... The handloom industry belongs to the traditional community of weavers.... Even after the advent of modern techniques and the growth of cooperative institutions the hereditary nature of the industry has hardly changed.
>
> (GoI, 1967, p. 17)

This was the case even by the 1980s; technological changes were found not to have fundamentally altered production organisation – with the household and family labour at the centre in most of the industry (Raman, 2010).

Hence, whether in migration or in the adoption of organisational and technical innovations, and whether in workshops or in households, family and community has always been the pillar around which handloom developed in most of India. In fact, we have seen in the literature that very often, adoption of these innovations subscribed to *family and community centrality*, even as far as 'externally' hired wage labour in the workshops went.

To reiterate the argument that sets the standard line in this analysis, community social capital and technology have often reinforced each other effectively and have shared a more or less symbiotic relationship in the handloom industry in India. If this is the case, it should therefore follow that for the Saliyars of Balaramapuram too, especially by virtue of being a migrant weaver community with official patronage and a multitude of other social and economic benefits, this harmony should have been long-lasting. But this has not been the case. So can their sustained downfall be due to bad industry conditions in the state? Is handloom a sick industry in Kerala, and, due to this, is weaving not the preferred activity for handloom-engaged households in the region? We answer this in the following section.

Participation in weaving in Kerala, compared to India on average

The handloom industry in India, as well as in Kerala state, is known for its uncertainties and fluctuations, as seen in production trends (Table 6.1).[7] But if we compare the situation in Kerala to the general situation across India, we see that many aspects of *participation in weaving* in Kerala have fared quite similarly to India in general. This prompts us to believe that the Saliyars operate in an environment that need not necessitate a permanent exit from the industry.

We will see from this section that despite high fluctuations in the industry in Kerala, participation in weaving in Kerala has been similar, or in some instances even better, than in India in general. We support this argument based on

Table 6.1 Production of cloth in the handloom sector in India and Kerala state

Year	Production in India (million square metres)	Growth in production in India (%)	Production in Kerala (million square metres)
2002–2003	5980	–	70.75
2003–2004	5490	–8.19	56.82
2004–2005	5722	4.23	–
2005–2006	6108	6.75	62.38
2006–2007	6536	7.01	62.48
2007–2008	6947	6.29	70.88
2008–2009	6677	–3.89	20.20
2009–2010	6806	1.93	23.95
2010–2011	6949	2.10	–

Source: based on Table 3.3 in MoT (2012) and GoK (various).

information in the *Handloom Census of India 2009–2010* (NCAER, 2010), a comprehensive and broad-ranging report on various aspects of the handloom industry in India. This is the third such census to be produced in India, the second having been undertaken in 1995/1996 (hence the frequent reference to this year) and the first in 1987/1988.

Let us first look at handloom at an all-India level. At an all-India level, the majority of households associated with handloom cloth production are engaged at the weaving stage. This is a large majority of around 82 per cent (numbering around 2.27 million households). In addition, most individuals weaving in these households are not elderly members of the family practising an outmoded economic activity; in fact, 70 per cent of the workforce is in the age group eighteen to forty-five. Although the population of weavers in India may have slightly declined, from 3.3 million in 1995/1996 to 2.9 million in 2009/2010, the proportion of *full-time* weavers among the total population of weavers has actually increased significantly, from around 44.3 per cent to around 63.5 per cent; this goes along with a decrease in the number of idle looms among total looms in the country, from 10 per cent in 1995/1996 to 4 per cent in 2009/2010.

Table 6.2 displays these and a few other indicators that show progressive figures. From these figures, we can judge that even if the handloom industry

Table 6.2 Comparison of selected indicators from the second and third handloom censuses

Indicator	Second census (1995–1996)	Third census (2009–2010)
Man days worked per weaver	197	234
Share of full-time weavers to total weavers	44%	64%
Share of idle handlooms	10%	4%
Share of weaver households reporting less than 1 metre of production per day	68%	46%

Source: based on Table 10.15 in MoT (2012).

faced fluctuations over the period 1995/1996 to 2009/2010, weaving itself has not become a redundant activity to permanently move away from.

Let us now move to some closer aspects. Data are available at the state level for Kerala and at the all-India level, but not at the district level for Kerala, which unfortunately prohibits us from viewing the situation in weaving in handloom at three levels: country, state and district. With this limitation in mind we move to Table 6.3, which shows that the proportion of weaver households among total handloom-engaged households is virtually the same in Kerala as it is in India in general.[8]

If we also look at the workforce among households engaged in handloom, we see from Table 6.4 that the proportion of weavers among total handloom workers in households is around three-quarters, well past an absolute majority, in both Kerala and India in general. In fact, Kerala even enjoys a very slightly higher proportion of weavers in handloom households.

However, it is doubted as to whether these weavers, who seem to comprise the majority of handloom workers in Kerala as well as in India in general, are engaged only on a part-time basis. If this is the case, we should be wary of the figures given in Table 6.4 and judge that the industry is populated by individuals who weave as a peripheral activity, besides engaging in other economic activities that may be more rewarding.

But Table 6.5 refutes this, as we see that almost the entire population of weavers in Kerala work full-time in this activity (as do allied workers, and handloom workers in general). In fact, this proportion is much greater in Kerala than in India on average (where it is 63.5 per cent). In addition, there are more part-time allied workers than part-time weavers in Kerala, suggesting that weaving in Kerala enjoys a greater full-time participation than allied activities in handloom production.

Table 6.3 Weaver or allied households as percentage of total handloom households (2009–2010)

	Weaver households (%)	*Allied households (%)*	*Others (%)*
Kerala	81.80	18.04	0.16
India	81.49	14.05	4.46

Source: own computations based on Table 3.1 by NCAER (2010).

Table 6.4 Proportion of weavers and allied workers to total workers in handloom in households (2009–2010)

	Proportion of weavers (%)	*Proportion of allied workers (%)*
Kerala	76.97	23.03
India	75.61	24.39

Source: own computations based on Table 4.2 by NCAER (2010).

Table 6.5 Handloom workers by nature of engagement as percentage of total workers in each category (2009–2010)

Category of worker	Engagement	Kerala (%)	India (%)
Handloom workers	Full time	97.37	64.26
	Part time	2.63	35.74
Weavers	Full time	99.02	63.49
	Part time	0.98	36.51
Allied workers	Full time	91.84	66.42
	Part time	8.16	33.58

Source: own computations based on tables 4.9, 4.10 and 4.11 by NCAER (2010).

Another indicator we can use to judge participation in handloom activity in Kerala is the number of workers in various categories of days worked per year. Here, in Table 6.6, we can see that this is the only indicator where Kerala performs a little below India on average, as the maximum proportion of handloom worker households (out of total – weaver and allied – households) feature in the category of 201 to 300 days worked per year, compared to the >300 category for an all-India level.

We can also see in Table 6.7 that the average number of person days worked per year in Kerala by weavers is actually more than that of allied workers, though the situation is the reverse for India as a whole. More broadly, the average person days worked per year by a handloom-engaged household is greater in Kerala than in India on average.

We now move on to a critical indicator of participation and performance of weaving households among handloom-engaged households: the average earnings per annum. Table 6.8 shows, very clearly, that weaver households in Kerala reported greater average earnings per year than allied households in the state, and far greater than either weaver or allied households at an all-India level. Contrary to what one might expect, weaver households in *rural* Kerala seem to report the highest average earnings among all categories (see Table 6.8).[9]

Hence, handloom – and particularly weaving – in Kerala has fared no worse than in the rest of India, and in some aspects even better.[10] Fluctuations in demand and other such problems plague the handloom industry as much as any

Table 6.6 Proportion of handloom worker households by number of days worked per year (2009–2010)

	<7	7–50	51–100	101–150	151–200	201–300	>300
Kerala	0%	1.08%	1.41%	3.14%	12.03%	61.97%	20.38%
India	0%	2.92%	15.49%	14.47%	16.30%	24.21%	26.55%

Source: based on Table 4.15 by NCAER (2010).

Table 6.7 Total and average number of person days worked per year (2009–2010)

	Average days per handloom-engaged household	Average days per weaver	Average days per allied worker
Kerala	296	246	214
India	264	183	217

Source: based on Table 4.13 by NCAER (2010).

other traditional industry in India, but weaving as a preferred profession in this industry has not taken a downturn in Kerala. In Balaramapuram too, weaving as a profession has survived among socially heterogeneous clusters of weavers who face the same industry conditions – good or bad – as the Saliyars. If pre- and post-weaving processes, or even non-weaving alternatives, were more attractive than weaving, there should have been a mass migration of communities out of weaving. But this has not been the case. Even if there has been a general outmigration towards other professions, it may be in the manner that was expounded by Mamidipudi *et al.* (2012), where exit from and re-entry into the profession characterise the migrations in and out of the industry. Weaver communities such as the Saliyars in Balaramapuram should not, ideally, have quit permanently but rather exercised a flexibility to exit and re-enter the profession such as what traditional weaver communities in other states in India have been doing. In other words, they should have actually shown resilience whereby they move out of the profession in bad times, but re-enter when conditions are better.

Mobility such as this, according to Mamidipudi *et al.* (2012), is the very basis of the maintenance of stability in handloom weaving and the sustainability of the networks within which it operates. So why did the Balaramapuram Saliyars, operating in a state whose participation in weaving is no worse off than the rest of India (and also having the advantage of a Geographical Indication Tag for the Balaramapuram *sari* and four other textile products, with Intellectual Property protection for ten years), choose to follow a one-way exit?

Table 6.8 Average earnings of weaver and allied households per annum (2009–2010)

		Weaver households (rupees per year)	Allied households (rupees per year)
Kerala	Rural	43,823	38,205
	Urban	31,242	29,571
	Total	**41,198**	**34,496**
India	Rural	38,260	29,693
	Urban	33,038	27,194
	Total	**37,704**	**29,300**

Source: based on Table 6.7 by NCAER (2010).

This chapter argues that it matters only secondarily whether the industry is performing well or not, as affiliation to a rigid network and traits of homophilous-embeddedness in the network can weaken even a seemingly prosperous community, even if that community is operating in a modestly performing (or maybe even well-performing) low-tech industry cluster.

Understanding the counter-example: the Saliyars of Balaramapuram

The Saliyars are evidently a counter-example to the standard line, and to understand why, we invoke the principal finding in the network study in the previous chapter – the presence of heavy homophilous-embeddedness in the Saliyars' networks, relative to the networks of other socially heterogeneous groups (such as the communities in the Payattuvila cluster). The property of homophilous-embeddedness in a network delivers its outcomes in a convoluted manner, working its way by distributing its implications on a range of economic and cultural factors. It has implications for informal information sharing in these localities, for information diffusion, and ultimately for technological progress.

To compare with the Saliyars, we outline how the other, socially heterogeneous, clusters in regions such as Payattuvila, which are currently enjoying a reasonable level of success, surged ahead over the decades primarily due to the absence of community cohesion and homophilous-embeddedness in their networks.

But before drawing these paths, we first trace the events that transpired in the handloom industry in Balaramapuram, around the Saliyar cluster, in the 1960s and 1970s, from whence the Saliyars reported that their decline commenced. We describe as follows a series of massive policy-prescribed developments from the 1960s onward in the Indian handloom industry. It is after describing these policy efforts that we trace the path by which the Saliyars' homophilous-embeddedness and their community cohesion have worked their way through an assortment of mechanisms in the economic choices and functioning of the Saliyars over the past four decades, bringing the community down to their current deteriorated condition, and ensuring a long-term status to that condition.

State support for organisational innovation and for the development and diffusion of innovative design

The purpose of the discussion that follows is to provide a taste of the various schemes and programmes developed by the state to serve what is probably the most important element in handloom – *design*. This section also summarises the state's efforts in modernising the industry and planning efficient networks for the innovation and diffusion of new information. Many of these schemes were opted out of by the Saliyars, in order to maintain their rigid networks and community cohesion.

Recalling from the previous chapter, production technology in weaving in Balaramapuram has remained essentially unchanged for around a century; and if there have been modifications at all, they have been only incremental and concern a few pre-loom activities such as spinning and winding/warping. The demand for the Balaramapuram variety of handloom textiles, to reiterate, finds its basis in the antiquity of production technology in weaving. The fly-shuttle loom was introduced in the Indian subcontinent about a century ago as an improvement over the pit loom, but both technologies operate side-by-side in this industry in Balaramapuram, each being used for different products. Despite weaving technology having remained more or less constant, knowledge has not remained static, and information networks have always occupied a decisive position in the industry.

The information that circulates in these interpersonal networks revolves around the most central element in weaving – *design*. Success, according to Saliyar community members and weavers at Payattuvila who were interviewed, is said to befall those who have quick access to information on the demands and trends in innovative designs. The individuals or groups who surge ahead are those who have access to vital nodes in the information networks (such as the Influential Information Actors (IIAs), referred to in the previous chapter) that carry the information on innovative design and the method of producing these designs on the cloth. This was in fact recognised by the state even in the 1950s, the first decade of policy planning in India following Independence. The government, at both central and state levels, felt the need to intervene in all three sectors of the handloom industry – cooperative societies, master-weavers and individual households – to promote design development and to universalise speedy access to innovative designs. The Government of India sought to do this by establishing two Institutes of Handloom Technology (IHTs – one in Varanasi in north India and another in Salem in south India) and several Weavers' Service Centres (WSCs – located all over the country), which were in turn advised to connect directly to the weavers and workshops in their respective regions. The locations of the WSCs were very carefully chosen in each state, ensuring proximity to the weaving hubs in that state. The government pursued the regular revision and reorganisation of syllabi at the IHTs which were at the apex of design development in the country, and which were to deliver the innovative designs to the WSCs through regular short-term training courses and exhibitions.

> [T]he Weavers Service Centre will be the nerve centre for the design development and the training of the weavers in the area for improving their output and enabling them to earn more.
>
> (MoC, 1974, p. 23)

The WSCs were instructed to maintain close contact with exporters and privately owned marketing organisations for information on modern fabric development, changing fashion demands, and other information. The IHTs and WSCs were to serve, in the language of our analysis, as state-led IIAs to assist in the efficient and ubiquitous diffusion of design information in their respective regions. The path that was charted for information on new design innovations was from the IHTs to WSCs, to proximate master-weavers and cooperatives, and then to the individual households who were connected in some capacity to the master-weavers and cooperatives. This was not without constant feedback between these actors and other significant private players in the industry.[11]

Besides this, the government also promoted modernisation and design development services for individual weavers who were outside the cooperative and master-weaver fold, as well as for underperforming master-weavers. A 'High Powered Team on the Problems of Handloom Industry' (whose report is in MoC, 1974) had in this regard recommended the organisation of twenty-five units, each comprising around 10,000 handloom weavers outside of the cooperative and master-weaver fold in handloom hubs around the country to receive training in new design and credit from nationalised banks, to benefit from marketing of output, and to strengthen linkages to WSCs.

In line with these propositions, by 1976 a Common Facility & Design Centre for weavers was set up in Kerala, in Balaramapuram. This had the explicit intent of promoting design innovations, providing training to weavers in design and technical advice in dyeing, printing and other pre- and post-loom processes (GoK, 1976). This had its roots not only in the vast programmes for handloom development discussed earlier, but also in the Government of Kerala's contribution to the Twenty Point Programme announced by the Prime Minister of India in 1975. The state government had proposed two projects in Kerala (in the north in Kannur district and in the south in Trivandrum district) for the intensive development of the handloom industry in the state, under the management of Hanveev (The Kerala State Handloom Development Corporation Ltd). These projects were infused with funds as large as Rs.1.85 million (in 1976 terms), mostly with assistance from the Government of India. This involved the organisation of almost 100 workshop-type weaving units, the establishment of 100 collective weaving centres, and their linkage with the two WSCs' training centres in the state for design evolution and other technical issues (GoK, 1976). During the same decade, a large volume of funds (to the tune of Rs.11 million in 1976 terms) in the form of cash credit was injected as working capital under the scheme of the Reserve Bank of India (the country's central bank), targeted not at household weaving units but primarily at those who were under the cooperative or the workshop/work-shed form of organisation (GoK, 1978). For individual weavers, commercial banks were directed, under the supervision of Hanveev, to provide aid under differential interest rate schemes. These projects and the financial assistance that they brought with them were continued beyond even the mid-1980s in Kerala (GoK, 1986).

In this manner, for around three decades – the 1950s, 1960s and 1970s – there was intensive involvement of state support in this industry, concentrated in and around the handloom hubs in each state in India, including Balaramapuram.

Although a variety of such recommendations were provided by the central and state governments with regard to the innovation and diffusion of design information, it was found by a study by the Planning Commission (GoI, 1967) that the fastest absorbers of new design information in the industry during the late 1950s and early 1960s were those who had also implemented the prescribed organisational innovations: namely the cooperatives and, more importantly, the *master-weavers* and the *workshops*. It was revealed also by MoC (1974) – the report brought out by the 'High Powered Study Team' – that though the *cooperative* mode of organisation was promoted by the government, the bulk of design development, the element that fuels the progress of the industry, came from the private sector, namely the master-weavers who operate the workshops and work-sheds and who were in close association with design development centres that were developed by the government during the 1950s and 1960s.[12] It was the master-weaver – in other words, the person who adopted the *workshop* or *work-shed* mode of organisation on a large scale – who was said to have played a leadership role in design innovation. Brief attempts to discourage this mode of organisation from some quarters in the government (based on certain accounts that there was rampant labour exploitation in these work-sheds and workshops) were put down consequent to surveys, which revealed that:

> it would be a serious mistake if at the present stage of development we try to abolish this [master-weaver] sector.... Till the cooperative sector is sufficiently developed and is able to give full service to its members and come up at least to the level which the master weavers have reached, it will be against the interests of weavers [for the state] to interfere with this sector.
>
> (MoC, 1974, p. 12)

In fact, even the earlier Planning Commission study (GoI, 1967) found through their analysis of a small sample of workshops in handloom producing regions such as Andhra Pradesh, Tamil Nadu and Maharashtra that it was the workshops rather than the individual households which effectively adopted many of the innovations in the industry:

> all of the 11 workshops had adopted one or more types of improved implements. Among different improved implements varnished/wire healds were adopted by all the workshops; steel reeds and warping machines in 9 out of 11 workshops. The majority of workshops adopted dobbies/jacquards and take-up-motion attachments.
>
> (GoI, 1967, p. 32)

Independent households, constituting the bulk of the industry, did absorb some innovations, but they evidently lagged behind households that had embraced other innovative forms of organisation – such as workshop and master-weaver arrangements. Independent households that excluded themselves from adapting to these organisational innovations also ended up missing out on the valuable training offered by state-sponsored agencies. The Planning Commission study provided some very interesting revelations regarding the self-exclusion of hereditary-weaving independent households who refused to participate in organisational innovations:

out of 1097 sample weaver households, 1068 had no trained member....
This means that a very few namely 29 sample households were reported to
have been trained under the training programme.... On the whole, weavers
did not generally take interest in getting themselves trained in the improved
methods of weaving.... A large majority of weaver households were not
even aware of the existence of training programmes.... About one-third of
the households felt considered that the training was *not necessary ... they
felt that their members engaged in the weaving establishments were already
trained because the occupation was hereditary, and as such they did not
require any particular training in the industry.*

(GoI, 1967, pp. 39–40, emphasis added)

To return very briefly to a historical instance, even in western India in the early
twentieth century, the workshops or *karkhanas* were the most enthusiastic actors in
adopting some of the crucial technological and organisational innovations in the
industry, while caste-weaver households were far more hesitant (Haynes, 2012).
Innovative products were said to have stemmed from those *karkhanas* who were
not opposed to the new machines and designs, and who were always on the lookout
for new markets in the region and beyond. At the same time, Haynes (2012) continues, many weaving households decided not to participate in these sweeping
changes; for instance, *Sali* and *Koshti* community weavers, who generally operated
in households, did not adopt the fly-shuttle as much as the *Padmasalis* did.

A school that had opened to spread new techniques among the Salis around
the same time simply failed to attract new students. In part because of their
difficulties in taking up the new methods, the Salis and Koshtis found it hard
to compete and eventually left for other occupations.

(Haynes, 2012, p. 217)

These revelations demonstrate that those who were willing to absorb organisational
innovations benefited from being at the forefront of design innovation, and, after
the 1950s, received enormous financial support from the state. But these findings
also provide a hint as to the attitudes among some closed communities. Although
the Planning Commission survey did not involve Balaramapuram, these results
give us very interesting leads towards the analysis that follows.[13]

The Saliyars were in some sense better than the communities that were surveyed
by GoI (1967), since they had adopted some smaller incremental innovations such
as the mechanisation of spinning. However, as detailed below, where they faltered
was in that they neither participated in absorbing and implementing organisational
innovations (hence depriving themselves of financial incentives and schemes
offered by the state in the 1960s and 1970s), nor had they effectively tapped design
innovations, which are possible to access through interpersonal networks. Both of
these exclusions had their roots in homophilous-embeddedness and community
cohesion, as we will see. The sections that follow are based on the illustration in
Figure 6.1.

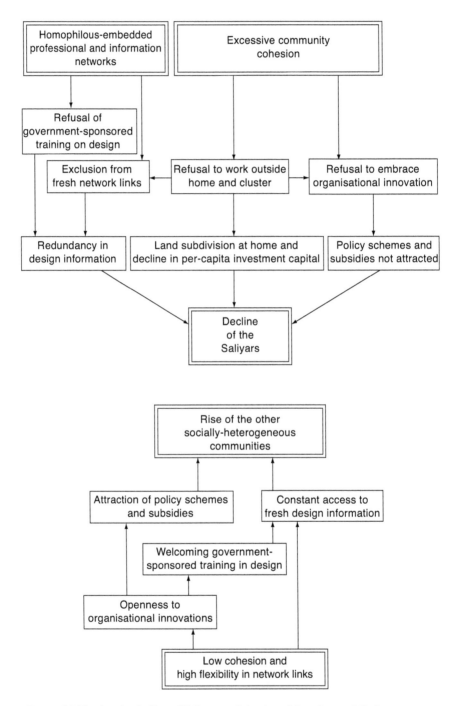

Figure 6.1 Tracing the decline of Saliyars and the rise of the other socially heterogeneous communities (source: based on fieldwork).

The decline of the Saliyars

According to a few Saliyar elders interviewed for this study, the first cause of the decline of the Saliyars may be attributed to the fact that their information on design was increasingly becoming redundant from the late 1970s and early 1980s onward, which happens to coincide with the period when the state and many other bodies were infusing finance and many schemes and programmes into the handloom industry in Kerala.

Redundancy in design information

During interviews with Saliyar elders, it was revealed that the Saliyars used to pride themselves on the designs they came up with and the innovative methods they developed to produce those designs on the final cloth; so much so that Saliyar weavers strove to keep information on these designs a community secret.

Designs were shared willingly within the community, but kept at close guard so as not to allow them to seep out until, of course, the final product went into the market. In this manner, though a mild and subtle competition existed among weavers within the community for innovative designs and innovative methods of generating those designs on the cloth, there was generally cooperation among Saliyar households to share information once a design had gained approval in the market. There was little input through information from the outside, since community cohesion was strong, and information networks were mostly tight-knit within the community.[14] This gives us pointers as to how and why redundancy in information began creeping into the Saliyars' information network.

Figure 6.1 illustrates that there are two main reasons why the Saliyars' information networks were plagued by redundant information: exclusion from fresh network links, and refusal to participate in government-sponsored training on design.

Let us look at the first reason. The exclusion from fresh network links was due to the fact that the Saliyars' information links were inherited generation after generation, and each Saliyar household was locked in from birth to a network of suppliers, customers and others, who were the chief sources of information on new design. Being a network clan (Bianchi and Bellini, 1991), tradition dictated whom to ask and whom to talk to. Interviews with Saliyar elders revealed that the community would frown upon those who abandoned these traditional links, by distancing the deviant individuals during social functions and for production issues. This ensured a rigid network, which over the long term fed into an incapability to access fresh information.

The exclusion from fresh network links could have been averted if weavers had more efficiently utilised the opportunity they had in migrating to another village called Amaravila in the vicinity of Balaramapuram.

Amaravila is a tiny village eight kilometres from Balaramapuram where a few Saliyar families established themselves from the 1970s onward. This movement was not unidirectional but to-and-fro, with many families shuttling between

Balaramapuram and Amaravila. By the late 1970s, Saliyar families in the Saliyar cluster at Balaramapuram had begun to suffer from a problem common to agriculture in India – land subdivision. The sense of family, strong among weaver communities in India in general, was particularly deep-seated in the Saliyars, so much so that Saliyar children would continue operating in the same household in which they grew up and where their parents wove. With the area of residence fixed, successive generations suffered from cramped households, and felt the need to move out of the cluster. When a Saliyar family moved out of the cluster, they wished to move only within the vicinity of Balaramapuram, and only to places where the community had possibilities to maintain a sense of identity and continue its religious and cultural practices. This was achievable where, for example, a temple with a favoured deity existed and where marriage relations were potentially possible with the existing inhabitants of their destination. Amaravila fitted these requirements very well, and so there was migration between this village and the Saliyar cluster at Balaramapuram.

But what went wrong had roots in the same reason. Amaravila was not uninhabited, and had a small number of weavers from various communities. But the Saliyar families that moved to Amaravila were still attached to the home cluster at Balaramapuram, sharing the same professional and information links. Hence, though there were a few weavers from different communities in Amaravila, the migrant Saliyars preferred to link with other Saliyars in their own home cluster at Balaramapuram. Links with these resident weavers of other communities could have begun the process of modifying the Saliyars' information network to include more out-of-community links, assisting them in slowly breaking out of their network rigidity; but the Saliyars missed this opportunity.

The move to Amaravila turned out to be a missed opportunity; it actually intensified the inflexibility of the Saliyar network, by virtue of being associated with the same homophilous-embedded networks of the home Saliyar cluster. Although a location change was undertaken with the intention of relieving oneself from land subdivision problems (which could have improved the structure and composition of the information network), the networks remained exactly the same, as did the design information. In every sense, the Saliyars ended up operating in nothing but a new location attached to the same homophilous-embedded networks, rather than evolving fresh networks that could have arisen from the new location. In this manner, homophilous-embeddedness and a sense of community cohesion characterised links with Amaravila and fuelled the exclusion of the Saliyars from fresh network links for information on design.

Another exclusion to which the Saliyars subjected themselves was the training given to weavers in Balaramapuram (Kerala in general) by agencies such as the state through training sessions organised by the nearest WSC as described above. This exclusion from training is interconnected with the refusal to embrace organisational innovations that attracted financial and technical support from the nodal agencies of the state, an issue that we will discuss below. The Saliyars willingly abstained from government-sponsored training workshops on design, detailed earlier in this chapter, as they had prided themselves on their capability to work as a community to come up with innovative designs and develop the expertise to weave those designs on the cloth. As one Saliyar elder put it: 'we didn't need anyone from outside to tell us what to do.'[15]

Very evidently, this standpoint maintained by the community, supported by social pressures not to participate, stemmed from an extreme sense of community cohesion. Hence, we see that homophilous-embeddedness in the Saliyars' networks and a sense of intense community cohesion was at the root of redundancy in information and thus impeded innovation in design, which is one reason that fed into the decline of the Saliyars.

Failure to adopt organisational innovations, and to attract policy schemes and funds

Another reason for the community's decline, stemming again from homophilous-embeddedness and community cohesion, was its failure to attract policy schemes and funding assistance from the state. These schemes were an integral part of the state's assistance to the handloom industry, which, as we have seen, continued for more than thirty years beginning from the mid-1950s and carrying on beyond the mid-1980s. As we have seen, the state had, for a long period, very systematically drawn out welfare schemes for training in design, funds for working capital and for the purchase of new looms and other equipment, and substantial financial and technical support for the embrace of organisational innovations such as workshops. Workshops, usually attached to a cooperative, were also introduced to schemes for marketing. Failure to enrol in these ways of functioning and in refusing to embrace certain key organisational innovations that characterised the handloom industry in Balaramapuram was another factor that founded the Saliyars' decline.

Organisational innovations mainly involved the adoption of the work-shed (or workshop), which was attached to local cooperatives, and within which wage labour was employed on numerous looms. Supervision in these work-sheds was supposed to be under a master-weaver who would or would not actually weave, and who played more of an administrative and advisory role, including the acquisition of new information on design and linking with the nodal agencies for design, either under the state or other private individuals. The master-weaver, as studies have often found, was the chief agent in design. It was revealed during interviews with the Saliyar elders that the work-shed and master-weaver arrangements were not really brand-new organisational innovations in the true sense of the term as there were similar master-weaver and workshop arrangements among the Saliyars (similar to the *karkhanas* within weaving communities in western India).[16] What was new in Balaramapuram was that organisational arrangements such as workshops, when introduced in this region, were prescribed as completely devoid of any community affiliation, an arrangement with which the Saliyars had little agreement.[17]

Until the 1970s there were, according to Saliyar elders, almost 300 Saliyar master-weavers in the community employing a handful of workers at looms in each of their homes. These weaving units with a cluster of looms were located within the Saliyars' homes, and employed labour from among the Saliyar community as well as from other communities. However, employees from the Saliyar community outnumbered those from outside by a large majority. Saliyar employees were, naturally, sourced from extended families or to maintain community relations and worked inside the homes of the Saliyar master-weavers. But the outsiders were allowed entry to, and operation from, only the backyard of the Saliyar home and not within the residence where household members and other Saliyar employees worked. Moreover, employees from the other communities were employed not in weaving but in pre- and post-loom activities, which meant that they were expected to offer little in terms of bringing in new information on the crucial element of design. Subdivision of land at home had shrunk space at home to operate one's own family's production activities, let alone operate master-weaver arrangements, and paying wage labour became more difficult. These issues led to the slow disappearance of these Saliyar master-weavers. Attempts to set up work-sheds outside of the cluster (where land was not scarce at the time) were rare, since most Saliyars reportedly did not want to leave the home cluster.

In addition, no Saliyar male was known to work for another community's master-weaver (for reasons of 'community pride' – this justification was cited consistently by those who were interviewed); and the Saliyar women who were employed at home for pre-loom tasks were in any case not permitted to work in handloom outside of the house. The Saliyars were very keen on sticking to their own organisational form – the household production unit with family/community division of labour – and their own cooperative societies were demarcated along community lines dense with homophilous-embeddedness.

Due to this environment in the Saliyar cluster, it was difficult for the Saliyars to break down their community cohesion in order to accept fully the work-shed form of organisation and production. Due to this non-acceptance, they were excluded from the links to the WSCs, in turn the IHTs, the loans and funds from the commercial banks, and the many other policy schemes and programmes on offer. The organisational innovations were simply not adopted, and the Saliyar master-weavers receded.

It should be noted that the Saliyars had no misgivings about adopting innovations such as electric spinning and winding machines, new forms and variants of dyes and yarn, and other such small incremental innovations in pre- and post-loom processes. This is because these innovations were not at odds with community structure and functioning, and did not expect movement out of the home and the cluster. But merely the acceptance of these innovations did not ensure any progress, as organisational innovations were also crucial for survival and sustenance. This major innovation was the one that the Saliyars had backed out of, due to community cohesion. Hence, once again, community cohesion stands out as being at the root of the refusal by Saliyars to adopt organisational innovations (as enthusiastically as the other socially heterogeneous clusters accepted them), leading to a failure in attracting policy schemes and funds.

Land issues at home and locally, and the decline of per capita investment capital

The Saliyars were endowed with large amounts of land when they were invited to Balaramapuram. This included not only their set of streets and their residences, but also large tracts of land spread across a couple of acres around their cluster. This extra land was for a long time a principal source of finance for investment into the handloom business, and a source of financial security for the family. However, two issues arose as the decades passed: first, the increasing difficulty in employing and financing wage labour to maintain the economic activities operating in the extra tracts of land; and second, the division and sale of sections of land for marriage- and dowry-related matters. Both of these factors were equally severe in depleting the stock of land that the families in this community owned. Other venues of sourcing investment included internal contributions from within the community such as borrowing and lending from relatives and other acquaintances. Banks and other financial institutions were seldom considered a source of investment capital, despite the fact that agriculture and traditional industry such as handloom were targeted with massive financial support by nationalised banks. This meant that from the 1970s onward there was an eventual diminution of sources for investment into the weaving business, adding to the difficulty in maintaining wage labour at home for weaving, and the eventual closure of Saliyar master-weaver units by the early 1980s. These extra tracts of land, if still available to the Saliyars, may have even allowed them to continue, and to set up new master-weaver units that might have attracted funds and state-led schemes. But by the time the schemes were developed in Kerala in the late 1960s and mid-1970s, the Saliyars had lost most of their extra tracts of land.

Yet another land-related issue, briefly visited earlier, was the subdivision and partitioning of the house to allow successive generations and their families to weave at home. A decrease in per capita land at home meant that per capita production also fell, followed in turn by a fall in per capita investment into weaving, pre-loom and post-loom activities. Naturally, expansions in weaving activity stopped and then began to decline, and handloom production among the Saliyars slowly began to incline towards pre-loom activities that required little investment and space to expand, compared to weaving. An extra loom, for instance, took up most of the floor area in one of the large rooms in an already crowded house, whereas an extra spinning machine took up very little space, as all that was needed was a small area on the side of a wall in a relatively smaller room. A yarn shop was easier to expand and the yarn business easier to invest in, given that extra bales of yarn took up very little space and the nature of the commodity's sale was fast moving (requiring less space requirements for inventory), compared to a master-weaver arrangement that took up many times the area of an entire yarn shop. An increase in intensity in spinning or other pre-loom activities could have improved the Saliyars' conditions, but an expansion in even these activities that required very little space had its own limits in an already small, and increasingly cramped, residence. Subsequent generations would set up a

loom or spinning wheel in another quarter of their respective homes, this practice naturally reaching a limit within two or three generations. Given that this
community was brought to Balaramapuram in the 1890s, one can picture that
there would have been at least two or even three generations in the house by the
1970s, all actively pursuing weaving and other activities simultaneously, in the
same small space of the home. Visits to Saliyar houses even today show spinning and plying activities in some Saliyar families literally jostling for space
with day-to-day living arrangements.

　　All these again point at one root cause – the community cohesion that did not
encourage (even if it did not strictly disallow) movement and operation out of
the home and outside of the Saliyar cluster. Movement out of the cluster only
meant towards Amaravila, the problems associated with which we have already
covered in the previous discussion.

Summing up

These three factors – (1) redundancy in information on innovative design, (2)
failure to attract state-sponsored schemes and funds by not embracing organisational innovations, and (3) diminishing land and investment capital – all appear
to have their roots in two very characteristic traits or attributes of the Saliyars:
homophilous-embedded networks and excessive community cohesion. As we
have seen, they are highly interconnected and often overlap. The Saliyars began
stagnating slowly by the late 1970s, and a crisis began to build up in the Saliyar
cluster from the early 1980s onward, intensifying by the late 1980s and through
the 1990s, and continuing even to the present day. This has its origins in the
unwarranted degree of community centrality displayed by the Saliyars, manifested and fed back by homophilous-embeddedness in their business and, more
importantly, in their information networks. The Saliyars had recognised that
their progeny had a choice between, on the one hand, inheriting the same networks, staying put in the home cluster with a household form of production
organisation and family/community division of labour, and avoiding tampering
with community relations; and, on the other hand, leaving weaving and handloom altogether. They seem to have chosen the latter.

The rise of the other socially heterogeneous communities

The depletion of resources for further investment and the redundancy in information on design brought about the stagnation of the Saliyars and the cooperative
societies with which they were associated. These Saliyar cooperatives, drawn on
community lines, became slow and backward in operation, many going defunct
and existing only on paper by the early 1980s. This is seen clearly in DoH
(1986), one of the works commissioned by the state government to assess the
performance of the schemes listed earlier in this chapter, and the performance of
the industry as such.[18] In this report it was seen that by 1984 the chief
cooperative society of the Saliyars, the 'Anchuwarnatheruvu HWCS Ltd',[19] was

listed as 'dormant' (DoH, 1986, p. 7). What is interesting is that this cooperative society was the *only* one that had a status listed as 'dormant', while the multitude of other cooperative societies in Balaramapuram – comprising socially hetero-geneous groups of weavers – were listed as 'working'.

This dormancy of the Saliyar cooperatives led to the next step – the takeover of these Saliyar cooperatives by the state and welcoming associations with weavers who belonged to all communities, not just the Saliyars. The remodelling of these societies was not simply by means of dissociation with the Saliyar com-munity and entry of the other communities, but by the systematic mediation of the government, playing an active role in reorganising the management of the societies, reworking their functioning and, most important of all, rewiring the networks in which they operated.

This brought about a 'secularising' of these formerly Saliyar-only cooperative societies, with all communities free to enter and participate. Of course, there were weaver households already in the areas around the Saliyar cluster long before the Saliyars came in, but these were (according to the Saliyars) small-time weavers and only a sprinkling in number, like any other village or town in India which had a small number of resident weavers. In addition, there were a few small coopera-tives in Balaramapuram besides the Saliyar cooperatives, but, according to the Saliyar elders interviewed, it was mainly after the state's remodelling and nurturing of the cooperative societies in a big way that the other socially heterogeneous clus-ters actually progressed from being modestly successful to thriving in the business. These socially heterogeneous clusters of weavers gained access to information from many external sources, and importantly from the state in its regular training sessions on design. They were subject to the WSC training sessions, links with exporters and other private players, funds and loan arrangements through the hand-loom development project in Trivandrum in the mid- and late 1970s, and many other progressive schemes. However, taking over the societies was just the initial step and the link with these state schemes was not the principal basis for the sus-tained rise of the other socially heterogeneous clusters in weaving. The coopera-tives that we refer to here also ended up in many quagmires over the decades, but the socially heterogeneous clusters continued to rise and sustain themselves in the business.[20] Although these linkages and the attraction of schemes and programmes boosted their businesses, their rise was due to two principal factors: (1) a convivial attitude towards organisational innovations (such as the work-sheds and master-weaver form of organisation); and (2) the flexibility in information network links. Both of these factors had roots in the fact that these communities operated in socially very heterogeneous environments which allowed little possibility for excessive cohesion.

The other socially heterogeneous clusters in Balaramapuram, whether as a part of the newly taken over cooperatives or not, had welcomed the organisa-tional innovations that were supported by the state through funds and training programmes.

This was the one crucial difference between the Saliyar cluster and the Payattuvila cluster. It was noted even during fieldwork that while the former was characterised by home-based family/community labour units, the latter was characterised by work-sheds (at home or near the residential area), which may have been owned by a family, but which employed wage labour sourced from the town regardless of caste, paid on a daily wage basis and attached to the local cooperative. The latter organisational form had drawn support from the state for the purchase of looms for work-sheds, incentives in terms of tax benefits, welfare benefits for workers (those handloom workers attached to cooperatives), the infusion of large amounts of working capital through nationalised banks, and many other such schemes. The other socially heterogeneous clusters had far better access to more flourishing domestic and other markets across India thanks to the associations with state-administered bodies such as the WSCs, and began supplying large upmarket showrooms[21] in Kerala and India in a capacity far greater than the Saliyars. With these sources and the regular training sessions in design organised by the WSCs, the other socially heterogeneous clusters in Balaramapuram were said to have surged ahead.

These communities, with no restrictions on network links and information sources, enjoyed a flexibility that the Saliyars had eschewed out of community cohesion and rigid inherited networks. The socially heterogeneous clusters had constant access to fresh information on designs and were always up to date on the latest trends in the market. They could associate and dissociate with agents in their networks as they wished, since they had no community or family obligations to bear. They had no restrictions preventing them from moving out of their homes and expanding whenever necessary, and no traditions directing them on how to operate their business. To reiterate: even when the handloom cooperatives in Kerala began languishing, clusters such as the one in Payattuvila enjoyed prolonged participation in the weaving business thanks to the welcoming attitude towards innovations, especially of the organisational variety, and a flexibility in linkage.

Even in western India a century ago, the family-run workshops or *karkhanas* were welcoming towards innovations and new designs. Reliability was an essential element in the workshops, for which community and family cohesion were depended upon. Innovation, on the other hand, required new information, and therefore periodically 'refreshed' network links. The workshop clusters of western India during this time appear to have taken advantage of both worlds – community cohesion in production relations inside the workshop, and external connections outside of the community with regard to contacting design innovators, looking to the state for financial incentives (when offered), new trade links and customers, and so on. Even divisions of family labour in these workshops were entrepreneurial. Members of the owner-family were involved in operations such as searching for new markets and customers, networking outside of the town, and furthering similar non-homophilous-embedded links. Embedded or homophilous links inside the workshop may have been safe, but the workshop-owning families knew that homophilous-embedded links outside of the workshop were dangerous. This was the crucial difference between the family-owned and community-based workshops in western India and Payattuvila on the one hand, and the Saliyar cluster on the other hand.

The machines and loom processes were never different (they still are not) between the Saliyars and a community such as Payattuvila. Both use the same kinds of looms (after all, the employment of this weaving technology is the very basis of demand in this industry), the same spinning machines, the same dyes, the same beaming techniques and so on. The big difference is in organisation of production activity and, importantly, network flexibility. In addition, a point to bear in mind is that the home retains centrality, even in Payattuvila where master-weaver arrangements thrive. Master-weavers in Payattuvila manage their work-sheds or workshops *in the vicinity of their homes* with considerable family involvement. The difference lies in the fact that they were not opposed to involving non-family employed labour in the workshops, welcoming towards organisational innovations, and, most important of all, operating in less homophilous-embedded information networks.

A key aspect therefore is whether the *networks* were flexible or not, and whether choosing expansion outside of the house and community was accepted by members of the community. A socially heterogeneous environment, with no community-related baggage, was (and still is) beneficial to maintaining the flexibility of the networks, and is also open to the possibility of migration outside of the house and the community. The possibility of a dangerous degree of community cohesion, and of homophilous-embedded in production and information networks, is very low in such environments, and was at the root of the rise of the socially heterogeneous clusters in handloom weaving in Balaramapuram.

Conclusion

The Saliyars have found themselves trapped. Although calamities in their cluster have come and gone in the past, the dilemmas that have sustained them and even exacerbated over the past thirty years are worse than in the decades prior to their decline. There is now too little community-sourced capital to invest among the Saliyars and risks of non-recovery of investment are very high. Diminished land resources have made it difficult to set up new work-sheds, and, even if they can be set up elsewhere, there is little source of finance for maintaining employed labour. In addition, outmigration of the youth has passed beyond a recoverable point, and most of the youth who could have stayed at home and attempted to recover business are gone. Handloom, and traditional industry in general, has always been infamous for the uncertainties and fluctuations that have often put its workers at grave risk. In fact, historically, too, in times of a crisis such as a famine, it has been noted by the literature that weavers were the first to starve (Roy, 1993, 2002), and hence the first to migrate. Those communities that migrated were found to display an excessive, sometimes unwarranted, amount of community cohesion and centrality to family. But this community and family spirit assisted and gave its own shape to the technology trajectory of handloom weaving in most of India. Inherited networks and community social capital overpowered the risks of adoption of new technologies and practices, and invigorated information flows. Community social capital and technological progress went hand-in-hand for the most part in the history of Indian handloom, as the former was used judiciously and not across all aspects of production and information seeking.

But while for the most part community cohesion has been historically congruent to technological progress and knowledge diffusion among community-based weaving clusters and groups in India, in the case of the Saliyars there has been disharmony. This does not require rethinking whether or not community social capital and technological progress share a healthy relation in low-tech industry clusters. We believe that they still do share such a relation, though only to a limit, after which the detriments of community social capital and rigidities associated with inherited networks set in, and hinder information diffusion and technological progress. The Saliyars are hence only a counter-example to the standard line, and not a case against it.

The empirical studies in Chapters 4, 5 and 6 have tackled the tasks that emerged from the results of the simulation model in Chapter 2. These tasks were to study: (1) the nature and characteristics of informal information sharing in a low-tech cluster with universal affinity among its agents; and (2) the effect of complex social relations on informal information sharing among agents where social groups and the divisions among them matter significantly and influence their information-sharing interaction decisions.

Notes

1 One could argue that the justification for caste censuses (as opposed to general population censuses or industry surveys) may be weak, since weavers may generally belong to particular castes, but *all* members of that caste may not weave. There is some truth in this argument, but one must bear in mind that there was a slim chance of finding weavers in other castes, especially during the period in history involved here. Hence, a pragmatic way to capture demographic information on weavers was to conduct surveys in and around weaver *castes*, even if all caste members were not weavers. We provide evidence later in this chapter (from Venkataraman, 1935) that even until the middle of the twentieth century, and despite the slow breakdown of caste and community monopolies in various occupations during the British Raj and after Independence, a large majority of weavers and handloom textile producers continued to hail from hereditary weaving communities.

2 Although Arasaratnam (1980) does not provide details of which communities exactly did this, he puts forward a very interesting argument that the weaver responses of the 1770s and 1780s in south India around the Carnatic region (most of modern-day Karnataka, Andhra Pradesh and Tamil Nadu states) were the first popular reactions against British rule in India.

3 This is reminiscent of the concept of ethnic enclaves.

4 This is very similar to the Saliyars of Balaramapuram, though they migrated at a much later period, and not out of circumstance but due to the invitation of the Maharaja of Travancore, under whose patronage they worked. The Maharaja on the one hand invited them to ensure his supply of Saliyar-woven high-quality clothing, and the Saliyars on the other hand, with his patronage, lived a lifestyle and observed community practices that were much higher than what the caste system had traditionally accorded them.

5 Venkataraman finds that the *Kaikolars, Devangas, Salés* (not related to the Saliyars at Balaramapuram) and *Sourashtras* were still the dominant weaving communities in the Madras Presidency, well into the twentieth century after the large-scale producing workshops began seeping into the handloom industry.

6 Note that the centrality of family in textile weaving was also prevalent in Japan. As explained by Dore (1983):

> there was intense coordination of activities of a large number of family enterprises.... The key family business was that of the merchant converter who contracted with the spinning company to turn its yarn into a certain type of cloth at a given contract price. The converter would send the yarn to another small family concern specialising in yarn dyeing, then it would go on to a specialist beamer who would wind it on to the warp beams in the desired pattern and also put the warp through the sizing process. Then it would be delivered to the weaver who might do his own weft preparation and the drawing-in (putting the harness on the beams ready for the looms) or might use other family businesses – contract winders or drawers in – for the process. And so on to the finishers who did the bleaching or texturising or over-printing.
>
> (Dore, 1983:462)

Family is also seen to be central in the Mercato footwear cluster in Ethiopia (Gebreyeesus and Mohnen, 2013), as is design innovation, an element that will occupy centre-stage in a later analysis in this chapter.

7 Production in Kerala appears to have faced a sudden and substantial drop after 2007/2008. This might prompt the allegation that industry conditions *are* indeed worse in Kerala than in the rest of India, which may actually be at the root of the permanent exit of the Saliyars. But this argument cannot be correct, as the Saliyar participation in weaving had already declined by then, and the community had largely exited handloom. If handloom had faced a sudden bad patch in Kerala during this period, or even in the past, the issue remains as to why it was mainly the Saliyars who left *en masse*, while others stayed and continued weaving. If there was a major decline in the industry, the Saliyars and other communities would have left in more or less equal proportions, other things remaining equal; but this has not been the case.

8 A *weaver household unit* is defined by NCAER (2010) as:

> one that has any member of the household who operated a loom even for one day in the last one year (preceding the survey date), either within the premises of the house (classifying the household as a 'with loom household') or outside the household premises (classifying the household as 'without loom household').

On the other hand, an *allied worker household unit* is defined by this census as:

> one that has any member of the household who has undertaken pre-loom (dyeing of yarn, warping/winding, weft winding, sizing, testing, etc.) and/or post-loom activities (dyeing of fabric/calendaring/printing of fabric, made-ups, etc.), even for one day in the last one year (preceding the survey date), either within the premises of the house or outside the household premises. These households did not have any members engaged in weaving activity within or outside the premises, nor did they have a loom within their premises.
>
> (NCAER, 2010, p. 6)

9 It must be noted that these figures, if calculated at a monthly level, appear quite low in absolute terms especially when considering rising living costs in both rural and urban India. However, the objective here is to demonstrate that even if weaving is not a lucrative option in terms of money earning, it still offers a better living for the most part in Kerala than in India on average, prompting us towards the larger question of

why Saliyars have made a permanent exit from weaving and from handloom altogether, unlike many other weaving communities in Kerala and India.

10 Although Kerala in some indicators shows a greater participation and intensity in
weaving compared to an all-India level, it is by no means the primary handloom
weaving state in India. Other states such as Andhra Pradesh, Maharashtra and Tamil
Nadu have far larger weaving industries compared to Kerala in terms of output,
export, etc. Evidence supporting this is considerable in NCAER (2010).

11 Today there are five IHTs (rechristened IIHTs – Indian Institutes of Handloom and
Textile Technology) in Varanasi, Salem, Guwahati, Jodhpur and Bargarh, as well as
twenty-five WSCs in almost all the states. In addition to the IIHTs managed by the
central government, there are, in addition, four handloom design and technology institutes managed by the state governments in central and south India, including in
Kannur in Kerala. There is also a National Centre for Textile Design (NCTD) in New
Delhi.

12 Eapen (1991) explains how active state involvement began in the mid-1950s, when
the handloom industry was assigned a major role in planned national development,
with a special emphasis on the *cooperative*, the government contributing to the share
capital of cooperatives and providing other financial assistance through loans and cash
credit arrangements.

13 In Balaramapuram, design innovations played a more significant role than technical
innovations, unlike in the towns surveyed by studies such as GoI (1967). Recall that
in Balaramapuram the very demand for the product was based on the constancy of its
weaving technology, and hence technical innovations were only very incrementally
absorbed whereas most information flows were around design innovations.

14 This recalls Burt (1992), who explained that redundancy of information leading to
obsolescence is indicated by cohesion and equivalence, which manifest in network
structure. Cohesive contacts, being strongly connected to one another, provide the
same information repeatedly. Equivalent contacts, connecting an agent to the same
third party, also direct the agent to receiving redundant information.

15 This is reminiscent of what was found by GoI (1967) in their survey, namely that
many hereditary caste-weaver households did not find the training 'necessary', by
virtue of handloom textile production being their hereditary profession.

16 The *karkhanas* of western India arrived more than a century earlier than in Balaramapuram, for one simple reason. While Balaramapuram was at the time a very small
village with a sprinkling of weaver households catering to a local and domestic
market, towns in the western part of the Indian subcontinent were at the heartland of
textile production in the subcontinent, producing for export to Britain and other
colonies.

17 Kochuthressia (1994) describes how for centuries the Saliyars as a community, even
outside of Balaramapuram, maintained their caste boundaries and community living,
which broke down after cooperative societies came into being.

18 DoH (1986) was an effort by the state government to list, in the form of a directory,
the primary handloom cooperative societies in Kerala state and their status at the
time.

19 'Anchuwarnatheruvu' is literally 'lane of five castes'. The Saliyars were invited to
Balaramapuram in the 1890s by the then Maharaja of Travancore, along with a few
families from four other Tamil-speaking communities. The main street on which the
Saliyars – the most populous and prominent among these communities – were located
was known as the 'lane of five castes'. HWCS is the Handloom Workers' Cooperative
Society.

20 Recall from the previous chapter that most registered cooperatives were found to exist
only on paper: in 2001, at least 250 out of the 366 listed cooperative societies in
Trivandrum district were found to be either non-existent or non-functional (Niranjana
and Vinayan, 2001). But despite the cooperatives stagnating, it was the adoption of

the workshop and work-shed form of organisation, operating under master-weavers and having flexible and dynamic information network links (i.e. a welcoming attitude to knowledge from the outside), that helped sustain these socially heterogeneous clusters, such as in Payattuvila, even today.
21 Recall again the influential information actors (IIA) from the previous chapter.

References

Arasaratnam, S., 1980. Weavers, Merchants and Company: The Handloom Industry in Southeastern India 1750–1790. *The Indian Economic and Social History Review*, 17(3), 257–281.

Bianchi, P. and Bellini, N., 1991. Public Policies for Local Networks of Innovators. *Research Policy*, 20(5), 487–497.

Borjas, G.J., 1992. Ethnic Capital and Intergenerational Mobility. *The Quarterly Journal of Economics*, 107(1), 123–150.

——, 1995. Ethnicity, Neighborhoods, and Human-Capital Externalities. *The American Economic Review*, 85(3), 365–390.

Coleman, J.S., 1988. Social Capital in the Creation of Human Capital. *American Journal of Sociology*, 94, S95–S120.

Dasgupta, P., 2005. Economics of Social Capital. *The Economic Record*, 81(255), S2–S21.

DoH, 1986. *Directory of Primary Handloom Cooperative Societies in Kerala.* Directorate of Handloom, Government of Kerala.

Dore, R., 1983. Goodwill and the Spirit of Market Capitalism. *The British Journal of Sociology*, 34(4), 459–482.

Eapen, M., 1991. 'Hantex: An Economic Appraisal', Working Paper 242, Centre for Development Studies, Trivandrum, India.

Gebreyeesus, M. and Mohnen, P., 2013. Innovation Performance and Embeddedness in Networks: Evidence from the Ethiopian Footwear Cluster. *World Development*, 41(c), 302–316.

GoI, 1967. *Study of Handloom Development Programme.* Programme Evaluation Organisation, Planning Commission, Government of India.

GoK, 1976. *Economic Review Kerala 1975.* Planning Board, Government of Kerala.

——, 1978. *Economic Review 1977.* Planning Board, Government of Kerala.

——, 1986. *Economic Review 1985.* Planning Board, Government of Kerala.

Haynes, D.E., 1996. The Logic of the Artisan Firm in a Capitalist Economy: Handloom Weavers and Technological Change in Western India, 1880–1947. In H. Stein and M.H. Subrahmanyam (eds) *Institutions and Economic Change in South Asia.* New Delhi: Oxford University Press.

——, 2001. Artisan Cloth-producers and the Emergence of Powerloom Manufacture in Western India 1920–1950. *Past & Present*, 172, 170–198.

——, 2012. *Small Town Capitalism in Western India.* Cambridge: Cambridge University Press.

Haynes, D.E. and Roy, T., 1999. Conceiving Mobility: Weavers' Migrations in Pre-colonial and Colonial India. *The Indian Economic and Social History Review*, 36(1), 35–67.

Kochuthressia, C.T., 1994. *Making of Women Workers: A Case Study of Women in the Traditional Weaving Streets of Chaliyas*, unpublished MPhil. thesis, School of Social Sciences, Mahatma Gandhi University, Kottayam, India.

Mamidipudi, A., Syamasundari, B. and Bijker, W., 2012. Mobilising Discourses: Hand-loom as a Sustainable Socio-technology. *Economic and Political Weekly*, 47(25), 41–51.

MoC, 1974. *Report of the High Powered Study Team on the Problems of Handloom Industry*. Ministry of Commerce, Government of India.

MoT, 2012. *Annual Report 2011–2012*, Ministry of Textiles, Government of India.

NCAER, 2010. *Handloom Census of India 2009–2010*. New Delhi: National Council for Applied Economic Research, Government of India.

Niranjana, S. and Vinayan, S., 2001. *Report on Growth and Prospects of Handloom Industry*, study commissioned by the Planning Commission, India.

Padgett, J.F. and Powell, W.W., 2012. The Problem of Emergence. In J.F. Padgett and W.W. Powell (eds) *The Emergence of Organizations and Markets*. Princeton, NJ, and Oxford: Princeton University Press.

Raman, V., 2010 *The Warp and the Weft: Community and Gender Identities among Banaras Weavers*. New Delhi, and Abingdon, Oxon: Routledge.

Roy, T., 1987. Relations of Production in Handloom Weaving in the Mid-Thirties. Working Paper 223. Centre for Development Studies, Trivandrum, India.

——, 1993. *Artisans and Industrialization: Indian Weaving in the Twentieth Century*. New Delhi, New York and Oxford: Oxford University Press.

——, 1996. Introduction. In T. Roy (ed.) *Cloth and Commerce: Textiles in Colonial India*. New Delhi, Thousand Oaks, CA, and London: Sage.

——, 1999. *Traditional Industry in the Economy of Colonial India*. Cambridge: Cambridge University Press.

——, 2002. Acceptance of Innovations in Early Twentieth Century Indian Weaving. *The Economic History Review*, 55(3), 507–532.

Venkataraman, K.S., 1935. *The Hand-loom Industry in South India*. Supplement to the Madras University Journal. Madras, India.

Walker, G., Kogut, B. and Shan W., 1997. Social Capital, Structural Holes and the For-mation of the Industry Network. *Organization Science*, 8(2), 109–125.

Wintrobe, R., 1995. Some Economics of Ethnic Capital Formation and Conflict. In A. Breton *et al.* (eds) *Nationalism and Rationality*. Cambridge: Cambridge University Press.

7 Conclusions and policy lessons

Summary

We have come to the end of this book. Let us summarise what this book was about, how it tried to achieve its goals, what it found, and to what future directions it contributes.

What this book was about

This book was about the nature and characteristics of information sharing by means of informal interaction among small producers in clusters, who operate using traditional and 'low' technologies. The aim of the book was to investigate interaction channels and dynamics for information sharing and technological progress among such producers, when their survival strategy is primarily defensive innovation. This objective was based on a number of motivations as follows. Small producers, especially low-tech small producers, need constantly to keep an eye on technological developments among their peers to make sure that they do not end up outmoded, especially since they are usually too small to work in isolation and cannot undertake R&D in the formal, conventional sense. It is important, if such producers wish to be proximate to their peers in terms of technological capability and knowledge stock, that they keep abreast of the velocity of technical change among their close allies or competitors. But the kind of learning and innovation that low-tech or traditional or rural producers perform is quite distinctive in that it involves a host of strategies beyond simply geographic proximity and networking, which need to be elaborated and closely studied. These strategies come under the umbrella of defensive innovation and learning, through observing, constantly communicating, interacting, informal information exchange, relying on social networks and so on. Defensive behaviour and collective invention are in most cases the first choice and not a last resort. Flexibility and geographical proximity are placed at the forefront, with local groups of producers and institutions agglomerating not simply for the convenience of production and for economies of scale, but to evolve a system rich with a constant 'buzz' of new knowledge and information. Strategies for networking for these purposes may or may not be influenced by complex social relations in the operating environment or location. That is, information sharing may be clean and untouched by any sort of social barriers, or may even arise as emergent properties of the social differences.

Hence, with this background, the two case studies in this book have attempted to disentangle oversimplified notions of spillovers and proximity that exist in the general approach to understanding innovation and learning by Indian innovation and technology policy, and to move deeper into investigations into the underlying mechanics of informal interactive behaviour. This is of special importance, since it is these kinds of economic agents and environments where social relations, either simple or complex, drive economic relations, and which constitute the vast majority of industrial and artisanal clusters in a developing country like India.

What was found, and how it contributes to the literature

The book tackled these objectives by employing two methods – simulation modelling and empirical study.

In the modelling and simulation of informal know-how sharing among co-located agents in a rural low-tech cluster coloured by various kinds of social relations, we saw how boundedly rational agents in a networked cluster shared information purely through informal means. This exercise tested whether the small-world network structure was the most favourable for information sharing, enquired as to what type of social relations regime was most conducive for information diffusion and equity of knowledge distribution in the cluster, and explored the effect of varying intensities of the influence of social relations and of network distance. It was found that the small-world network structure may still be the best network structure for high performance, but not for most equitable knowledge distribution, when information sharing is undertaken in environments of complex social relations in a cluster. In addition, it was confirmed that the highest and most equitable knowledge distribution, with informal information sharing among networked agents in a cluster, was achieved when there was universal affinity among the agents.

With this confirmation, we undertook the empirical study of an actual case of a cluster characterised by universal affinity among its members, and studied its attempt to adapt to an innovation purely through informal information sharing. The empirical study of the coir cluster was motivated by the necessity to explore interaction mechanisms and channels in a low-tech cluster, to investigate the importance of information flows and learning processes within such clusters in their attempt to learn and adapt to technological change, and the institutional terrain within which these mechanisms and dynamics operate. Lessons from this descriptive case study, in terms of the importance of interpersonal affinity in a cluster, provided possible answers as to why some innovations, even with full financial and institutional backing, may not have diffused effectively across their target regions, or may not have been completely adapted within a region, causing divergent experiences among regions in an industry.

The book then moved on to a more complicated environment, characterised by informal information sharing heavily influenced by the complex social relations in the region. We clearly saw that when information sharing through informal interaction in a cluster is demarcated by social group, and involvement of social capital is intensive for an extended period of time, the emergent path that the cluster takes in terms of economic activity and its position in the market is certainly noteworthy. A network analysis of the Saliyar cluster provided evidence that it is not just embeddedness alone, but its *combination* with homophily in various intensities that is detrimental to clusters relying on information sharing chiefly through informal interaction. Consequently, the study demonstrated how it was imperative to disentangle social embeddedness into homophilous- and non-homophilous-embeddedness. That is, the conceptual ambit of embeddedness has to broaden out to recognise that social embeddedness comes in various 'homophilies'. The study of the Saliyars proceeded to argue that affiliation to a rigid network and traits of homophilous-embeddedness can weaken even a seemingly prosperous group, regardless of industry performance. We saw how complex social relations influence economic relations and technological progress, when these relations are relayed across generations.

This book aims to contribute to three main areas: (1) the literature on defensive innovation; (2) the literature on the role of networks in technological innovation and knowledge diffusion; and (3) policy studies of Indian small firm and traditional technology clusters. The contributions of this book in all three areas of literature may be placed under one umbrella – its endeavour to study the *economic-sociology* of informal information sharing among small units in defensively innovating clusters, which are set in scenarios characterised by complex social relations impinging upon economic and innovation relations. All three areas above, and the body of literature devoted to them, have not adequately enquired into this direction, which the book has endeavoured to fulfil. We now move on to some specific policy lessons.

A few lessons for policy

Let us bring back an issue discussed in Chapter 1 concerning the thought that despite several studies on informal information, Powell and Grodal (2005) and Maharajh and Kraemer-Mbula (2010) lament that there has been scarce empirical research on linking informal ties to the innovation process, probably due to the fact that informal innovation activities are not captured by innovation surveys (Gault and von Hippel, 2009) and there is generally a bias by quantitative survey-based research and policy deliberations towards innovation processes involving formal scientific and technical knowledge, such as formal R&D (Jensen *et al.*, 2007; Maharajh and Kraemer-Mbula, 2010). It may not actually be the case that studies linking informal ties with the innovation process are numerically 'few'. What Powell and Grodal may be referring to is the fact (suggested also by Jensen *et al.* (2007) and Maharajh and Kraemer-Mbula (2010)) that attention given to free information sharing in the literature is disproportionate to its occurrence, relative to the attention given to formal R&D and formal methods of diffusion of information. Taking this lead, and parallel to what Spielman *et al.* (2008) recommended, policy must recognise the existence of multiple sources of innovation and be inclusive of those sources. Hence, these proportions (between policy attention in India given to information sourced through free information sharing, and attention given to more formal sources and methods) must be more balanced and sensitive to one another, this being the first policy lesson from this study.

To understand the importance of the first policy lesson, let us take, for example, the Danish experience outlined by Lundvall *et al.* (2002). The Danish system of innovation comprises a large low-tech sector characterised by incremental and experience-based innovations, as much as by radical or science-based innovation in its high-tech sector. The Danish system of innovation, in its policy framework, has, according to Lundvall *et al.* (2002), deeply appreciated the low-tech and traditional variety of innovation and information diffusion practices and has remained an important priority for industrial policy. The rush for high-tech and ICTs has not overtaken the importance given to 'everyday learning and innovation' in Denmark, an example worthy of providing lessons for India where traditional and low-tech industries form the foundation of rural and semi-urban economies. The lesson from the Danish illustration in Lundvall *et al.* (2002) is that a narrow innovation system focusing on R&D and high-tech or science-based systems will not make much sense in the south (within which rural India may easily be included).[1]

In fact, the science, technology and innovation policy of the Government of India (DST, 2003, 2013) is stunted as far as attention to sources of innovation from non-R&D routes is concerned. Mani (2013) criticises this series of policy documents for having regularly associated innovation with formal R&D activities alone. This is a display of severe ignorance on the part of policy in a country where technological change is sourced from (and constantly provoked by) an industrial sector that consists of mostly small and medium-sized units operating on low- and medium-level technologies, without in-house R&D departments. This book hence adds support to Mani's (2013) call for the science, technology and innovation policy in India to appreciate the non-R&D routes to innovation as well, and to develop indicators to measure activities along these routes.

A second policy lesson for India is the appreciation of proximity, which is not altogether forgotten, but not yet comprehensive in the manner that it should be. The notion of proximity is not simple and monolithic (as we have discussed in Chapter 1). Policy must appreciate that for informal interactive information sharing to occur, geographic proximity is essential but not enough – also in need of inclusion in policy construction are the recognition of cognitive proximity among actors in the innovation system, organisational proximity in production and knowledge capacities, and, very importantly, social proximity as embedded in social relations (Graf, 2006).

The third policy lesson for India calls for the recognition that proximity in these various perspectives – cognitive, organisational, geographical and social – must not be overemphasised, as excessive cohesion can lead to lock-in and insulation. This has been illustrated through the study of the Saliyars. Actors cannot be close in all directions, lest ties that bind become 'ties that blind' (Grabher, 1993; Graf, 2006). Weak links outside, coupled with their fair share of strong links within the cluster are optimal (Granovetter, 1973) to gain the benefits of proximity as well as new information from outside. For new information to come from outside, agents within the cluster must develop relations based on reciprocity and trust towards external agents, which take time and effort to mature (Graf, 2006).

A recent World Bank study on agricultural innovation systems suggests, in one of its modules (Ekboir, 2012), that one very effective strategy where public funding can be put to deliver effective results is to direct investments towards financing what are called 'catalytic agents'. These agents (which might include NGOs, research organisations and so on) essentially perform the task of assembling potential actors (firms, individuals) in the cluster who can benefit from information sharing with one another. Catalytic agents must be funded and encouraged, as they play the role, in network theory terminology, of 'filling structural holes'. In other words, these are agents that can play a central role in bringing together actors (or groups of actors) who were formerly not connected, and who would benefit from information sharing from one another. The catalytic agents by themselves may not provide new information but they fulfil the important task of bridging missing network links between actors or clusters of actors. Ekboir (2012) suggests building capabilities among actors willing to be these catalytic agents, who may be individuals or dedicated organisations that foster the sharing of ideas. In a study on rural innovation systems and networks among Ethiopian agricultural smallholders (Spielman *et al.*, 2008), the public service provider itself was found to be the catalyst and the central node in information sharing, but this may not always be the case. These catalysts, called 'civic entrepreneurs' by Cooke (2002), are proposed in his study as catalysts for creating regional economy and community relationships operating across boundaries; such leaders are usually business or community actors with strong and widespread personal networks among diverse constituencies. In the coir cluster study we saw that a catalytic agent or civic entrepreneur was not an individual but a forum, Kudumbasree, which served, unintentionally, as the central nodal point for actors in the cluster to come together and meet others with whom they would not interact in the ordinary course of the day. Kudumbasree is but one example, and many arenas in clusters such as these can be funded and supported for the sole purpose of bringing together agents who could potentially share know-how with one another.

The fourth policy lesson for India therefore is to support and fund central nodes, the catalysts and the common arenas, besides the innovation itself.[2] This supplements the third policy lesson in helping to tone down the detriments of cohesion by allowing fresh information to seep in and diffuse.

The appreciation of information sharing by means of interaction through social networks is no longer peripheral in the small firms literature, but it must percolate into policy making in India where the appreciation of this behaviour is still only superficial and where economic- and information-acquiring interactions thrive in scenarios of complex social relations. Formal knowledge generation mechanisms, in the form of R&D labs run by the state, or even policy think-tanks and government organisations, must achieve a balance between research on 'formal' technological output – embodied artefacts such as machinery – and informal information transfer mechanisms. An appreciation must be made of the fact that merely providing nodal points at various locations to disseminate the 'hardware' of technologies is not sufficient (though necessary) and the 'software' of the technology should be disseminated as well, taking into full account the mesh in which local actors are placed. Clusters with weakly tied actors may require a completely different information dissemination strategy as compared to a cluster with very strong internal ties; while for the former, the policy-making body must regularly set up arenas where actors can come together to discuss problems and solutions around everyday experiences of the technology, for the latter, the policy-making body must provide avenues to source information on links outside of the thickly interconnected cluster to ensure that obsolescence does not result.

To achieve all of this, policy makers must involve network indicators along with other conventional socio-economic indicators while evolving pro-grammes. Network indicators can expand policy makers' ability to predict future developments in markets and technologies; they are useful in devising 'early warning systems' to create information concerning changes in the technological and industrial landscape, allowing for maximisation of gain or mitigation of loss from the fallout of these changes, and also allowing for the assessment of whether or not certain portions of a sector or industry that are weak or isolated require an increase in social capital (Malerba and Vonortas, 2009). As cooperation and competition among agents are both economic forms of social capital in which trust and learning are centrally involved, a key concern of policy should be to study missing ingredients of social capital in the region, which should be addressed by programmes in support of net-working (Cooke, 2002); this is also where network indicators come into use. One must recognise that a network is a locus for innovation (and learning), as it provides timely access to external knowledge and resources while also testing internal expertise and learning abilities by virtue of the fact that an agent's linkages involve not only diverse formal contracts but also informal sharing of information (Vonortas, 2009). This is particularly important for many sectors where R&D plays a relatively minor role and learning experi-ences that are not easily visible are hard to grasp, where the part of the eco-nomics of knowledge that remains unknown is far greater than the part that is known (Foray, 2004).

The systems of innovation approach and the 'learning regions' framework treat the cluster or agglomeration as not just a set of co-located actors but as a milieu for collective learning and innovation with strong interpersonal ties within. Policy making in India with regard to dissemination of technologies in rural industrial clusters must take into account the vast wealth of information and lessons provided by this literature (such as the Danish example given earlier) to strengthen learning capability building in order to mobilise collective learning in 'localised innovation systems' such as low-tech clusters. The final policy lesson for India, therefore, is that the network perspective must seep into techno-logy and development policy. Network science and the network paradigm have become relevant across disciplinary boundaries, whose application has revolu-tionised research across disciplines (Brandes *et al.*, 2013). Network analysis today takes on a leading role in various fields, but it must seep into Indian policy making and industry studies as well.

Supporting an economic-sociology approach to understanding knowledge diffusion and learning

The general mainstream approach to science and technology and innovation for development in India comprises two views – a top-down policy prescription view, and a high-tech preference view. This book aims at an understanding that is much broader than the limited approach these aspects take, by projecting innovation and learning as being more inclusive and *social* processes than the mainstream view perceives them to be; a perspective that is essential while craft-ing development policy for an economy like India that is trying to tap its innov-ative potential.

Hence, at a broader level, this book contributes towards the larger theme of the economic-sociology of knowledge diffusion and technological learning. Economic-sociology (for an understanding of which we draw from Swedberg (1990, 2003)) is the application of the sociological tradition to economic phe-nomena in an attempt to explain them, wherein the analysis of economic inter-ests is combined with an analysis of social relations. That is, though economic-sociology shares most of the concerns and goals of economic analysis, it departs from convention in that the role of social relations and institutions is kept central to the analysis (Swedberg, 2003).[3] From Granovetter's (1985) concept of embedded action, for example, sociology has provided a systematic approach to predicting economic behaviour from the structure of social ties (Vedres and Stark, 2010).

There are a number of studies that have already used an economic-sociology understanding of innovation and learning as their principal undercurrent, such as Arora (2009), Akçomak (2009), Mamidipudi *et al.* (2012), and the collection of studies in Adam and Westlund (2012) on an understanding of innovation and learning in a socio-cultural context.

Whether in the simulation model in Chapter 2, or in the coir cluster study in Chapter 4, or the study of the Saliyars in Chapters 5 and 6, the central pillar of analysis and understanding on this has always been rooted within an under-standing of social relations that have a bearing on economic relations. Each of the analyses in this book has been around concerns of learning, innovation and knowledge diffusion which are generally 'economics' concepts but have been dealt with here with essentially sociological perspectives.[4] This is because as much as they are economic interests, knowledge diffusion and learning are *sociological interests* too. These interests are as much conceptualised, expressed and realised in social terms and in social relations (Swedberg, 2003) as they are in economic terms and production relations in a conventional sense. We see evidence of this in the empirical analyses in this book as well. The Saliyars were very particular about effective information diffusion in their community not only for business interests but also for community interests. The women in the coir cluster in Manappuram were seen to be effective collective learners not only for resilience against the possibilities of a quick downfall within a problematic traditional low-tech industry, but also to reinforce 'neighbourly' relations within their cluster. In the simulation model too, rewards were given to teachers who doled out information to learners within their own social group, in order to maintain community dominance in the cluster. We have also relied, though not in its most rigorous sense, on an economic history approach to understanding why network rigidity among the Saliyars is a phenomenon rooted in their long-standing community cohesion and inherited networks.

Had we used a purely conventional economics approach, we would have understood only the purely *economic* mechanics behind the stories of the coir cluster or the Saliyars. Using an economic-sociology approach, we have understood the processes in these clusters as *socially conditioned* processes, i.e. actions by these agents are driven by economic *and* social interests, and orientation towards other agents in the vicinity (Swedberg, 2003). As Swedberg (2003) has argued, economic actors often orient themselves towards other actors in multiple ways, and the social structure as a motive and consequence always becomes a pivotal part of that analysis. In the analysis of information diffusion and learning through informal information sharing, this book has mainly subscribed to this approach, maintaining social structure and social relations as central to the economics of knowledge diffusion and learning.

Throughout the second and third quarters of the twentieth century, this obvious and necessary bond between sociology and economics was cast largely aside. A revival was begun in the last two decades of the century, which Akçomak (2009) views as an *awakening* of the sociology-economics bond that was forgotten in the neoclassical tradition. That this is a revival or awakening, and not a novel development in social science, has to be emphasised, since this bond was alive and thriving for centuries, even until the 1930s, with contributions from figures such as Adam Smith, Karl Marx, Max Weber, and finally Schumpeter and Polanyi, who wrote extensively on economic issues with an economic-sociology approach. The application of this economic-sociology approach to understanding information diffusion and technological learning is what this book essentially aims at contributing towards. This approach is of the essence, whether in the study of high-tech formal innovation and learning, or informal information sharing in low-tech settings.

Notes

1 At the same time, Lundvall *et al.* (2002) say, we must also take into consideration aspects of *power* in its role in economic development:

> The focus on interactive learning – a process in which agents communicate and even cooperate in the creation and utilisation of new economically useful knowledge – may lead to an underestimation of the conflicts over income and power, which are also connected to the innovation process. It may be more common in the South than in the North that interactive learning possibilities are blocked and existing competences destroyed (or de-learnt) for political reasons related to the distribution of power.
>
> (Lundvall *et al.*, 2002, p. 226)

2 However, such central nodes or catalysts must be set up with due recognition of the kinds of networks that map the cluster in question, as they may not be relevant in cases such as the Saliyar clusters where there is strong cohesiveness. The introduction of a catalyst node in a network having one or more highly cohesive components may be futile, as those components may simply disregard the catalyst.

3 An approach encapsulated in the discussion across the second half of Chapter 1 in this book.

4 It is useful to note at this point that the chief methodology of this book, namely social network analysis, seeks the understanding of an issue keeping *relational connectivity* and *dependence* as central concerns (Brandes *et al.*, 2013). This understanding has been applied in the treatment of all elements – simulation modelling as well as empirical study – in this book.

References

Adam, F. and Westlund, H., 2012. *Innovation in Socio-cultural Context*. New York, and Abingdon, Oxon: Routledge.

Akçomak, İ.S., 2009. *The Impact of Social Capital on Economic and Social Outcomes*. PhD. UNU-MERIT and Universiteit Maastricht, The Netherlands.

Arora, S., 2009. *Knowledge Flows and Social Capital: A Network Perspective on Rural Innovation*. PhD. UNU-MERIT and Universiteit Maastricht, The Netherlands.

Brandes, U., Robins, G., McCranie, A. and Wasserman, S., 2013. What is Network Science? *Network Science*, 1(1), 1–15.

Cooke, P., 2002. *Knowledge Economies: Clusters, Learning and Cooperative Advantage*. New York and London: Routledge.

DST, 2003. *Science and Technology Policy 2003*. Department of Science and Technology, Ministry of Science and Technology, Government of India.

——, 2013. *Science, Technology and Innovation Policy 2013*. Department of Science and Technology, Ministry of Science and Technology, Government of India.

Ekboir, J., 2012. How to Build Innovation Networks. Thematic Note 2 in *Agricultural Innovation Systems: An Investment Sourcebook*. Washington, DC: The World Bank.

Foray, D., 2004. *The Economics of Knowledge*. Cambridge, MA: MIT Press.

Gault, F. and von Hippel, E., 2009. The Prevalence of User Innovation and Free Innovation Transfers: Implications for Statistical Indicators and Innovation Policy. 4722–09. MIT Sloan School Working Paper.

Grabher, G., 1993. The Weakness of Strong Ties: The Lock-in of Regional Development in the Ruhr Area. In G. Grabher (ed.) *The Embedded Firm: On the Socioeconomics of Industrial Networks*. London and New York: Routledge.

Graf, H., 2006. *Networks in the Innovation Process: Local and Regional Interactions.* Cheltenham, UK, and Northampton, USA: Edward Elgar.

Granovetter, M., 1973. The Strength of Weak Ties. *American Journal of Sociology*, 78(6), 1360–1380.

——, 1985. Economic Action and Social Structure: The Problem of Embeddedness. *American Journal of Sociology*, 91(3), 481–510.

Jensen, M.B., Johnson, B., Lorenz, E. and Lundvall, B-Å., 2007. Forms of Knowledge and Modes of Innovation. *Research Policy*, 36(5), 680–693.

Lundvall, B-A., Johnson, B., Andersen, E.S. and Dalum, B., 2002. National Systems of Production, Innovation, and Competence Building. *Research Policy*, 31(2), 213–231.

Maharajh, R. and Kraemer-Mbula, E., 2010. Innovation Strategies in Developing Countries. In E. Kramer-Mbula and W. Wamae (eds) *Innovation and the Development Agenda.* Canada: IRDC, Organization for Economic Cooperation and Development (OECD).

Malerba, F. and Vonortas, N.S., 2009. Innovation Networks in Industries with Sectoral Systems: An Introduction. In F. Malerba and N.S. Vonortas (eds) *Innovation Networks in Industries.* Cheltenham, UK, and Northampton, USA: Edward Elgar.

Mamidipudi, A., Syamasundari, B. and Bijker, W., 2012. Mobilising Discourses: Handloom as a Sustainable Socio-Technology. *Economic and Political Weekly*, 47(25), 41–51.

Mani, S., 2013. The Science, Technology and Innovation Policy 2013: An Evaluation. *Economic and Political Weekly*, 48(10), 16–19.

Powell, W.W. and Grodal, S., 2005. Networks of Innovators. In J. Fagerberg *et al.* (eds) *The Oxford Handbook of Innovation.* Oxford: Oxford University Press.

Spielman, D.J., Davis, K.E., Negash, M. and Ayele, G., 2008. Rural Innovation Systems and Networks: Findings from a Study of Ethiopian Smallholders. IFPRI Discussion Paper 00759, International Food Policy Research Institute (IFPRI), Washington, DC.

Swedberg, R., 1990. *Economics and Sociology: Redefining their Boundaries: Conversations with Economists and Sociologists.* Princeton, NJ: Princeton University Press.

——, 2003. *Principles of Economic Sociology.* Princeton, NJ, and Oxford: Princeton University Press.

Vedres, B. and Stark, D., 2010. Structural Folds: Generative Disruption in Overlapping Groups. *American Journal of Sociology*, 115(4), 1150–1190.

Vonortas, N.S., 2009. Innovation Networks in Industry. In F. Malerba and N.S. Vonortas (eds) *Innovation Networks in Industries.* Cheltenham, UK, and Northampton, USA: Edward Elgar.

Appendix
The Saliyars of Balaramapuram

For a brief note on the Saliyars, we refer throughout to Ramaswamy (2006), a monumental work on the textile producers of medieval south India. The word *shalika* in Sanskrit for 'weaver' (Singh, 1988) is the most likely etymology of the caste name *Sale* or *Saliga*, one among the many weaver castes in the Tamil-speaking regions of medieval southern India. This caste was known by various other names in southern peninsular India, verified by inscriptions in old temples across the region, and by the common worship of the deity *Salisvara*. However, there was considerable division of the old caste by region, practices, beliefs, economic position and so on through time. The Saliyars, as they are known today, belonging to the *Vaishya* tier of the caste system (Singh, 1988), were the prominent weaving community in south India during the reign of the powerful Chola Empire between the tenth and fourteenth centuries CE.[1] Weavers in general settled in and around the immediate precincts of a large temple, and had their own exclusive quarters supported by royalty and religious bodies of the time. Economic privileges and high ritual positions with vital responsibilities characterised these communities of weavers, sometimes even extending to monetary and managerial responsibilities during major ceremonies and rituals in the big temples. During the Chola reign, they were even conferred the august title *Choliya Saliyar* and a suffix *Chetti* (a suffix usually held by prosperous merchants), and were often granted considerable land on the condition that they supplied clothes to the image of the deity and other smaller idols on various ccasions every year.

But with the foundation of the Vijayanagar Empire after the fourteenth century, they seem to have lost their dominance to other weaver castes across southern India, and were said to eventually migrate further south into Kerala, residing there – noted by Duarte Barbosa, the Portuguese writer and officer in India – as upper castes with low social status due to low economic status and a clientele of lower caste consumers. Niranjana (2006) reiterates Ramaswamy's argument that weavers' social position was determined ultimately not by their ritual position in the traditional caste hierarchy but by their location and position in local economic networks.

The Saliyars of Balaramapuram in Kerala, however, originated not from the groups observed by Barbosa but from those based at the southernmost tip of the neighbouring state of Tamil Nadu (who may, of course, have been descended from groups of Saliyar families who never left Tamil Nadu). According to a legend, in the seventeenth century the Maharaja of Travancore imported a handful of silk- and cotton-weaver families into what was then Kottar village in the Nagercoil region at the southernmost tip of present-day Tamil Nadu (Rajagopalan, 1986). The Saliyars may have been a part of this group, and were invited in the 1890s into southern Kerala, along with a few members from four other Tamil-speaking communities, at the behest of the Maharaja of Travancore to locate at Balaramapuram town. Although there were already many other Malayalam-speaking weaving communities already operating in that location (Rajagopalan, 1986), the Saliyars were to serve as weavers to the royal family, with official patronage. They were settled on a set of streets, which were, and still are, surrounded by socially heterogeneous agglomerations of other weaving communities. They operated as the dominant weaving community in the region for many years, at least until the 1970s according to an elderly member of the Saliyar community there, and held no animosity towards other Tamil- or Malayalam-speaking communities. The community included, as it still does today, weavers, plyers, spinners, dyers, beamers, yarn sellers, finished product sellers, wholesalers, retailers and so on. But what changed dramatically over the past forty years, besides position, is that the population of Saliyars engaged in weaving, or for that matter any handloom-related activity, declined. This community is no longer 'synonymous' with the product.

Note

1 Occupations at the time were hereditary and based almost entirely on caste, and professional guilds were developed in India, similar to the artisanal guilds in medieval Europe. However, south Indian guilds differed from their European counterparts in that the former did not maintain uniform standards in products and prices (Ramaswamy, 2006, p. 38).

References

Niranjana, S., 2006. Many Threads of a Story. *Economic and Political Weekly*, 41(49), 5050–5051.
Rajagopalan, V., 1986. *The Handloom Industry in North and South Kerala: A Study of Production and Marketing Structures.* MPhil. Centre for Development Studies, Trivandrum, India.
Ramaswamy, V., 2006. *Textiles and Weavers in South India*, 2nd edn. New Delhi: Oxford University Press.
Singh, K.S., 1998. *India's Communities N–Z.* People of India Series Volume VI, Anthropological Survey of India. New Delhi and Oxford: Oxford University Press.

Index

Page numbers in **bold** denote figures.

For Product Safety Concerns and Information please contact our EU
representative GPSR@taylorandfrancis.com
Taylor & Francis Verlag GmbH, Kaufingerstraße 24, 80331 München, Germany